Profiles of Nobel Prize-Winning Scientists

Shah Rukh

Published by Shah Rukh, 2024.

PROFILES OF NOBEL PRIZE-WINNING SCIENTISTS

First edition. May 14, 2024.

ISBN: 979-8224604418

Written by Shah Rukh.

Table of Contents

Prologue

The Nobel Prize represents the pinnacle of achievement in various fields of science, honoring individuals or groups who have made significant contributions that have profoundly impacted our understanding of the world. Since its inception in 1901, the Nobel Prize has become synonymous with groundbreaking discoveries, pioneering research, and the relentless pursuit of knowledge. It is awarded in recognition of work that not only advances our grasp of complex scientific phenomena but also often paves the way for future innovations.

In this book, "Profiles of Nobel Prize-Winning Scientists," we embark on a journey through the lives and achievements of some of the most brilliant minds in history. From Albert Einstein's revolutionary theories of relativity to Marie Curie's discovery of radioactivity, these scientists have dared to push the boundaries of what was thought possible, often at great personal risk and against substantial odds. Their stories are not just about scientific achievement; they are also about perseverance, curiosity, and an unyielding desire to uncover the mysteries of our universe.

Each chapter delves into the lives of these remarkable individuals and teams, exploring not only their Nobel-winning discoveries but also the journeys that led them to those moments of triumph. We will examine the challenges they faced, the inspirations that drove them, and the broader impacts their work has had on science and society. Whether it is the quest to understand the fundamental laws of physics, the structure of DNA, or the intricacies of chemical reactions, the contributions of these scientists have shaped our world in ways that continue to resonate today.

As you read through these profiles, you will not only learn about the scientific breakthroughs that earned these individuals the highest honors but also gain insight into the human stories behind the science. You will meet pioneers who challenged the status quo, innovators who brought new ideas to life, and visionaries who looked beyond the present to explore the possibilities of the future.

This book is an homage to the relentless spirit of inquiry and the quest for knowledge. It is a celebration of those who have dared to ask the big questions and, in doing so, have provided answers that continue to enlighten, inspire, and transform our understanding of the universe. Welcome to a world of discovery and inspiration, where science meets the human spirit, and where every profile tells a story of extraordinary achievement.

Let us begin our journey through the lives and legacies of the Nobel Prize-winning scientists who have changed the world.

Chapter 1: Albert Einstein

Albert Einstein, one of the most iconic figures in the history of science, was born on March 14, 1879, in the city of Ulm, in the Kingdom of Württemberg in the German Empire. His contributions to physics, particularly the development of the theory of relativity, have profoundly impacted the way we understand the universe. Einstein's early life was marked by curiosity and a deep fascination with the natural world. Although he initially struggled in school, particularly with the rigid, rote learning methods prevalent in the German education system, his interest in mathematics and science grew stronger over time. By the age of 12, Einstein had already taught himself geometry from a textbook and had begun to delve into calculus, demonstrating an exceptional aptitude for abstract thinking.

Einstein's formal education continued at the Swiss Federal Polytechnic in Zurich, where he initially sought to study electrical engineering. However, his focus soon shifted entirely to mathematics and physics, subjects in which he excelled. Despite his brilliance, Einstein faced significant challenges in his academic career, often clashing with professors due to his unconventional thinking and reluctance to follow strict academic protocols. After graduating in 1900, he struggled to find a teaching position and ultimately took a job as a patent examiner at the Swiss Patent Office in Bern. This seemingly mundane job allowed Einstein ample time to think deeply about scientific problems, leading to one of the most productive periods of his life.

In 1905, often referred to as his "miracle year" (Annus Mirabilis), Einstein published four groundbreaking papers in the journal *Annalen der Physik*, each of which would have been enough to establish his place in history. The first of these papers provided an explanation for the photoelectric effect, a phenomenon where light striking a metal surface generates an electric current. Einstein proposed that light could be thought of as a stream of particles, or "quanta," which later became known as photons. This idea challenged the traditional wave theory of light and laid the groundwork for quantum mechanics, a field that would revolutionize physics in the 20th century. For this work, Einstein was awarded the Nobel Prize in Physics in 1921, though by then, he was already world-renowned for other contributions.

The second paper, on Brownian motion, offered a theoretical explanation for the erratic movement of particles suspended in a fluid, a phenomenon observed by botanist Robert Brown decades earlier. Einstein's analysis provided empirical evidence for the existence of atoms and molecules, which were still debated at the time, and offered a way to determine their size and the number of molecules in a given volume. This work further solidified the atomic theory of matter and had far-reaching implications in statistical mechanics and thermodynamics.

However, it was Einstein's third and fourth papers from 1905 that would forever change the landscape of physics. The third paper introduced the special theory of relativity, a radical departure from classical mechanics that redefined concepts of space and time. Einstein postulated that the laws of physics are the same for all observers in uniform motion and that the speed of light is constant regardless of the observer's motion. This led to the revolutionary idea that time and space are interwoven into a single four-dimensional continuum known as spacetime. One of the most famous consequences of this theory is the equation $E = mc^2$, which asserts the equivalence of mass and energy. This equation suggested that a small amount of mass could be converted into a vast amount of energy, a principle later confirmed in nuclear reactions.

The fourth paper, which was an extension of his special relativity theory, delved into the equivalence of mass and energy. It was in this context that Einstein proposed the mass-energy equivalence formula, $E = mc^2$, which became one of the most famous equations in science. This equation implied that mass could be converted into energy and vice versa, a concept that would later become crucial in understanding nuclear fission and fusion. Einstein's theory of special relativity challenged the Newtonian mechanics that had dominated physics for centuries and opened the door to new ways of thinking about the universe.

Following his work on special relativity, Einstein continued to explore the implications of his theories, eventually leading to the development of the general theory of relativity, published in 1915. While special relativity dealt with objects moving at constant speeds, general relativity addressed objects moving under the influence of gravity. Einstein proposed that gravity was not a force, as Isaac Newton had described, but rather a curvature of spacetime caused by mass. Massive objects, such as stars and planets, bend the fabric of spacetime around them, and this curvature is what we perceive as gravity. One of the most dramatic predictions of general relativity was the bending of light around massive objects, a phenomenon known as gravitational lensing. This prediction was spectacularly confirmed during a solar eclipse in 1919, when light from stars was observed to bend as it passed near the sun. This confirmation made Einstein an international celebrity and cemented his place as one of the greatest scientists of all time.

Einstein's general theory of relativity also predicted the existence of black holes, regions of space where the curvature of spacetime becomes so extreme that not even light can escape. Although Einstein himself was skeptical of the physical reality of black holes, his equations suggested their inevitability, and subsequent observations have confirmed their existence. General relativity has since become one of the cornerstones of modern physics, with applications ranging from cosmology to the Global Positioning

System (GPS), which must account for the effects of general relativity to maintain accuracy.

Despite his monumental contributions to theoretical physics, Einstein was also deeply engaged with philosophical and ethical questions, particularly in the context of the turbulent political landscape of the 20th century. Born into a secular Jewish family, Einstein became increasingly concerned with the rise of nationalism and anti-Semitism in Europe. His pacifist and internationalist views were well known, and he was an outspoken critic of militarism and war. As the Nazi regime gained power in Germany, Einstein, who was already living in the United States at the time, renounced his German citizenship and accepted a position at the Institute for Advanced Study in Princeton, New Jersey. He remained in the United States for the rest of his life, becoming a U.S. citizen in 1940.

During World War II, Einstein's concerns about the potential misuse of his theories became a reality. In 1939, he signed a letter to President Franklin D. Roosevelt, warning that Nazi Germany might be developing an atomic bomb and urging the United States to begin its own research into nuclear weapons. This letter led to the establishment of the Manhattan Project, which ultimately developed the atomic bombs dropped on Hiroshima and Nagasaki in 1945. Although Einstein was not directly involved in the project, he later expressed deep regret about his role in its inception and became an advocate for nuclear disarmament.

In the years following the war, Einstein continued to work on theoretical physics, although he became increasingly isolated from the mainstream scientific community, which was moving in new directions with the development of quantum mechanics. Despite his early contributions to quantum theory, Einstein was deeply troubled by its implications, particularly its probabilistic nature, which he famously criticized with the phrase, "God does not play dice with the universe." He spent much of his later life searching for a unified field theory that would reconcile general relativity and quantum mechanics, but this quest remained unfulfilled at the time of his death.

Beyond his scientific achievements, Einstein was also a passionate advocate for civil rights and social justice. He was a member of the NAACP and worked closely with African American leaders like W.E.B. Du Bois and Paul Robeson to combat racial discrimination in the United States. He was also an early supporter of Zionism, although he envisioned a peaceful coexistence between Jews and Arabs in Palestine and was opposed to the establishment of a Jewish state that did not guarantee equal rights for all its inhabitants.

Einstein's personal life was complex and marked by both triumphs and tragedies. He was married twice, first to Mileva Marić, with whom he had two sons, and later to his cousin Elsa Löwenthal. His relationships with his family were often strained, particularly with his first wife and their eldest son, Hans Albert. Despite these difficulties, Einstein maintained close friendships with many of the leading intellectuals of his time and was known for his wit, humor, and love of music, particularly the violin.

Albert Einstein died on April 18, 1955, in Princeton, New Jersey, leaving behind a legacy that continues to shape our understanding of the universe. His work laid the foundation for many of the technological advancements of the 20th and 21st centuries, from nuclear energy to GPS, and his theories continue to be tested and confirmed by new observations and experiments. Einstein's contributions to science and his moral and philosophical reflections on the role of science in society have made him a symbol of intellectual curiosity, creativity, and the pursuit of knowledge. His image, with his unruly hair, kind eyes, and thoughtful expression, has become synonymous with genius, and his life story continues to inspire generations of scientists, philosophers, and thinkers around the world.

Chapter 2: Max Planck

Max Planck, a towering figure in the history of physics, was born on April 23, 1858, in Kiel, Germany. He is best known as the father of quantum theory, a revolutionary concept that transformed our understanding of atomic and subatomic processes. Planck's work laid the foundation for a new era in physics, influencing generations of scientists and reshaping the trajectory of scientific thought. His contributions to the field of physics are immense and varied, and his legacy continues to be felt in both theoretical and applied sciences.

Planck's early life was marked by a strong family background in education and intellectual pursuits. His father, Johann Julius Wilhelm Planck, was a professor of law at the University of Kiel, and his grandfather and great-grandfather were also academics. This environment fostered a deep appreciation for learning in young Max. Although he showed talent in music and was an accomplished pianist, Planck chose to pursue a career in physics, a decision that would have profound implications for the scientific community.

Planck enrolled at the University of Munich in 1874, where he studied under Philipp von Jolly, who introduced him to the principles of thermodynamics. Planck was particularly fascinated by the second law of thermodynamics, which states that the entropy, or disorder, of a closed system tends to increase over time. This principle would play a central role in his later work. After completing his doctorate in 1879, Planck continued his studies in Berlin, where he was influenced by prominent physicists such as Hermann von Helmholtz and Gustav Kirchhoff. Although he was deeply inspired by these figures, it was his own independent thinking that led to his groundbreaking discoveries.

Planck began his academic career as a lecturer at the University of Munich in 1880. His early work focused on thermodynamics, particularly the concept of entropy. However, it was his investigation into blackbody radiation that would lead to his most significant contribution to physics. Blackbody radiation refers to the spectrum of light emitted by an idealized, perfect emitter (a blackbody) that absorbs all incident radiation. In the late 19th century, the study of blackbody radiation posed a significant challenge to classical physics. The prevailing theories, based on classical mechanics and electromagnetism, failed to accurately predict the observed spectrum of blackbody radiation, especially at high frequencies, where they predicted an "ultraviolet catastrophe"—a divergence to infinite energy.

In 1900, Planck made a bold and revolutionary proposal that would change the course of physics. He suggested that the energy of electromagnetic waves is quantized, meaning that it could only be emitted or absorbed in discrete amounts, or "quanta." Planck introduced a fundamental constant, now known as Planck's constant (h), which relates the energy of a quantum of radiation to its frequency through the equation $E = h\nu$, where "E" is the energy, "h" is Planck's constant, and "ν" is the frequency of the radiation. This hypothesis was radical at the time, as it challenged the classical view that energy could vary continuously. Planck's quantization of energy marked the birth of quantum theory, a field that would later be expanded by other great minds such as Albert Einstein, Niels Bohr, and Werner Heisenberg.

Planck's introduction of the quantum concept was not immediately accepted by the scientific community. Even Planck himself viewed his proposal as a mathematical tool rather than a fundamental physical truth. However, the implications of his work were profound. By quantizing energy, Planck was able to derive a formula, now known as Planck's law, that accurately described the blackbody radiation spectrum across all frequencies. This was a major breakthrough, as it resolved the discrepancies between classical theory and experimental observations, and it marked the beginning of a new era in physics.

In 1905, Albert Einstein applied Planck's quantum hypothesis to explain the photoelectric effect, providing further evidence for the quantization of energy and laying the groundwork for the development of quantum mechanics. Einstein's work on the photoelectric effect, for which he would later receive the Nobel Prize, demonstrated that light could be thought of as consisting of particles, or "photons," each carrying a quantum of energy proportional to its frequency. This was a direct extension of Planck's ideas and further solidified the concept of quantization in the realm of electromagnetic radiation.

Planck's work on quantum theory did not end with his blackbody radiation law. He continued to explore the implications of quantization in various areas of physics, contributing to the development of quantum mechanics, which would emerge as a fully-fledged theory in the 1920s. Although Planck remained somewhat skeptical of the broader philosophical implications of quantum mechanics, particularly the probabilistic nature of the theory as formulated by Heisenberg and others, he recognized the significance of the quantum revolution and supported its development.

In addition to his contributions to quantum theory, Planck made significant advances in other areas of physics. He worked on thermodynamics, including studies on the irreversibility of physical processes and the nature of entropy. His work on the second law of thermodynamics was particularly influential, as it provided a deeper understanding of the relationship between energy and entropy in physical systems. Planck also made important contributions to the theory of heat radiation and to the understanding of the thermodynamic properties of gases and solids.

Planck's achievements were widely recognized during his lifetime. In 1918, he was awarded the Nobel Prize in Physics for his discovery of energy quanta. This honor solidified his status as one of the most important physicists of the 20th century. Planck also held numerous prestigious positions, including serving as the president of the German Physical Society from 1905 to 1909 and again from 1915 to 1918. He was also a member of the Prussian Academy of Sciences and was later elected as its president.

Despite his scientific successes, Planck's personal life was marked by significant hardship and tragedy. He married Marie Merck in 1887, and the couple had four children. However, their first child, Karl, died in infancy, and Marie herself passed away in 1909. Planck later remarried, to Marga von Hoesslin, and they had one son, Hermann. The tragedies in Planck's life did not end there. His son Erwin was executed by the Gestapo in 1945 for his involvement in the plot to assassinate Adolf Hitler, and his daughter Grete died during childbirth, as did her twin sister Emma a few years later.

Planck's life was also profoundly affected by the political turmoil of his time. He lived through both World Wars and the rise of the Nazi regime in Germany. Planck was a man of deep moral convictions, and he opposed the Nazi ideology, particularly its anti-Semitic policies. He was a friend and supporter of many Jewish scientists, including Albert Einstein, and he advocated for their rights and safety during the Nazi era. However, Planck faced significant challenges in navigating the political landscape of the time. As the president of the Prussian Academy of Sciences, he struggled to maintain the integrity of the institution while resisting the pressures of the Nazi government. His efforts to protect Jewish colleagues were often met with limited success, and he was forced to make difficult compromises.

During the Second World War, Planck's home in Berlin was destroyed in an air raid, and many of his scientific papers and personal belongings were lost. Despite these hardships, Planck continued to work on his scientific research, even as he endured personal and professional challenges. His resilience and dedication to science were remarkable, and he remained active in the scientific community until his death.

Max Planck passed away on October 4, 1947, in Göttingen, Germany, at the age of 89. His death marked the end of an era, but his legacy continues to influence the field of physics. Planck's constant remains a fundamental constant of nature, essential to the formulation of quantum mechanics and modern physics. The Planck units, a system of natural units based on his constant, are used in various fields of theoretical physics, including cosmology and quantum gravity. Planck's work laid the foundation for the development of quantum mechanics, which has since become one of the most successful and widely tested theories in the history of science.

Beyond his scientific achievements, Planck's life and career exemplify the virtues of intellectual curiosity, perseverance, and moral integrity. He was a man who remained committed to the pursuit of knowledge even in the face of personal and professional adversity. His contributions to science were not only groundbreaking in their own right but also paved the way for future generations of physicists to explore the mysteries of the quantum world.

Planck's influence extends far beyond the confines of theoretical physics. His work has had a profound impact on a wide range of scientific disciplines, from chemistry and material science to information theory and computer science. The principles of quantum mechanics, which Planck helped to establish, underpin much of modern technology, including semiconductors, lasers, and quantum computers. In this way, Planck's legacy is not only a testament to his intellectual achievements but also a reminder of the far-reaching consequences of scientific discovery.

Moreover, Planck's philosophical reflections on the nature of science and the role of the scientist have left an enduring mark on the scientific community. He believed that science was a pursuit of truth, guided by empirical evidence and rational inquiry, but he also recognized the limitations of human knowledge and the need for humility in the face of the unknown. Planck's insights into the nature of scientific progress, including his famous observation that "a new scientific truth does not triumph by convincing its opponents and making them see the light, but rather because its opponents eventually die, and a new generation grows up that is familiar with it," continue to resonate with scientists and philosophers alike.

Max Planck's life and work represent the epitome of scientific achievement, characterized by a relentless pursuit of understanding and a commitment to advancing human knowledge. His contributions to quantum theory have reshaped our understanding of the universe, and his legacy continues to inspire scientists and thinkers across the world. As we continue to explore the frontiers of physics, from the behavior of subatomic particles to the nature of the cosmos, we do so standing on the shoulders of giants like Max Planck, whose vision and determination have illuminated the path forward.

Chapter 3: Werner Heisenberg

Werner Heisenberg, one of the most influential physicists of the 20th century, was a central figure in the development of quantum mechanics. Born on December 5, 1901, in Würzburg, Germany, Heisenberg made groundbreaking contributions that reshaped our understanding of the microscopic world. His most famous achievement, the uncertainty principle, remains a cornerstone of quantum theory, fundamentally altering the way we perceive the nature of reality.

Heisenberg grew up in an intellectually stimulating environment. His father, August Heisenberg, was a professor of classical philology, and his family placed a strong emphasis on education and scholarly pursuits. From an early age, Heisenberg showed a keen interest in mathematics and physics, fields that would soon dominate his life. He received his early education in Munich, where he excelled in his studies and demonstrated an extraordinary aptitude for theoretical thinking.

In 1920, Heisenberg entered the University of Munich, where he studied physics under Arnold Sommerfeld, one of the leading physicists of the time. Sommerfeld was known for his pioneering work in atomic theory and quantum mechanics, and his influence on Heisenberg was profound. Under Sommerfeld's guidance, Heisenberg delved into the study of quantum phenomena, developing a deep understanding of the emerging field of quantum theory.

Heisenberg's academic journey took him to the University of Göttingen, where he worked with Max Born, another luminary in the field of quantum mechanics. Göttingen was a hub of theoretical physics at the time, attracting some of the brightest minds in the world. Here, Heisenberg was exposed to the cutting-edge ideas and debates that were shaping the future of physics. He also encountered

Niels Bohr, the Danish physicist whose work on atomic structure and quantum theory would have a lasting impact on Heisenberg's own research.

It was during his time in Göttingen that Heisenberg made his first major contribution to physics. In 1925, at the age of 23, he developed matrix mechanics, the first complete and consistent formulation of quantum mechanics. This was a revolutionary approach that differed significantly from the classical mechanics developed by Isaac Newton and later refined by other physicists. In classical mechanics, the position and momentum of a particle could be precisely determined at any given time, allowing for the prediction of its future behavior. However, Heisenberg's matrix mechanics introduced a new way of thinking about these quantities.

In matrix mechanics, physical quantities such as position and momentum are represented by matrices, which are mathematical objects that generalize the concept of numbers and can have multiple components. Heisenberg's approach suggested that these quantities do not have definite values simultaneously, but rather are related by a set of probabilistic rules. This was a radical departure from the deterministic view of classical physics and marked the beginning of a new era in theoretical physics.

Heisenberg's matrix mechanics was initially met with skepticism by some physicists, as it was a highly abstract and mathematically complex formulation. However, it soon gained recognition for its ability to accurately describe a wide range of quantum phenomena, including the behavior of electrons in atoms. Heisenberg's work provided a powerful mathematical framework for understanding the quantum world, and it laid the foundation for further developments in quantum theory.

In 1927, Heisenberg made his most famous contribution to physics: the uncertainty principle. This principle, which is sometimes called the Heisenberg uncertainty principle, states that there is a fundamental limit to the precision with which certain pairs of physical quantities, such as position and momentum, can be simultaneously known. Specifically, the more precisely the position of a particle is determined, the less precisely its momentum can be known, and vice versa. Mathematically, the uncertainty principle is expressed as $\Delta x \cdot \Delta p \geq \hbar/2$, where "$\Delta x$" is the uncertainty in position, "Δp" is the uncertainty in momentum, and "$\hbar$" is the reduced Planck's constant.

The uncertainty principle had profound implications for the philosophy of science and our understanding of the nature of reality. In classical physics, it was assumed that with sufficient information, one could predict the future behavior of any physical system with arbitrary precision. However, Heisenberg's uncertainty principle challenged this notion, suggesting that there are intrinsic limits to what can be known about the physical world. This introduced an element of indeterminacy into the fabric of reality, leading to a new interpretation of the quantum world.

The uncertainty principle also played a key role in the development of the Copenhagen interpretation of quantum mechanics, which Heisenberg helped to formulate along with Niels Bohr. According to the Copenhagen interpretation, the wave function of a quantum system represents the probabilities of different outcomes rather than definite physical properties. This interpretation emphasizes the role of the observer in the measurement process, suggesting that the act of measurement itself affects the system being observed. The Copenhagen interpretation remains one of the most widely accepted interpretations of quantum mechanics, though it has been the subject of much debate and discussion over the years.

Heisenberg's contributions to quantum mechanics earned him widespread recognition and numerous accolades. In 1932, at the age of 31, he was awarded the Nobel Prize in Physics "for the creation of quantum mechanics, the application of which has, inter alia, led to the discovery of the allotropic forms of hydrogen." This was a remarkable achievement for such a young scientist, and it solidified Heisenberg's place among the great physicists of his time.

Despite his success, Heisenberg's career was not without controversy. During World War II, he became involved in the German atomic bomb project, also known as the Uranverein (Uranium Club). This project aimed to develop nuclear weapons for Nazi Germany, and Heisenberg's role in it has been the subject of much scrutiny and debate. Some historians argue that Heisenberg deliberately slowed down the project or even sabotaged it, while others believe that he was genuinely committed to the research but was hampered by a lack of resources and the chaotic state of wartime Germany.

Heisenberg's involvement in the Uranverein raises complex ethical questions about the responsibilities of scientists in times of war. After the war, Heisenberg and several other German scientists were detained by Allied forces and held at Farm Hall in England, where their conversations were secretly recorded. These recordings, known as the Farm Hall transcripts, reveal that Heisenberg and his colleagues were surprised by the news of the atomic bombings of Hiroshima and Nagasaki, suggesting that they had not made significant progress toward developing a bomb themselves.

After his release from detention, Heisenberg returned to Germany, where he played a leading role in the postwar reconstruction of German science. He became director of the Max Planck Institute for Physics, where he continued his research in theoretical physics. In the years following the war, Heisenberg shifted his focus to the study of cosmic rays, nuclear physics, and the unified field theory. He also became increasingly involved in scientific policy and international cooperation, advocating for the peaceful use of nuclear energy and the importance of scientific collaboration across national boundaries.

Heisenberg's later years were marked by his continued influence on both physics and the broader scientific community. He was a prolific writer and lecturer, and he published numerous books and papers on a wide range of topics in theoretical physics. His work on quantum field theory, particularly the development of the S-matrix (scattering matrix) theory, was influential in the study of particle physics. Heisenberg also made significant contributions to the understanding of symmetry principles in physics, which are central to modern theories of fundamental particles and forces.

In addition to his scientific achievements, Heisenberg was deeply interested in the philosophy of science. He explored the philosophical implications of quantum mechanics and the nature of scientific knowledge, often drawing on ideas from classical philosophy. Heisenberg was particularly influenced by the works of Immanuel Kant, and he believed that the uncertainty principle had important philosophical ramifications. He argued that the principle revealed fundamental limitations in our ability to know and predict the behavior of nature, challenging the deterministic worldview that had dominated science since the time of Newton.

Heisenberg's reflections on the relationship between science and philosophy culminated in his book "Physics and Philosophy: The Revolution in Modern Science," published in 1958. In this work, Heisenberg discussed the philosophical challenges posed by quantum mechanics and the need for a new understanding of the nature of reality. Heisenberg's insights into the interplay between science and philosophy continue to be studied and debated by philosophers and scientists alike, and his contributions to the philosophy of science have left a lasting legacy.

Throughout his life, Heisenberg was recognized with numerous honors and awards. In addition to the Nobel Prize, he received the

Max Planck Medal, the Matteucci Medal, and the Wilhelm Exner Medal, among others. He was also a member of several prestigious scientific academies, including the Royal Society of London and the American Academy of Arts and Sciences. Heisenberg's impact on the field of physics and his contributions to our understanding of the quantum world have earned him a place among the greatest scientists in history.

Werner Heisenberg passed away on February 1, 1976, in Munich, Germany, at the age of 74. His death marked the end of an era in theoretical physics, but his legacy continues to shape the field. The uncertainty principle, matrix mechanics, and the Copenhagen interpretation remain central to the study of quantum mechanics, and Heisenberg's ideas continue to influence the way physicists think about the nature of reality.

Heisenberg's life and work embody the spirit of scientific inquiry and the quest for knowledge. He was a scientist who was not afraid to challenge established ideas and who made bold strides into the unknown. His contributions to quantum mechanics opened new avenues of exploration and fundamentally altered our understanding of the universe. Moreover, Heisenberg's engagement with the philosophical implications of his work reflects a deep commitment to understanding the broader meaning of scientific discoveries.

Heisenberg's legacy is not confined to his scientific achievements alone. He was also a mentor and educator who inspired a new generation of physicists. His students and collaborators, many of whom went on to become prominent scientists in their own right, were profoundly influenced by his ideas and approach to physics. Heisenberg's teaching emphasized the importance of rigorous thinking, creativity, and a willingness to question assumptions—all qualities that are essential to the advancement of science.

In the years since Heisenberg's death, the field of quantum mechanics has continued to evolve, with new discoveries and theoretical developments building on the foundations he helped to establish. The uncertainty principle, in particular, has been explored in greater depth, leading to new insights into the nature of quantum systems and the limits of measurement. Heisenberg's work has also found applications in fields beyond physics, including information theory, cryptography, and even philosophy, where his ideas continue to resonate.

As we look to the future, the challenges and mysteries of quantum mechanics remain as compelling as ever. The quest to understand the fundamental nature of reality, to unravel the secrets of the quantum world, and to explore the limits of human knowledge continues to drive scientific inquiry. In this ongoing endeavor, Werner Heisenberg's contributions stand as a testament to the power of human curiosity, the importance of intellectual courage, and the enduring impact of great scientific minds. His legacy reminds us that science is not just a collection of facts and theories, but a dynamic and ever-evolving process of discovery, driven by the pursuit of truth and the desire to understand the world around us.

Chapter 4: Marie Curie

Marie Curie, one of the most remarkable scientists in history, stands as a towering figure in the world of science and beyond. Born Maria Sklodowska on November 7, 1867, in Warsaw, Poland, she rose from humble beginnings to become a pioneering physicist and chemist whose work not only revolutionized our understanding of radioactivity but also paved the way for significant advancements in medicine, physics, and chemistry. Her life and achievements are a testament to her extraordinary intellect, unwavering determination, and profound impact on science and society.

Marie Curie's early life was marked by hardship and perseverance. She was the youngest of five children in a family that valued education but struggled financially after the loss of her mother to tuberculosis when Marie was just ten years old. Her father, a teacher of mathematics and physics, instilled in her a love for learning, especially in the sciences. Despite the challenging circumstances, Marie excelled academically, demonstrating an exceptional aptitude for mathematics and physics from a young age.

In the late 19th century, opportunities for women in higher education were severely limited, particularly in her native Poland, which was then under Russian control. Determined to pursue her education, Marie moved to Paris in 1891 to attend the Sorbonne, one of the few universities in Europe that admitted women. There, she adopted the French form of her name, Marie, and immersed herself in her studies, focusing on physics and mathematics. Despite the difficulties of living in poverty and the challenges of studying in a foreign language, Marie Curie graduated at the top of her class in physics in 1893 and obtained a second degree in mathematics the following year.

It was at the Sorbonne that Marie met Pierre Curie, a physicist whose work on crystallography had already earned him a solid reputation in the scientific community. The two married in 1895, forming not only a personal partnership but also one of the most famous scientific collaborations in history. Their shared passion for research led them to work together on groundbreaking experiments that would change the course of science.

Marie Curie's most famous work began with her doctoral research, which focused on the mysterious phenomenon of radioactivity, a term she herself coined. In 1896, Henri Becquerel had discovered that uranium emitted rays that could expose photographic plates, but little was understood about this phenomenon. Marie Curie was intrigued by this discovery and chose to investigate it further for her doctoral thesis. She hypothesized that the rays were not merely a result of molecular interactions but were instead a property of the atoms themselves, suggesting that the source of this energy was something fundamental to the nature of matter.

To test this hypothesis, Marie Curie conducted meticulous experiments, measuring the strength of the rays emitted by different substances. She soon discovered that the intensity of the rays was proportional to the amount of uranium present, regardless of the form of the compound. This led her to conclude that the emission of radiation was an atomic property. Her research extended to other elements, and in 1898, Marie Curie discovered that thorium also emitted similar rays, thus confirming her theory that radioactivity was not unique to uranium but was a property of certain elements.

Driven by curiosity and a desire to understand the nature of this new phenomenon, Marie Curie continued her experiments, focusing on a mineral called pitchblende, which exhibited even higher levels of radioactivity than uranium. Working under extremely difficult conditions—using makeshift laboratories and handling large quantities of radioactive materials with little knowledge of the potential dangers—Marie and Pierre Curie isolated two previously unknown elements from pitchblende: polonium, named after Marie's native Poland, and radium. The discovery of these elements was a monumental achievement, revealing the existence of powerful new forces within atoms and opening up new fields of research in both physics and chemistry.

The Curies' work on radioactivity earned them widespread recognition and acclaim. In 1903, Marie Curie was awarded the Nobel Prize in Physics, shared with Pierre Curie and Henri Becquerel, for their joint research on radiation phenomena. This made her the first woman to win a Nobel Prize, breaking significant barriers in the male-dominated scientific community. The recognition of her work brought not only prestige but also much-needed funding, allowing the Curies to continue their research.

Tragically, Pierre Curie's life was cut short in 1906 when he was struck by a horse-drawn carriage and killed instantly. The loss of her husband was a devastating blow to Marie, but she remained steadfast in her commitment to science. Despite her grief, she took over Pierre's teaching position at the Sorbonne, becoming the first woman to teach at the institution. Her lectures were well-attended, and she continued to advance her research on radioactivity, further solidifying her reputation as a leading scientist.

Marie Curie's work on radium and its compounds led to significant developments in the field of medicine, particularly in the treatment of cancer. Radium's ability to destroy diseased cells made it a valuable tool in radiation therapy, and Marie Curie became an advocate for its medical applications. She also recognized the potential dangers of radioactive materials, though the full extent of the risks was not yet understood at the time. Marie and her colleagues frequently handled radioactive substances without protective measures, and the long-term effects of this exposure would later take a toll on her health.

In 1911, Marie Curie was awarded her second Nobel Prize, this time in Chemistry, for her discovery of radium and polonium and her investigation of their properties. She became the first person to win Nobel Prizes in two different scientific fields, an extraordinary accomplishment that underscored her unparalleled contributions to science. The award also came during a period of personal turmoil, as she faced intense scrutiny and criticism from the public and press due to a scandal involving her relationship with a married colleague, Paul Langevin. Despite the challenges, Marie Curie remained focused on her work, demonstrating remarkable resilience and dedication.

During World War I, Marie Curie applied her scientific expertise to the war effort, developing mobile X-ray units known as "Little Curies" that were used to diagnose injuries on the battlefield. She personally oversaw the installation of these units and trained technicians, including her daughter Irène, who would later become a Nobel laureate herself. Marie Curie's contributions to the war effort saved countless lives and further solidified her legacy as a scientist committed to the practical application of her discoveries.

After the war, Marie Curie continued her research and advocacy for science. She played a key role in establishing the Radium Institute in Paris, which became a leading center for research on radioactivity. Her work at the institute focused on the chemical properties of radioactive elements and their medical applications. She also traveled extensively, raising funds for scientific research and promoting international collaboration among scientists. Her efforts helped to establish the Curie Foundation, which continues to support cancer research and treatment to this day.

Marie Curie's health began to decline in the 1920s, likely due to her prolonged exposure to high levels of radiation. She suffered from various ailments, including cataracts and chronic fatigue, but she remained active in her research and public engagement until her final years. On July 4, 1934, Marie Curie passed away from aplastic anemia, a condition caused by bone marrow failure, likely a result of her extensive work with radioactive materials.

Marie Curie's legacy is profound and enduring. Her pioneering research on radioactivity not only revolutionized the fields of physics and chemistry but also had far-reaching implications for medicine and industry. The discovery of radium and polonium opened new avenues of scientific inquiry, leading to the development of nuclear energy and advancements in cancer treatment. Her work laid the foundation for the modern understanding of atomic structure and the forces that govern the behavior of matter at the most fundamental level.

Beyond her scientific achievements, Marie Curie is remembered as a trailblazer who broke down barriers for women in science. Her success in a male-dominated field challenged prevailing gender norms and inspired generations of women to pursue careers in science and technology. She was a role model not only for her scientific brilliance but also for her determination, perseverance, and commitment to the betterment of humanity through science.

Marie Curie's influence extends far beyond her own lifetime. Her contributions to science have been recognized through numerous honors and awards, including the naming of the chemical element curium in her honor. Her life and work continue to inspire scientists, educators, and students around the world. The Curie Institutes in Paris and Warsaw, which she helped to establish, remain leading centers for medical research and treatment, carrying forward her legacy of scientific excellence and humanitarian service.

In the broader context of scientific history, Marie Curie's work represents a turning point in our understanding of the natural world. Her discovery of radioactivity challenged existing theories of matter and energy, leading to a paradigm shift that has had a lasting impact on science and society. Her research demonstrated the power of curiosity-driven inquiry and the importance of perseverance in the face of adversity. Marie Curie's life is a testament to the idea that science knows no gender, and her legacy continues to inspire those who seek to push the boundaries of human knowledge.

Marie Curie's story is not just one of scientific achievement; it is also a story of courage, resilience, and the relentless pursuit of knowledge. She faced numerous obstacles, from financial hardship and personal loss to societal discrimination, yet she remained unwavering in her commitment to her work. Her determination to overcome these challenges and her ability to make groundbreaking discoveries in the face of adversity make her one of the most admired figures in the history of science.

As we reflect on the life and contributions of Marie Curie, it is important to recognize the broader impact of her work on the world. Her research on radioactivity has had a profound effect on numerous fields, from medicine to energy production, and her pioneering spirit continues to inspire innovation and discovery. The principles she embodied—curiosity, perseverance, and a commitment to the greater good—are as relevant today as they were in her time. Marie Curie's legacy is a reminder of the power of science to transform our understanding of the world and to improve the human condition, and her life serves as an enduring example of the extraordinary potential of the human mind when driven by a passion for discovery.

Chapter 5: Hans Bethe

Hans Bethe was one of the most influential physicists of the 20th century, whose contributions to science spanned numerous fields, from nuclear physics to astrophysics, quantum mechanics, and solid-state physics. Born in Strasbourg, Germany, on July 2, 1906, Bethe's early life and education were marked by his prodigious talent and intellectual curiosity, traits that would lead him to make groundbreaking discoveries that would shape the course of modern physics and have profound implications for both science and humanity.

Bethe's childhood was steeped in an environment that encouraged academic excellence. His father, a physiologist, and his mother, a music teacher, nurtured his early interest in science. Bethe attended the University of Frankfurt and later the University of Munich, where he studied under the renowned physicist Arnold Sommerfeld. Sommerfeld's mentorship had a lasting impact on Bethe, who quickly distinguished himself as a brilliant student. He completed his doctorate in 1928 at the age of 22, with a dissertation on electron diffraction in crystals, a topic that would later prove foundational to the field of solid-state physics.

In the years following his doctorate, Bethe held positions at several prestigious institutions, including the University of Munich, the University of Stuttgart, and the University of Tübingen. However, the rise of the Nazi regime in Germany in 1933 forced Bethe, who was of Jewish descent, to leave his homeland. He moved to England, where he worked at the University of Manchester under Patrick Blackett and the Cavendish Laboratory at the University of Cambridge. During this period, Bethe's research began to focus more intensely on nuclear physics, an area in which he would make some of his most significant contributions.

Bethe's work in nuclear physics reached new heights after he moved to the United States in 1935. He accepted a position at Cornell University, where he would spend the majority of his career. It was at Cornell that Bethe developed the theoretical framework for nuclear reactions, which would later be instrumental in understanding the processes that power the sun and other stars. His work culminated in the formulation of the Bethe-Weizsäcker cycle, also known as the CNO (carbon-nitrogen-oxygen) cycle, a key mechanism in stellar nucleosynthesis.

The CNO cycle, along with the proton-proton chain reaction, explained how stars convert hydrogen into helium, releasing enormous amounts of energy in the process. This work was revolutionary, providing the first comprehensive explanation of how stars generate energy and thus laying the foundation for modern astrophysics. Bethe's insights into nuclear reactions were not only crucial for understanding stellar processes but also had far-reaching implications for the development of nuclear energy and weapons.

Bethe's expertise in nuclear physics made him a natural choice for involvement in the Manhattan Project during World War II. In 1942, he was invited to join the project at Los Alamos Laboratory, where he was appointed head of the theoretical division. At Los Alamos, Bethe played a central role in the development of the atomic bomb. His leadership and deep understanding of nuclear processes were critical to the success of the project, particularly in solving complex problems related to the bomb's design and function.

One of Bethe's major contributions to the Manhattan Project was his work on the implosion mechanism used in the "Fat Man" bomb, which was dropped on Nagasaki. His theoretical calculations helped optimize the efficiency of the bomb, ensuring that it would achieve the desired explosive yield. While Bethe's work on the atomic bomb was scientifically remarkable, it also placed him at the center of one of the most morally complex issues of the 20th century—the use of nuclear weapons.

After the war, Bethe became a vocal advocate for the peaceful use of nuclear energy and for arms control. He was deeply aware of the devastating power of the weapons he had helped create and was committed to preventing their use in the future. Bethe's efforts in this regard were multifaceted. He was a key figure in the development of the hydrogen bomb, although he later expressed deep reservations about its deployment. He also played a significant role in the scientific community's efforts to promote nuclear disarmament and was an outspoken critic of the arms race during the Cold War.

Bethe's contributions to science extended far beyond his work on nuclear weapons. In the post-war years, he returned to Cornell University and continued to make groundbreaking contributions to a wide range of fields. His work on quantum electrodynamics, for example, was pivotal in advancing our understanding of the interactions between charged particles and electromagnetic fields. Bethe's calculation of the Lamb shift, a small difference in energy levels in hydrogen atoms, provided crucial experimental confirmation of quantum electrodynamics and earned him widespread acclaim in the scientific community.

In 1967, Bethe was awarded the Nobel Prize in Physics for his work on the theory of nuclear reactions, particularly his discoveries concerning the energy production in stars. The Nobel Committee recognized the profound impact of his research on our understanding of the universe and the fundamental processes that govern the behavior of matter at the atomic level. Bethe's Nobel Prize was a fitting recognition of his contributions to physics, but it was also just one of many honors he received during his illustrious career.

Throughout his life, Bethe remained deeply engaged with both scientific research and public policy. He was a passionate advocate for the responsible use of scientific knowledge and often spoke out on issues of national security, arms control, and energy policy. Bethe was instrumental in the scientific advisory process for the U.S. government, providing guidance on issues ranging from nuclear strategy to the peaceful use of atomic energy. His work in these areas reflected his belief that scientists had a moral obligation to consider the broader implications of their work and to use their expertise for the betterment of society.

Bethe's intellectual contributions were matched by his dedication to teaching and mentoring the next generation of physicists. At Cornell, he was known for his rigorous yet supportive approach to teaching, inspiring countless students to pursue careers in science. Many of Bethe's students went on to become prominent physicists, and his influence can be seen in the work of subsequent generations of scientists. His ability to convey complex ideas with clarity and precision made him a beloved teacher and a respected figure in the academic community.

Even in his later years, Bethe remained actively involved in research, continuing to publish papers and engage with new developments in physics well into his 90s. His work on supernovae, for example, provided important insights into the processes that lead to the explosive death of massive stars. Bethe's curiosity and passion for discovery never waned, and his contributions to science continued to grow, cementing his legacy as one of the most important physicists of the 20th century.

Hans Bethe passed away on March 6, 2005, at the age of 98, leaving behind a legacy that continues to resonate in the scientific community and beyond. His life and work exemplify the power of scientific inquiry to expand our understanding of the universe and to shape the course of history. Bethe's contributions to nuclear physics, astrophysics, and quantum mechanics have had a lasting impact on science, while his commitment to the ethical use of scientific knowledge has inspired generations of scientists to think critically about the implications of their work.

Bethe's story is one of intellectual brilliance, moral integrity, and a deep commitment to both science and humanity. His contributions to the Manhattan Project and his subsequent efforts to promote arms control highlight the complex relationship between science and society, while his groundbreaking research in nuclear physics and astrophysics continues to influence the field to this day. As we reflect on Hans Bethe's life and legacy, we are reminded of the importance of scientific inquiry, the need for ethical responsibility, and the enduring impact of those who dedicate their lives to the pursuit of knowledge.

Chapter 6: Richard Feynman

Richard Feynman, born on May 11, 1918, in Queens, New York, was an American physicist whose contributions to science, particularly in the field of quantum mechanics, have left an indelible mark on modern physics. Feynman was a scientist, educator, philosopher, and a man with an insatiable curiosity for the world around him. His life and work epitomize the intersection of genius, creativity, and a passion for understanding the fundamental laws that govern the universe. Feynman's journey from a precocious child in New York to one of the most celebrated physicists of the 20th century is a story of brilliance, unconventional thinking, and a relentless pursuit of knowledge.

Feynman's early years were shaped by his father's encouragement to think critically and to question everything. His father, Melville Feynman, was a uniform salesman with a deep interest in science, and he instilled in his son a love for learning and a skepticism of accepted norms. Feynman's mother, Lucille, contributed to his sense of humor and ability to connect with others, qualities that would later make him a beloved teacher and public figure. Feynman's intellectual gifts were evident from a young age. By the time he was a teenager, he had already taught himself advanced mathematics, including calculus, and had begun to delve into the complexities of physics.

After high school, Feynman attended the Massachusetts Institute of Technology (MIT), where he earned his bachelor's degree in 1939. His time at MIT was marked by a deepening interest in theoretical physics, and he quickly established himself as a prodigious talent. From MIT, Feynman went on to pursue his doctorate at Princeton University, where he studied under John Archibald Wheeler, one of the leading physicists of the time. At Princeton, Feynman worked on a variety of problems in quantum mechanics and electromagnetism, developing the ideas that would eventually lead to his Nobel Prize-winning work.

Feynman's doctoral thesis introduced the path integral formulation of quantum mechanics, a novel approach that provided a new way of understanding the behavior of particles at the quantum level. This formulation, which involved summing over all possible paths that a particle could take between two points, was a radical departure from the traditional methods of quantum mechanics and showcased Feynman's ability to think outside the box. His work on path integrals laid the groundwork for much of his later research and has become a standard tool in quantum field theory.

During World War II, Feynman was recruited to work on the Manhattan Project at Los Alamos Laboratory, where he contributed to the development of the atomic bomb. Feynman was one of the youngest scientists on the project, but his contributions were significant. He worked on various aspects of the bomb's design and safety mechanisms, and his work in calculating the explosive yields of nuclear materials was crucial to the success of the project. Despite the gravity of his work, Feynman approached the project with his characteristic curiosity and enthusiasm, often finding creative solutions to complex problems. His experiences at Los Alamos also exposed him to the moral and ethical dilemmas of scientific research, issues that would continue to influence his thinking throughout his life.

After the war, Feynman took a position as a professor at Cornell University, where he began to develop many of the ideas that would later define his career. It was during this time that he introduced the concept of Feynman diagrams, a graphical representation of the interactions between particles in quantum electrodynamics (QED). These diagrams provided a visual and intuitive way to understand the complex calculations involved in QED and became an essential tool for physicists working in the field. Feynman's work on QED, for which he shared the 1965 Nobel Prize in Physics with Julian Schwinger and Sin-Itiro Tomonaga, was a major achievement in theoretical physics and provided one of the most accurate descriptions of the interactions between light and matter.

Feynman's contributions to QED were part of a broader effort to reconcile the predictions of quantum mechanics with the principles of special relativity. His approach was characterized by a deep understanding of the underlying physical principles, combined with a willingness to challenge established ideas and explore new methods. Feynman's work not only advanced the field of quantum mechanics but also influenced a wide range of other areas in physics, from particle physics to condensed matter theory.

In 1950, Feynman accepted a position at the California Institute of Technology (Caltech), where he would spend the remainder of his career. At Caltech, Feynman continued to push the boundaries of physics, exploring new ideas and mentoring a generation of students who would go on to become leading scientists in their own right. His teaching style was legendary—Feynman was known for his ability to explain complex concepts in simple, intuitive terms, often using everyday examples to illustrate abstract ideas. His lectures were filled with humor, insight, and a contagious enthusiasm for science, and they attracted students from all disciplines.

Feynman's approach to teaching was perhaps best exemplified by the famous "Feynman Lectures on Physics," a series of introductory physics lectures he delivered at Caltech between 1961 and 1963. These lectures were later compiled into a three-volume set that has become one of the most popular and widely-read physics books of all time. The Feynman Lectures are renowned for their clarity, depth, and the way they convey the beauty and elegance of physics. They reflect Feynman's belief that science should be accessible to everyone and that complex ideas can be understood by anyone with the curiosity and willingness to learn.

In addition to his work in physics, Feynman was a polymath with interests in a wide range of subjects, from biology to philosophy, art, and music. He was an accomplished bongo player, a skilled safecracker (a hobby he picked up at Los Alamos), and a passionate advocate for the importance of scientific skepticism and critical thinking. Feynman's curiosity about the world was boundless, and he approached every subject with the same rigorous, yet playful, mindset that he brought to physics.

One of Feynman's most famous contributions to science outside of his work in quantum mechanics was his role in investigating the Space Shuttle Challenger disaster in 1986. Feynman was appointed to the Rogers Commission, which was tasked with determining the cause of the accident. His independent and unconventional approach to the investigation, which involved demonstrating the failure of the O-rings with a simple experiment using ice water, played a crucial role in uncovering the root cause of the disaster. Feynman's findings, and his insistence on the importance of honesty and transparency in science and engineering, were instrumental in highlighting the failures in NASA's decision-making process that led to the tragedy.

Throughout his life, Feynman remained a vocal advocate for the integrity of science. He often spoke out against pseudoscience, emphasizing the importance of evidence, experimentation, and skepticism. His famous lecture "Cargo Cult Science," delivered at Caltech in 1974, is a powerful critique of scientific practices that lack rigor and an admonition to always question assumptions and seek truth. Feynman's commitment to the scientific method and his disdain for dogma and authority made him a role model for scientists and educators around the world.

Feynman's influence extended beyond the scientific community. He became a cultural icon, known for his wit, humor, and unique perspective on life. His autobiographical books, "Surely You're

Joking, Mr. Feynman!" and "What Do You Care What Other People Think?" became bestsellers and introduced a wider audience to the life and thoughts of one of the most brilliant minds of the 20th century. These books, filled with anecdotes from Feynman's life, capture his playful spirit, his love of learning, and his unorthodox approach to both science and life.

Despite his many accolades and achievements, Feynman remained humble and grounded. He often downplayed his own contributions, preferring to focus on the joy of discovery rather than the recognition that came with it. Feynman's love of teaching and his ability to inspire others to think critically and creatively are perhaps his greatest legacies. His impact on the field of physics is immeasurable, but his influence on the way we think about science and the world around us is equally profound.

Feynman passed away on February 15, 1988, after a battle with cancer. His death marked the end of an era in physics, but his ideas and his approach to science continue to inspire generations of scientists, educators, and curious minds. Richard Feynman's life was a testament to the power of curiosity, the importance of questioning everything, and the joy that comes from exploring the unknown. He once said, "I would rather have questions that can't be answered than answers that can't be questioned." This philosophy guided his work and his life, and it is a philosophy that continues to resonate with those who seek to understand the world in all its complexity and wonder.

Feynman's contributions to science, his unique teaching style, and his infectious enthusiasm for learning have left an indelible mark on both the scientific community and popular culture. He was a man who reveled in the mysteries of the universe and who found joy in the process of discovery. His legacy is not only the groundbreaking work he did in quantum mechanics and other fields, but also the spirit of curiosity and skepticism he instilled in those who followed in his footsteps. Richard Feynman was a true original, a scientist who embraced the unknown and inspired others to do the same. His life reminds us that science is not just a collection of facts and equations, but a way of thinking, a way of seeing the world, and, above all, a way of finding joy in the exploration of the unknown.

Chapter 7: James Watson, Francis Crick, & Maurice Wilkins

James Watson, Francis Crick, and Maurice Wilkins are three towering figures in the history of science, whose collaboration and individual contributions led to one of the most groundbreaking discoveries of the 20th century—the structure of DNA. Their work revolutionized our understanding of genetics, laying the foundation for modern molecular biology, and has had far-reaching implications in medicine, biotechnology, and our understanding of life itself. The story of how these three scientists came together, along with Rosalind Franklin, to uncover the double helix structure of DNA is a tale of brilliance, competition, collaboration, and the relentless pursuit of knowledge.

James Dewey Watson was born on April 6, 1928, in Chicago, Illinois. He was a precocious child with a keen interest in birds and natural history, but it was during his college years that he discovered his passion for genetics. Watson attended the University of Chicago at the age of 15, where he was influenced by the work of the geneticist Hermann Joseph Muller. After earning his bachelor's degree in zoology, Watson went on to pursue his Ph.D. at Indiana University under the supervision of Salvador Luria, a leading figure in bacteriophage research. Watson's early research focused on the effects of X-rays on bacteriophage multiplication, but he soon became interested in the structure of DNA, inspired by Erwin Schrödinger's book *What is Life?*, which speculated on the molecular basis of heredity.

Francis Harry Compton Crick was born on June 8, 1916, in Northampton, England. Crick's path to molecular biology was not straightforward. He initially studied physics at University College London, but his studies were interrupted by World War II, during which he worked on the development of magnetic mines for the British Admiralty. After the war, Crick switched fields, driven by a desire to understand the fundamental principles of life. He began his Ph.D. work at Cambridge University, focusing on the physical properties of cytoplasm, but like Watson, he was captivated by the question of how genetic information is stored and transmitted in living organisms. Crick's background in physics equipped him with a unique perspective on biological problems, and he soon became interested in the structure of proteins and nucleic acids.

Maurice Hugh Frederick Wilkins was born on December 15, 1916, in Pongaroa, New Zealand. Wilkins' early life was spent in England, where he pursued his education in physics at St. John's College, Cambridge. During World War II, Wilkins worked on radar technology and later on the development of the atomic bomb as part of the Manhattan Project. After the war, he turned his attention to biology, joining the Biophysics Unit at King's College London, where he began to study the physical properties of DNA using X-ray crystallography. Wilkins was among the first to suggest that X-ray diffraction could be used to determine the structure of DNA, a method that would prove crucial in the discovery of the double helix.

The story of the discovery of DNA's structure is inextricably linked with that of Rosalind Franklin, whose work at King's College London provided critical evidence that led to Watson and Crick's model of the double helix. Franklin was an expert in X-ray crystallography, and her meticulous work produced some of the clearest images of DNA ever obtained. One of these images, known as Photograph 51, was shown to Watson and Crick without her knowledge by Maurice Wilkins. This photograph provided key insights into the helical structure of DNA, particularly the dimensions of the helix and the arrangement of its components.

Watson and Crick were working together at the Cavendish Laboratory at the University of Cambridge. They had been trying to solve the structure of DNA using model building, an approach that involved creating physical models of the molecule based on available experimental data. Their first attempts were unsuccessful, largely because they were working with incorrect assumptions about the structure of the molecule. However, once they saw Franklin's Photograph 51 and Wilkins' accompanying data, they were able to refine their model, leading to their historic breakthrough in 1953.

On February 28, 1953, Watson and Crick famously walked into The Eagle pub in Cambridge, where Crick announced that they had "found the secret of life." Their model of DNA, a double helix composed of two strands of nucleotides twisted around each other, was not only elegant but also immediately suggested how genetic information could be replicated and passed from one generation to the next. The key to their model was the pairing of the nitrogenous bases—adenine with thymine, and guanine with cytosine—held together by hydrogen bonds. This complementary base pairing explained how DNA could carry genetic information in its sequence of bases and how it could be accurately copied during cell division.

Watson and Crick's model was published in the April 25, 1953, issue of *Nature* in a brief paper titled "Molecular Structure of Nucleic Acids: A Structure for Deoxyribose Nucleic Acid." This paper, less than a page long, changed the course of biological science. In the same issue of *Nature*, two additional papers were published: one by Maurice Wilkins and his colleagues, and another by Rosalind Franklin and her student Raymond Gosling. These papers provided the experimental evidence that supported Watson and Crick's model, particularly the X-ray diffraction data that revealed the helical structure of DNA.

The discovery of the DNA double helix was not without controversy. Rosalind Franklin, who had produced the critical X-ray diffraction data, did not receive the recognition she deserved during her lifetime. Franklin died of ovarian cancer in 1958, four years before Watson, Crick, and Wilkins were awarded the Nobel Prize in Physiology or Medicine in 1962. The Nobel Prize is not awarded posthumously, so Franklin was not eligible, but many have argued that her contributions were not sufficiently acknowledged by Watson, Crick, or Wilkins in their Nobel lectures or in the years that followed.

The implications of the discovery of the DNA double helix were profound and far-reaching. It provided the foundation for the field of molecular biology, leading to our understanding of the genetic code, the process of transcription and translation, and the mechanisms of genetic inheritance. The knowledge of DNA's structure paved the way for the development of modern genetics, including the Human Genome Project, gene therapy, and the biotechnology industry. It also raised important ethical questions about the manipulation of genetic material, questions that continue to be debated today.

James Watson went on to have a distinguished career in science, becoming the first director of the Human Genome Project, which successfully mapped the entire human genome. Watson's later years, however, were marred by controversy due to his remarks on race and intelligence, which led to his resignation from his position at Cold Spring Harbor Laboratory and a tarnished legacy. Despite this, his contributions to the discovery of DNA's structure remain a cornerstone of modern biology.

Francis Crick continued his research at the Medical Research Council (MRC) Laboratory of Molecular Biology in Cambridge, where he turned his attention to the genetic code and the process by which DNA is translated into proteins. Crick proposed the "central dogma" of molecular biology, which describes the flow of genetic information from DNA to RNA to protein. In his later years, Crick shifted his focus to neuroscience, particularly the study of consciousness, a field he pursued until his death in 2004.

Maurice Wilkins remained at King's College London, where he continued his work on the structure of DNA and other biological molecules. Wilkins' contributions to the discovery of the DNA double helix were recognized with the Nobel Prize, but he lived a relatively quiet life compared to Watson and Crick. Wilkins' later work included studies on the structure of RNA and chromatin, and he remained active in the scientific community until his death in 2004.

The discovery of the DNA double helix is a testament to the power of collaboration and the importance of combining different scientific disciplines—physics, chemistry, and biology—to solve complex problems. It is also a story of the human side of science, with all its rivalries, ethical dilemmas, and moments of brilliance. Watson, Crick, and Wilkins, along with Rosalind Franklin, unlocked the molecular secrets of life, a discovery that has transformed our understanding of biology and continues to shape the future of science and medicine. Their work stands as one of the greatest achievements in the history of science, a discovery that has fundamentally changed our understanding of who we are and how life operates at the most basic level.

Chapter 8: Albert A. Michelson

Albert Abraham Michelson, a pioneering figure in the field of physics, holds a distinguished place in the annals of scientific history for his groundbreaking work in the precise measurement of the speed of light and for the development of the Michelson interferometer. His meticulous experiments and innovative contributions to optical physics not only earned him the Nobel Prize in Physics in 1907, making him the first American scientist to receive this honor, but also laid the groundwork for future advancements in the study of light and the nature of space and time. Michelson's life and work are emblematic of the transformative power of science and the relentless pursuit of knowledge.

Born on December 19, 1852, in Strelno, Prussia (now Strzelno, Poland), Michelson immigrated to the United States with his family when he was just a child. His early life in California was marked by modesty, but his keen intellect quickly set him apart. At the age of 17, he entered the United States Naval Academy in Annapolis, Maryland, where he began his formal education in the sciences. Although his initial focus was on navigation and naval engineering, Michelson's interest in physics, particularly optics, soon took precedence. His fascination with the properties of light would define his career and lead him to explore some of the most fundamental questions in physics.

Upon graduating from the Naval Academy in 1873, Michelson was appointed an instructor of physics and chemistry there, a position that allowed him to pursue his interest in the measurement of the speed of light. The speed of light had been a subject of intense scientific inquiry since the time of Galileo, but by the 19th century, it had become clear that more precise measurements were needed. Michelson, with his meticulous nature and innovative thinking, was well-suited to this task. In 1877, he conducted his first experiments on the speed of light using a modified version of Léon Foucault's rotating mirror apparatus. His measurements, conducted with a level of precision previously unattained, were more accurate than any that had been made before. Michelson's early work caught the attention of the scientific community and set the stage for his future achievements.

In 1880, Michelson left the Navy to study in Europe, where he worked with some of the most prominent physicists of the time, including Hermann von Helmholtz in Berlin and Gustav Kirchhoff in Heidelberg. During his time in Europe, Michelson continued to refine his techniques for measuring the speed of light and developed the interferometer, an instrument that would become central to his most famous experiments. The Michelson interferometer, which uses the interference of light waves to measure very small distances, was a revolutionary tool that allowed for unprecedented precision in the measurement of wavelengths and distances.

The interferometer's most famous application came in 1887 when Michelson, along with his colleague Edward Morley, conducted what is now known as the Michelson-Morley experiment. This experiment was designed to detect the presence of the "aether," a hypothetical medium through which light was thought to propagate, much like sound waves travel through air. The concept of the aether was widely accepted at the time, as it was believed to be the substance that filled the void of space and provided a medium for the transmission of electromagnetic waves.

The Michelson-Morley experiment was ingeniously simple in its design but profound in its implications. By comparing the speed of light in perpendicular directions—one parallel to the presumed motion of the Earth through the aether and the other perpendicular to it—Michelson and Morley expected to observe a difference in the speed of light, which would provide evidence for the existence of the aether. However, the results of their experiment were entirely unexpected: no such difference was observed. The speed of light was found to be the same in all directions, regardless of the Earth's motion. This null result was a monumental finding, as it contradicted the aether theory and challenged the prevailing understanding of light and space.

The implications of the Michelson-Morley experiment were not immediately understood, but it eventually became one of the key pieces of evidence leading to the development of Albert Einstein's theory of special relativity. Einstein's theory, which revolutionized physics, proposed that the speed of light is constant in all inertial frames of reference and that time and space are not absolute but relative to the observer's motion. The rejection of the aether concept and the affirmation of the constancy of the speed of light were foundational to Einstein's work, making the Michelson-Morley experiment one of the most significant experiments in the history of physics.

Michelson's contributions to science, however, were not limited to this singular experiment. Throughout his career, he continued to innovate and refine techniques for optical measurement. His work extended to the measurement of the wavelengths of spectral lines and the precise determination of the standard meter in terms of the wavelength of light. Michelson's determination of the speed of light, which he measured repeatedly throughout his life, set a new standard for precision in scientific measurement and remained the most accurate value for decades.

In 1892, Michelson became a professor at the University of Chicago, where he would spend the rest of his career. His tenure at Chicago was marked by continued experimentation and theoretical work in optics and spectroscopy. He also played a significant role in establishing the university as a leading center for scientific research in the United States. Michelson's influence on his students and colleagues was profound, and he became a mentor to a generation of physicists who would go on to make their own significant contributions to the field.

In 1907, Michelson was awarded the Nobel Prize in Physics "for his precision optical instruments and the spectroscopic and metrological investigations carried out with their aid." This recognition was a testament to the significance of his work and his contributions to the advancement of science. Michelson's Nobel Prize was particularly noteworthy as it marked the first time an American scientist had received this prestigious honor, signaling the emergence of the United States as a major center of scientific research.

Michelson's later years were dedicated to even more ambitious projects. One of his final achievements was the measurement of the diameter of the star Betelgeuse using an interferometer attached to a telescope at the Mount Wilson Observatory. This was the first time the size of a star other than the Sun had been measured, and it demonstrated the power of interferometry in astronomical observations. Michelson's work in this area paved the way for future developments in the field of observational astronomy and the study of celestial bodies.

Albert Michelson passed away on May 9, 1931, but his legacy endures. His contributions to the precise measurement of light and the development of instruments that could measure distances with extraordinary accuracy have had a lasting impact on physics. The Michelson interferometer remains a fundamental tool in physics laboratories around the world, used in a wide range of applications from studying gravitational waves to testing the limits of quantum mechanics.

Michelson's life and work exemplify the relentless pursuit of scientific knowledge and the importance of precision in experimental science. His experiments, characterized by their meticulous design and execution, pushed the boundaries of what was possible in the measurement of light and laid the foundation for some of the most important developments in modern physics. Albert A. Michelson's legacy is not just in the discoveries he made, but in the rigorous approach to scientific inquiry that he exemplified, an approach that continues to inspire physicists and scientists to this day.

Chapter 9: Ramakrishnan, Steitz, & Yonath

Venkatraman Ramakrishnan, Thomas A. Steitz, and Ada Yonath are three prominent scientists who have made monumental contributions to the field of molecular biology, specifically in understanding the structure and function of the ribosome. Their work, which culminated in a shared Nobel Prize in Chemistry in 2009, has profoundly advanced our knowledge of the molecular machinery that drives life at its most fundamental level: the synthesis of proteins. The ribosome, a complex molecular machine within the cell, is responsible for translating genetic information encoded in messenger RNA (mRNA) into proteins, which are essential for virtually all cellular processes. By elucidating the structure of the ribosome at an atomic level, Ramakrishnan, Steitz, and Yonath provided critical insights into how this process works, paving the way for numerous advances in medicine, genetics, and biotechnology.

The story of their work is one of perseverance, innovation, and collaboration, spanning decades of research and countless hours in the laboratory. The ribosome is one of the most complex and vital structures within living cells, and understanding its function has been a challenge for scientists for many years. The ribosome is composed of two subunits, each made up of ribosomal RNA (rRNA) and proteins. The larger subunit catalyzes the formation of peptide bonds, linking amino acids together to form proteins, while the smaller subunit is responsible for decoding the mRNA sequence. The precise arrangement of these components and their interactions during protein synthesis was not fully understood until the advent of advanced techniques in X-ray crystallography, which allowed researchers to visualize the ribosome's structure at an unprecedented level of detail.

Ada Yonath, an Israeli crystallographer, was a pioneer in the effort to determine the structure of the ribosome. Born in 1939 in Jerusalem, Yonath showed an early interest in science, despite the challenges she faced growing up in a modest family during turbulent times. Her determination led her to pursue a career in biochemistry and structural biology, fields that were still relatively undeveloped in Israel at the time. Yonath's early work focused on the crystallization of biological molecules, a crucial step in determining their three-dimensional structures using X-ray crystallography. However, the ribosome presented an enormous challenge for crystallographers due to its large size and complexity.

Yonath's breakthrough came in the late 1970s and early 1980s when she developed a novel method for crystallizing the ribosome by using ribosomes from extremophiles—organisms that thrive in extreme environments. These ribosomes were more robust and stable, making them more amenable to crystallization. Yonath's innovative approach led to the first successful crystallization of ribosomal subunits, a feat that had eluded scientists for decades. This achievement was a critical first step in the journey to determine the ribosome's structure, as it provided the necessary material for X-ray diffraction experiments.

Around the same time, Thomas A. Steitz, an American biochemist, was also making significant strides in the study of the ribosome. Born in 1940 in Milwaukee, Wisconsin, Steitz developed an early passion for chemistry, which he pursued throughout his education. After completing his Ph.D. at Harvard University, Steitz became a leader in the field of structural biology, particularly in the study of large molecular complexes using X-ray crystallography. His work on the structure of enzymes and nucleic acids set the stage for his later focus on the ribosome.

Steitz's approach to understanding the ribosome involved not just crystallization but also the development of advanced computational methods to interpret the data obtained from X-ray diffraction experiments. These techniques allowed for the construction of detailed models of the ribosome's structure, revealing how the ribosomal RNA and proteins were arranged and how they interacted with mRNA and transfer RNA (tRNA) during protein synthesis. Steitz's work was instrumental in demonstrating how the ribosome functions as a highly coordinated molecular machine, with each component playing a specific role in the translation process.

Venkatraman Ramakrishnan, an Indian-born American structural biologist, also made critical contributions to the study of the ribosome. Born in 1952 in Chidambaram, India, Ramakrishnan was initially trained as a physicist before transitioning to biology, a move that allowed him to apply his expertise in physics and mathematics to the study of complex biological systems. After completing his Ph.D. in physics at Ohio University, Ramakrishnan shifted his focus to structural biology, recognizing the potential of X-ray crystallography to unravel the mysteries of large biological molecules.

Ramakrishnan's work on the ribosome was characterized by his innovative use of cryo-electron microscopy and X-ray crystallography to obtain high-resolution images of the ribosomal subunits. His research provided crucial insights into the structure of the small ribosomal subunit, which is responsible for reading the mRNA sequence and ensuring that the correct amino acids are incorporated into the growing protein chain. Ramakrishnan's findings illuminated the intricate details of how the ribosome discriminates between different tRNAs and how antibiotics can target bacterial ribosomes to inhibit protein synthesis.

The combined efforts of Yonath, Steitz, and Ramakrishnan led to a series of groundbreaking discoveries that culminated in the complete atomic-level structures of both the small and large ribosomal subunits. These structures revealed the precise arrangement of the ribosomal RNA and proteins, showing how they interact to perform the complex task of translating genetic information into proteins. The researchers also uncovered the mechanisms by which the ribosome catalyzes peptide bond formation, a fundamental reaction in biology that links amino acids together to form proteins.

One of the most significant outcomes of their work was the discovery of the ribosome's role as a ribozyme—a type of RNA molecule that has catalytic activity. This finding was revolutionary because it challenged the long-held view that proteins were the only biological molecules capable of catalysis. The realization that the ribosome's catalytic core is made up of RNA, not protein, provided strong evidence for the "RNA world" hypothesis, which suggests that early life forms may have relied on RNA for both genetic information storage and catalytic functions before the evolution of proteins.

The implications of the work of Yonath, Steitz, and Ramakrishnan extend far beyond basic science. The detailed knowledge of ribosomal structure has had a profound impact on the development of antibiotics. Many antibiotics work by targeting the bacterial ribosome, disrupting protein synthesis and thereby killing or inhibiting the growth of bacteria. Understanding the structure of the ribosome has allowed scientists to design new antibiotics that are more effective and have fewer side effects, a critical development in the fight against antibiotic-resistant bacteria.

In addition to their scientific achievements, Yonath, Steitz, and Ramakrishnan have served as mentors and role models for countless young scientists around the world. Their work exemplifies the power of collaboration and the importance of perseverance in scientific research. Despite the many challenges they faced, including technical difficulties and the skepticism of some in the scientific community, they remained committed to their goal of understanding the ribosome at the most fundamental level.

The Nobel Prize in Chemistry awarded to Yonath, Steitz, and Ramakrishnan in 2009 was a fitting recognition of their monumental contributions to science. The Nobel Committee cited their work as a "milestone in the life sciences" that has transformed our understanding of one of the most essential processes in biology. The award also highlighted the international nature of scientific research, as the three laureates came from different backgrounds and worked in different parts of the world, yet their efforts converged on a shared goal.

Ada Yonath's pioneering work in ribosome crystallization, Thomas Steitz's leadership in structural biology, and Venkatraman Ramakrishnan's innovative use of cryo-electron microscopy and X-ray crystallography have collectively advanced our understanding of the molecular basis of life. Their discoveries have opened new avenues of research in molecular biology, genetics, and medicine, and their legacy continues to inspire future generations of scientists. The story of Ramakrishnan, Steitz, and Yonath is not just one of scientific achievement, but also one of the power of curiosity, determination, and collaboration in the quest to understand the fundamental mechanisms of life.

Chapter 10: Sauvage, Stoddart, & Feringa

Jean-Pierre Sauvage, Sir Fraser Stoddart, and Bernard Feringa are three distinguished scientists who were jointly awarded the Nobel Prize in Chemistry in 2016 for their groundbreaking work in the design and synthesis of molecular machines. These tiny devices, made of molecules, represent a revolutionary step forward in nanotechnology and hold the potential to transform numerous fields, including medicine, materials science, and electronics. The trio's pioneering efforts have pushed the boundaries of chemistry, leading to the creation of molecules that can perform mechanical tasks, an achievement that seemed almost unimaginable just a few decades ago. Their work is a testament to human ingenuity and the relentless pursuit of knowledge, as they each played a crucial role in transforming the dream of molecular machines into reality.

The story of their achievements begins with Jean-Pierre Sauvage, a French chemist born in 1944. Sauvage's early work in chemistry was influenced by his mentor, Jean-Marie Lehn, who won the Nobel Prize in Chemistry in 1987 for his work on supramolecular chemistry. Supramolecular chemistry, the study of non-covalent interactions between molecules, provided the foundation for Sauvage's later work. In 1983, Sauvage made a significant breakthrough by successfully synthesizing a catenane, a molecule consisting of two interlocked rings. This achievement was groundbreaking because it demonstrated the possibility of creating mechanically interlocked molecules, which are essential components of molecular machines. The interlocking rings in a catenane are not chemically bonded but are linked in such a way that they cannot be separated without breaking the rings. This interlocking structure allows for relative motion between the rings, a feature that Sauvage recognized could be harnessed to perform mechanical work at the molecular level.

Sauvage's work on catenanes laid the groundwork for the development of more complex molecular machines. He and his team continued to explore the potential of interlocked molecules, creating molecular systems that could undergo controlled movements. In the 1990s, Sauvage successfully synthesized a molecular system in which a copper ion moved between different positions within a molecule, effectively creating a molecular switch. This work was a significant step towards the creation of functional molecular machines, as it demonstrated that molecules could be designed to perform specific tasks when triggered by external stimuli, such as light or heat.

While Sauvage was pioneering the field of interlocked molecules, Fraser Stoddart, a Scottish chemist born in 1942, was making his own groundbreaking contributions to the field of molecular machines. Stoddart's work focused on the development of rotaxanes, another type of mechanically interlocked molecule. A rotaxane consists of a molecular "ring" that is threaded onto a molecular "axle," with bulky groups at either end of the axle preventing the ring from slipping off. This setup allows the ring to move back and forth along the axle, much like a bead on a string. Stoddart's innovation was to harness this motion to create molecular machines that could perform mechanical tasks.

In the 1990s, Stoddart and his team developed the first molecular "shuttle," a rotaxane in which the ring moved between two different stations on the axle. This movement could be controlled by external stimuli, such as changes in pH or the presence of certain chemicals. Stoddart's work demonstrated that it was possible to create molecular systems that could perform controlled, reversible movements, a key requirement for the development of functional molecular machines. His research opened up new possibilities for the design of molecular devices, including molecular elevators, switches, and motors.

One of Stoddart's most significant achievements was the development of a molecular motor, a rotaxane-based system that could convert chemical energy into mechanical work. This molecular motor operated by using the energy released from a chemical reaction to drive the movement of the ring along the axle, much like how a traditional motor converts electrical energy into mechanical motion. Stoddart's work on molecular motors represented a major advance in the field of nanotechnology, as it provided a blueprint for how molecular machines could be powered and controlled.

Meanwhile, Bernard Feringa, a Dutch chemist born in 1951, was also making significant contributions to the development of molecular machines. Feringa's work focused on the design and synthesis of molecular motors and rotary switches, systems that could undergo controlled rotational movements. In 1999, Feringa achieved a major breakthrough by creating the first molecular motor that could rotate in a single direction when exposed to light. This molecular motor consisted of a molecule with a chiral center, which allowed it to rotate in a specific direction when exposed to ultraviolet light. The motor could complete a full rotation in four steps, with each step being triggered by a pulse of light.

Feringa's molecular motor was a remarkable achievement, as it demonstrated that it was possible to design and build a molecular system that could perform a continuous, directional motion. This work opened up new possibilities for the development of nanoscale machines that could perform complex tasks, such as moving cargo, pumping fluids, or assembling other molecules. Feringa's motor was also notable for its efficiency, as it could complete millions of rotations per second, making it one of the fastest molecular machines ever created.

The contributions of Sauvage, Stoddart, and Feringa to the field of molecular machines have had far-reaching implications for science and technology. Their work has paved the way for the development of new materials and devices with applications in medicine, electronics, and energy. For example, molecular machines could be used to deliver drugs to specific cells in the body, improving the precision and effectiveness of treatments. They could also be used to create new types of sensors, switches, and memory devices that operate at the nanoscale, leading to advances in computing and information storage.

The potential applications of molecular machines are vast, and scientists are just beginning to explore the possibilities. The work of Sauvage, Stoddart, and Feringa has provided the foundation for this burgeoning field, and their innovations continue to inspire new research and development. Their contributions have also highlighted the importance of interdisciplinary collaboration in science, as their work drew on principles from chemistry, physics, and materials science to achieve its goals.

The awarding of the Nobel Prize in Chemistry to Sauvage, Stoddart, and Feringa in 2016 was a recognition of their pioneering work in the field of molecular machines. The Nobel Committee praised their "design and synthesis of molecular machines" as an achievement that "takes chemistry to a new dimension." The award also underscored the importance of creativity and imagination in scientific research, as the development of molecular machines required not only technical skill but also a visionary approach to problem-solving.

The work of Sauvage, Stoddart, and Feringa has also had a significant impact on the broader scientific community, inspiring new generations of researchers to explore the possibilities of molecular machines. Their achievements have demonstrated that it is possible to create functional devices at the molecular level, a concept that was once considered the realm of science fiction. Their work has also highlighted the potential of chemistry to address some of the most pressing challenges facing society, from developing new materials and technologies to advancing our understanding of the fundamental processes of life.

In addition to their scientific achievements, Sauvage, Stoddart, and Feringa have been influential mentors and educators, training and inspiring many young scientists who have gone on to make their own contributions to the field. Their work has also been characterized by a spirit of collaboration and openness, as they have freely shared their knowledge and expertise with the scientific community. This collaborative approach has been crucial to the success of the field of molecular machines, as it has allowed researchers to build on each other's work and make rapid progress.

The story of Jean-Pierre Sauvage, Fraser Stoddart, and Bernard Feringa is a testament to the power of scientific inquiry and the potential of chemistry to transform our understanding of the world. Their work on molecular machines has opened up new frontiers in science and technology, and their legacy will continue to shape the field for years to come. As researchers continue to explore the possibilities of molecular machines, they will build on the foundation laid by these three pioneering scientists, whose contributions have fundamentally changed the way we think about chemistry and its role in the modern world.

The field of molecular machines is still in its early stages, but the work of Sauvage, Stoddart, and Feringa has provided a clear roadmap for future research. Scientists are now exploring ways to integrate molecular machines into larger systems, such as nanorobots or smart materials, that can perform complex tasks in response to environmental cues. These systems could have a wide range of applications, from targeted drug delivery to the creation of adaptive materials that can change their properties in response to external stimuli.

As the field of molecular machines continues to evolve, the work of Sauvage, Stoddart, and Feringa will remain a cornerstone of the discipline. Their pioneering contributions have not only advanced our understanding of the fundamental principles of chemistry but have also opened up new possibilities for innovation and discovery. The potential of molecular machines to revolutionize technology and improve human life is immense, and the work of these three scientists has laid the foundation for this exciting and rapidly developing field. Their legacy will continue to inspire future generations of scientists as they explore the possibilities of the molecular world and seek to harness its potential for the benefit of society.

Chapter 11: Arthur Ashkin

Arthur Ashkin, born on September 2, 1922, in Brooklyn, New York, was a physicist whose groundbreaking work in the field of optics and laser technology earned him a share of the Nobel Prize in Physics in 2018. His most notable contribution to science is the invention of optical tweezers, a technology that uses laser beams to manipulate microscopic particles, including biological molecules, without physical contact. This invention revolutionized several fields of research, particularly in biology and medicine, by enabling scientists to study and manipulate cells, viruses, and other tiny entities with unprecedented precision.

Ashkin's journey into the world of physics began with his education at Columbia University, where he earned a bachelor's degree in physics in 1947. He then went on to pursue graduate studies at Cornell University, earning a Ph.D. in nuclear physics in 1952. After completing his education, Ashkin joined Bell Laboratories, where he began his research career. Although his early work at Bell Labs focused on microwave technology and non-linear optics, it was his later work on lasers that would lead to his most significant contributions.

In the 1960s, lasers were still a relatively new technology, and researchers were just beginning to explore their potential applications. Ashkin was fascinated by the possibilities lasers offered and began investigating how light could be used to exert forces on small particles. He was particularly interested in the concept of radiation pressure, a phenomenon where light exerts a force on objects due to the momentum carried by photons. While radiation pressure had been known since the early 20th century, it had not been widely explored as a practical tool for manipulating objects.

Ashkin's breakthrough came in 1970 when he discovered that laser light could be used to trap and move microscopic particles. By focusing a laser beam into a narrow point, Ashkin found that he could create a region of intense light that would exert a force on small particles, pulling them towards the center of the beam. This force was strong enough to hold the particles in place, effectively trapping them in a small region of space. Ashkin's discovery was revolutionary, as it demonstrated that light could be used not just to illuminate or measure objects, but also to physically manipulate them.

Ashkin initially called his invention "optical traps," but the technology later became known as "optical tweezers" due to its ability to pick up and move tiny objects, much like a pair of tweezers. Optical tweezers quickly gained recognition as a powerful tool in physics, allowing researchers to study small particles and forces at the microscopic level with unprecedented precision. The ability to trap and manipulate particles using light opened up new possibilities in many areas of science, from studying the properties of atoms and molecules to exploring the behavior of biological cells.

One of the most significant applications of optical tweezers is in the field of biophysics, where they have been used to study the mechanical properties of biological molecules such as DNA and proteins. By attaching microscopic beads to molecules and then using optical tweezers to stretch or manipulate them, scientists can measure the forces involved in various biological processes, such as the folding and unfolding of proteins or the interactions between DNA and other molecules. This ability to study molecular mechanics at such a fine scale has provided invaluable insights into the fundamental processes of life and has advanced our understanding of diseases and potential treatments.

In addition to their applications in biology, optical tweezers have also been used in other fields, such as chemistry and material science. For example, they have been employed to manipulate and assemble microscopic structures, allowing researchers to build complex nanoscale devices and materials. The precision offered by optical tweezers makes them ideal for tasks that require the manipulation of individual molecules or particles, such as sorting different types of cells or assembling molecular machines.

Ashkin's invention of optical tweezers is widely regarded as one of the most important technological advancements in modern science. It has not only enabled new research possibilities but has also led to the development of new techniques and tools that have become essential in laboratories around the world. The impact of optical tweezers on science and technology cannot be overstated, as they have transformed our ability to study and manipulate the microscopic world.

Despite the significance of his invention, Ashkin's work went largely unrecognized by the broader scientific community for many years. It was not until much later in his career that he began to receive the recognition he deserved. In 2018, at the age of 96, Ashkin was awarded the Nobel Prize in Physics, becoming the oldest person to ever receive the prestigious award. The Nobel Committee recognized Ashkin for his "groundbreaking inventions in the field of laser physics," specifically highlighting his development of optical tweezers.

Ashkin's contributions to science extend beyond the invention of optical tweezers. Throughout his career, he made significant contributions to the field of nonlinear optics, particularly in the study of second-harmonic generation, a process in which two photons of the same frequency interact with a material to produce a new photon with twice the frequency of the original photons. His work in this area laid the foundation for many advances in laser technology and optical communications.

In addition to his scientific achievements, Ashkin was known for his relentless curiosity and passion for discovery. Even in his later years, he continued to conduct research in his home laboratory, driven by a deep desire to explore the mysteries of the universe. His work ethic and dedication to science were an inspiration to many, and his legacy continues to influence researchers around the world.

Ashkin's invention of optical tweezers has had a profound impact on numerous fields, leading to new discoveries and advancements in our understanding of the natural world. The ability to manipulate and study microscopic particles with such precision has opened up new avenues of research that were previously unimaginable. The implications of his work are vast, with potential applications in medicine, biology, chemistry, and beyond.

One area where optical tweezers have shown great promise is in the study of single molecules and molecular interactions. By using optical tweezers to manipulate individual molecules, researchers can investigate the forces and dynamics involved in molecular processes with unprecedented detail. This has led to new insights into the mechanics of enzymes, the behavior of molecular motors, and the interactions between DNA and proteins. Such research is crucial for understanding the fundamental processes that underlie life and could lead to the development of new therapies for diseases.

In the field of medicine, optical tweezers have been used to study the mechanical properties of cells and tissues, providing valuable information about how cells respond to different stimuli and how diseases such as cancer affect cellular behavior. This research has the potential to improve our understanding of disease progression and could lead to the development of new diagnostic tools and treatments. For example, by measuring the stiffness of cancer cells, researchers can gain insights into how the disease spreads and identify potential targets for therapy.

Optical tweezers have also been used in the development of new materials and nanotechnology. By manipulating nanoparticles and assembling them into complex structures, scientists can create new materials with unique properties, such as enhanced strength, conductivity, or reactivity. These materials could have a wide range of applications, from more efficient solar cells to advanced drug delivery systems. The precision offered by optical tweezers makes them ideal for assembling nanoscale devices and materials, paving the way for future innovations in technology and engineering.

Another exciting application of optical tweezers is in the study of quantum mechanics. By trapping and manipulating individual atoms or particles, researchers can explore the fundamental principles of quantum physics and test theories that are difficult to investigate using traditional methods. This research could lead to new discoveries in the field of quantum computing and quantum information, with potential applications in secure communication, cryptography, and other areas of technology.

Ashkin's work on optical tweezers has also inspired the development of related technologies, such as optical traps for atoms and ions, which are used in experiments involving cold atoms and quantum optics. These technologies have opened up new possibilities for studying the behavior of matter at extremely low temperatures, leading to advances in our understanding of quantum phenomena and the development of new quantum technologies.

Throughout his career, Ashkin remained a humble and dedicated scientist, driven by a deep curiosity about the natural world. His contributions to science have had a lasting impact, influencing countless researchers and leading to new discoveries and innovations. His invention of optical tweezers is a prime example of how fundamental research can lead to transformative technologies that have far-reaching implications for society.

In addition to his scientific achievements, Ashkin's life and career serve as a reminder of the importance of perseverance and dedication in the pursuit of knowledge. His work ethic, creativity, and passion for discovery continue to inspire scientists around the world, and his legacy will undoubtedly endure for generations to come.

Arthur Ashkin's contributions to the field of optics and laser technology have forever changed the landscape of modern science. His invention of optical tweezers has provided researchers with a powerful tool for exploring the microscopic world, leading to new discoveries and advancements in a wide range of fields. The impact of his work is felt not only in the scientific community but also in the broader society, as the technologies and knowledge he helped develop continue to shape our understanding of the world and drive progress in medicine, technology, and beyond.

Chapter 12: Stanley Prusiner

Stanley Ben Prusiner, born on May 28, 1942, in Des Moines, Iowa, is a neurologist and biochemist whose groundbreaking work on prions earned him the Nobel Prize in Physiology or Medicine in 1997. Prusiner's discovery of prions—infectious proteins that cause neurodegenerative diseases—revolutionized our understanding of disease pathology and challenged long-held beliefs in molecular biology. His work not only shed light on the mechanisms underlying several devastating brain diseases but also opened new avenues of research into protein misfolding and its implications for human health.

Prusiner's journey into the world of medical research began with his education at the University of Pennsylvania, where he earned his bachelor's degree in chemistry in 1964. He continued his studies at the same institution, receiving his M.D. in 1968. Following his medical degree, Prusiner completed an internship in internal medicine at the University of California, San Francisco (UCSF), before moving on to the National Institutes of Health (NIH) in Bethesda, Maryland, where he worked as a clinical associate. It was during his time at the NIH that Prusiner developed a deep interest in the brain and its diseases, which would eventually lead him to the field of neurology.

In the early 1970s, Prusiner returned to UCSF to complete his residency in neurology. It was here that he encountered a patient with Creutzfeldt-Jakob disease (CJD), a rare and fatal neurodegenerative disorder. This encounter sparked Prusiner's interest in understanding the disease's underlying cause, a curiosity that would drive his research for years to come. At the time, the prevailing scientific consensus was that infectious agents, such as bacteria or viruses, were responsible for diseases like CJD. However,

Prusiner's research would ultimately challenge this view and propose a radical new concept in biology.

In 1982, Prusiner published a seminal paper in which he introduced the term "prion" (derived from "proteinaceous infectious particle") to describe a novel class of infectious agents composed solely of protein, with no nucleic acid component like DNA or RNA. Prions were unlike any other known pathogens; they were simply misfolded proteins that could induce normal proteins in the brain to misfold as well, leading to a cascade of protein misfolding and aggregation. This process resulted in the formation of insoluble amyloid plaques in the brain, which are characteristic of prion diseases.

Prusiner's prion hypothesis was initially met with skepticism and resistance from the scientific community. The idea that a protein, without any genetic material, could cause an infectious disease went against the central dogma of molecular biology, which held that nucleic acids were the carriers of genetic information and the agents of infection. Despite the criticism, Prusiner continued to amass evidence supporting his hypothesis, conducting meticulous experiments to demonstrate that prions could replicate and transmit disease in the absence of nucleic acids.

One of the key pieces of evidence for Prusiner's prion hypothesis came from studies of scrapie, a neurodegenerative disease affecting sheep and goats. Scrapie had been known for centuries, but its cause remained a mystery. Prusiner and his colleagues were able to show that the infectious agent responsible for scrapie was a misfolded protein that could induce the misfolding of the normal prion protein (PrP) in the brains of infected animals. This finding provided strong support for the idea that prions were the causative agents of neurodegenerative diseases.

Further research by Prusiner and others revealed that prion diseases were not limited to animals. In addition to scrapie and CJD, prions were implicated in a range of other neurodegenerative disorders, including bovine spongiform encephalopathy (BSE), also known as "mad cow disease," and its human equivalent, variant Creutzfeldt-Jakob disease (vCJD). These diseases are characterized by the progressive degeneration of brain tissue, leading to symptoms such as dementia, motor dysfunction, and, ultimately, death. The discovery of prions provided a unifying explanation for these diseases, linking them to a common molecular mechanism involving protein misfolding.

Prusiner's work also had broader implications for our understanding of other neurodegenerative diseases, such as Alzheimer's, Parkinson's, and Huntington's diseases. Although these conditions are not caused by prions in the strict sense, they share similar pathological features, including the accumulation of misfolded proteins in the brain. This realization has led to the concept of "prion-like" mechanisms in these diseases, where misfolded proteins propagate by inducing the misfolding of their normal counterparts, much like prions do. This has opened new avenues of research aimed at understanding the role of protein misfolding in a wide range of neurodegenerative conditions and has highlighted the potential for developing therapies that target these processes.

In recognition of his pioneering work, Stanley Prusiner was awarded the Nobel Prize in Physiology or Medicine in 1997. The Nobel Committee acknowledged his discovery of prions as a major breakthrough in our understanding of infectious diseases and neurodegeneration. The award was not only a personal triumph for Prusiner but also a validation of his persistence and commitment to challenging established scientific dogma. His work has since become a cornerstone of modern neuroscience and has inspired countless researchers to explore the mysteries of prion diseases and protein misfolding.

Beyond his Nobel Prize, Prusiner's contributions to science have been recognized with numerous other awards and honors, including the Albert Lasker Award for Basic Medical Research, the Wolf Prize in Medicine, and the National Medal of Science. He has also held prominent academic positions, including serving as the director of the Institute for Neurodegenerative Diseases at UCSF, where he has continued to lead research on prions and related diseases.

Prusiner's discovery of prions has had profound implications for public health and disease prevention. The recognition that prions are responsible for diseases like BSE and vCJD has led to significant changes in food safety regulations, particularly in the beef industry, to prevent the spread of prion-contaminated products. It has also spurred the development of diagnostic tests to detect prion diseases in humans and animals, as well as research into potential therapies to treat or prevent these diseases.

Despite the progress that has been made, prion diseases remain incurable, and much about them is still not fully understood. The challenge of developing effective treatments for prion diseases is compounded by the fact that prions are highly resistant to traditional methods of sterilization and decontamination, making them particularly difficult to eliminate from infected tissues or environments. Moreover, the long incubation period of prion diseases means that individuals may be infected for years or even decades before symptoms appear, complicating efforts to diagnose and treat the diseases early.

One of the most pressing questions in prion research is understanding the precise molecular mechanisms by which prions induce protein misfolding and how this process leads to neurodegeneration. Researchers are also investigating whether similar mechanisms are involved in other neurodegenerative diseases and whether targeting these mechanisms could provide new therapeutic strategies. The study of prions has also raised important questions about the nature of protein structure and function, challenging our understanding of how proteins fold, maintain their shapes, and interact with other molecules in the cell.

In addition to his scientific work, Stanley Prusiner has been an outspoken advocate for increased funding and support for research on neurodegenerative diseases. He has emphasized the importance of basic research in uncovering the fundamental mechanisms of disease and has called for greater investment in the development of new treatments and diagnostic tools. Prusiner's advocacy has helped to raise awareness of the devastating impact of prion diseases and has contributed to efforts to find cures for these and other neurodegenerative conditions.

Prusiner's legacy extends beyond his scientific discoveries to his role as a mentor and educator. Throughout his career, he has trained and inspired numerous students, postdoctoral fellows, and junior faculty members, many of whom have gone on to make significant contributions to the field of neuroscience. His commitment to fostering the next generation of scientists reflects his belief in the importance of curiosity-driven research and the pursuit of knowledge for its own sake.

In conclusion, Stanley Prusiner's discovery of prions represents one of the most significant advances in modern medicine and molecular biology. His work has transformed our understanding of infectious diseases and neurodegeneration, challenging long-held assumptions and opening new avenues of research. The implications of his research continue to be felt across multiple fields, from neuroscience and biochemistry to public health and food safety. Despite the challenges that remain, Prusiner's contributions have laid the foundation for future discoveries that may one day lead to effective treatments and cures for prion diseases and other neurodegenerative disorders. His dedication to science and his willingness to challenge established ideas serve as an enduring example of the power of innovation and perseverance in the pursuit of knowledge.

Chapter 13: Dorothy Crowfoot Hodgkin

Dorothy Crowfoot Hodgkin was a pioneering British chemist and crystallographer whose groundbreaking work in the field of X-ray crystallography significantly advanced our understanding of the structures of biological molecules. Born on May 12, 1910, in Cairo, Egypt, Hodgkin's early life was marked by her deep fascination with the natural world, a passion that would guide her through a lifetime of scientific inquiry and discovery. Her achievements in the study of complex organic compounds, including the structures of penicillin, vitamin B12, and insulin, earned her the Nobel Prize in Chemistry in 1964, making her one of the most prominent scientists of the 20th century.

Hodgkin's journey into the world of science began at an early age. She was the eldest of four daughters in a family deeply rooted in education and scholarship. Her parents, John Winter Crowfoot and Grace Mary Hood, were both archaeologists, and their academic interests undoubtedly influenced Hodgkin's intellectual development. Despite spending much of her childhood in the United Kingdom, she was born in Cairo due to her father's work as an educational administrator in Egypt. The family's frequent travels across Europe and the Middle East exposed young Dorothy to various cultures and ideas, fostering her curiosity and desire to understand the world around her.

Hodgkin's formal education began at Sir John Leman Grammar School in Beccles, Suffolk, where she developed a strong interest in chemistry. Her fascination with crystals and minerals was sparked when she received a chemistry set as a gift, and this interest deepened when she attended a lecture on X-ray crystallography by John Desmond Bernal, a pioneering physicist and crystallographer, during her time at Oxford High School for Girls. Bernal's work on the diffraction of X-rays by crystals introduced Hodgkin to a method that would become central to her future research.

In 1928, Hodgkin enrolled at Somerville College, Oxford, to study chemistry. Her time at Oxford was transformative, as she quickly immersed herself in the study of crystallography under the guidance of her mentor, H.M. Powell. During her undergraduate years, Hodgkin was one of the first students to use X-ray crystallography to investigate the structure of organic compounds. Her early research focused on sterols, a class of organic molecules, and she successfully determined the structure of cholesterol iodide, which was a significant achievement at the time.

After graduating from Oxford with first-class honors in chemistry in 1932, Hodgkin continued her studies at the University of Cambridge, where she worked in the laboratory of John Desmond Bernal, who had by then become a leading figure in the field of X-ray crystallography. Under Bernal's mentorship, Hodgkin honed her skills in crystallography and began to explore the structures of increasingly complex organic molecules. It was during her time at Cambridge that Hodgkin collaborated with Bernal on the first X-ray diffraction studies of a protein, pepsin, marking a significant milestone in the field of molecular biology.

In 1934, Hodgkin returned to Oxford, where she embarked on a remarkable research career that would span several decades. She joined the faculty at Somerville College, eventually becoming a fellow and tutor in chemistry. Hodgkin's work at Oxford was characterized by her relentless pursuit of understanding the structures of biologically important molecules, using X-ray crystallography as her primary tool. Her meticulous approach to research and her ability to tackle complex problems set her apart from her peers.

One of Hodgkin's most significant contributions to science came in the 1940s when she began working on the structure of penicillin, a groundbreaking antibiotic discovered by Alexander Fleming in 1928. Despite penicillin's importance in treating bacterial infections, its chemical structure remained unknown, which hindered efforts to synthesize it and produce it on a larger scale. Hodgkin's work on penicillin was fraught with challenges, as the molecule's complex structure made it difficult to analyze using the techniques available at the time.

Undeterred, Hodgkin applied her expertise in X-ray crystallography to unravel the structure of penicillin. She meticulously analyzed the diffraction patterns produced when X-rays were passed through crystals of penicillin, gradually piecing together the molecule's three-dimensional structure. After years of painstaking work, Hodgkin and her team succeeded in determining the exact structure of penicillin in 1945. This discovery was a major breakthrough, as it provided crucial insights into how the antibiotic functioned and paved the way for the development of synthetic penicillin, which could be produced on a larger scale to meet the growing demand for the drug during and after World War II.

Hodgkin's success in solving the structure of penicillin cemented her reputation as a leading crystallographer, but her most celebrated achievement was yet to come. In the 1950s, Hodgkin turned her attention to another complex molecule—vitamin B12, an essential nutrient involved in the production of red blood cells and the maintenance of the nervous system. The structure of vitamin B12 was even more intricate than that of penicillin, and its determination would require Hodgkin to push the limits of X-ray crystallography to new heights.

The project to determine the structure of vitamin B12 was a monumental undertaking that involved collaboration with researchers from around the world. Hodgkin and her team at Oxford faced numerous technical challenges, as the molecule's large size and complexity made it difficult to obtain clear diffraction patterns. However, Hodgkin's persistence and ingenuity eventually paid off. In 1956, after more than five years of research, she successfully determined the structure of vitamin B12, revealing the molecule's unique corrin ring structure, which was unlike anything previously seen in organic chemistry.

The discovery of the structure of vitamin B12 was a scientific tour de force that earned Hodgkin widespread acclaim. Her work provided critical insights into the molecule's function and its role in the human body, and it also demonstrated the power of X-ray crystallography as a tool for elucidating the structures of complex biological molecules. The significance of this achievement was recognized with numerous awards and honors, culminating in Hodgkin's receipt of the Nobel Prize in Chemistry in 1964.

Hodgkin's Nobel Prize marked the pinnacle of a career dedicated to the pursuit of knowledge and the advancement of science. However, she did not rest on her laurels. In the 1960s, Hodgkin embarked on what would become the most challenging project of her career—the determination of the structure of insulin, a hormone critical for regulating blood sugar levels in the body. Insulin was of immense medical importance, particularly for the treatment of diabetes, but its structure had eluded scientists for decades due to its complexity.

Hodgkin had first begun working on insulin in the 1930s, but the project had to be set aside as she focused on penicillin and vitamin B12. By the time she returned to insulin in the 1960s, advances in technology had made it possible to tackle the problem with renewed vigor. Hodgkin and her team applied the latest techniques in X-ray crystallography to analyze insulin crystals, slowly but surely building up a detailed picture of the molecule's structure.

The determination of the structure of insulin was a long and arduous process that spanned several decades. It required Hodgkin to combine her deep understanding of chemistry with innovative approaches to crystallography, as well as the support of a dedicated team of researchers. Despite the difficulties, Hodgkin remained committed to the project, driven by her belief in the importance of understanding the molecular basis of biological processes.

Finally, in 1969, after more than 30 years of work, Hodgkin and her team succeeded in determining the three-dimensional structure of insulin. This achievement was a testament to Hodgkin's perseverance and her ability to overcome the formidable challenges posed by one of the most complex molecules ever studied. The structure of insulin provided crucial insights into how the hormone interacts with its receptor and regulates blood sugar levels, laying the groundwork for future research in diabetes and endocrinology.

Throughout her career, Dorothy Hodgkin was known not only for her scientific achievements but also for her commitment to mentoring and supporting the next generation of scientists. She was a beloved teacher and mentor to many students at Oxford, inspiring them with her passion for research and her unwavering dedication to the pursuit of knowledge. Hodgkin was also an advocate for women in science, and she worked tirelessly to promote gender equality in a field that was, at the time, dominated by men. Her own success as a female scientist in a male-dominated world made her a role model for aspiring women scientists around the globe.

In addition to her scientific work, Hodgkin was deeply committed to social and humanitarian causes. She was an active member of the Pugwash Conferences on Science and World Affairs, an international organization dedicated to reducing the threat of nuclear war and promoting peaceful resolutions to global conflicts. Hodgkin's involvement in Pugwash reflected her belief in the responsibility of scientists to use their knowledge for the betterment of humanity and to work towards a more just and peaceful world.

Hodgkin's contributions to science were recognized with numerous awards and honors throughout her lifetime. In addition to the Nobel Prize, she received the Copley Medal from the Royal Society in 1976, becoming the first woman to be awarded this prestigious honor. She was also made a member of the Order of Merit, one of the highest honors in the United Kingdom, in 1965, and she received honorary degrees from several universities around the world. Despite these accolades, Hodgkin remained modest and unassuming, always emphasizing the collaborative nature of scientific research and the contributions of her colleagues and students.

Dorothy Crowfoot Hodgkin passed away on July 29, 1994, at the age of 84. Her legacy as one of the most influential scientists of the 20th century endures, and her contributions to the field of X-ray crystallography continue to have a profound impact on the study of biological molecules. Hodgkin's work not only advanced our understanding of the structures of some of the most important molecules in biology but also demonstrated the power of crystallography as a tool for uncovering the mysteries of life at the molecular level.

Hodgkin's life and work are a testament to the power of curiosity, determination, and intellectual rigor. Her achievements in science broke new ground and paved the way for future discoveries in chemistry, biology, and medicine. Moreover, her commitment to mentoring young scientists and advocating for social justice has left a lasting imprint on the scientific community and beyond. Today, Dorothy Crowfoot Hodgkin is remembered not only as a brilliant chemist and crystallographer but also as a pioneering woman who blazed a trail for future generations of scientists. Her story is an inspiration to all who seek to understand the natural world and to use that knowledge to make a positive impact on society.

Chapter 14: Modrich, Sancar, & Lindahl

Paul L. Modrich, Aziz Sancar, and Tomas Lindahl are three prominent scientists whose groundbreaking work in the field of DNA repair mechanisms earned them the Nobel Prize in Chemistry in 2015. Their research collectively unveiled the intricate molecular processes by which cells maintain the integrity of their genetic information, safeguarding it from the damage that can occur due to environmental factors, cellular metabolism, and errors during DNA replication. This trio's contributions to our understanding of DNA repair not only provided profound insights into the fundamental workings of life but also had significant implications for cancer research, aging, and the development of novel therapeutic approaches.

The story of their research begins with the realization that DNA, the molecule that carries genetic information in all living organisms, is remarkably vulnerable to damage. DNA is constantly exposed to potentially harmful agents such as ultraviolet (UV) light, ionizing radiation, and chemical mutagens, all of which can cause changes to its structure. Additionally, the very process of DNA replication—essential for cell division—can introduce errors into the genetic code. If left unrepaired, these errors and damages can lead to mutations, which can disrupt the function of genes, potentially leading to diseases like cancer or contributing to the aging process. Understanding how cells detect and repair these errors became a central question in molecular biology, and it was within this context that Modrich, Sancar, and Lindahl made their pioneering contributions.

Paul L. Modrich, an American biochemist, was born on June 13, 1946, in Raton, New Mexico. Modrich's interest in science was nurtured from a young age, particularly by his high school chemistry teacher, who recognized his talent and encouraged him to pursue a career in scientific research. After earning a bachelor's degree in biology from the Massachusetts Institute of Technology (MIT) in 1968, Modrich went on to complete his Ph.D. in biochemistry at Stanford University in 1973, where he worked under the guidance of Arthur Kornberg, a Nobel laureate known for his work on DNA replication.

Modrich's Nobel-winning research focused on a specific DNA repair mechanism known as mismatch repair (MMR). Mismatch repair is crucial for correcting errors that occur during DNA replication, a process that duplicates the cell's genetic material before cell division. During replication, the DNA polymerase enzyme synthesizes a new strand of DNA by copying the existing strand. However, this process is not foolproof, and occasionally the enzyme incorporates the wrong nucleotide, resulting in a mismatch—where the newly added nucleotide does not correctly pair with the corresponding nucleotide on the original strand. If these mismatches are not corrected, they can lead to permanent mutations in the DNA sequence.

Modrich's work elucidated the molecular mechanisms by which cells recognize and repair these mismatches. He discovered that the mismatch repair system involves a series of proteins that work together to identify the mismatch, remove the incorrectly paired nucleotide, and replace it with the correct one. This system is highly efficient, correcting more than 99% of replication errors, thereby ensuring the fidelity of DNA replication and the stability of the genome. Modrich's research not only clarified how mismatch repair works in bacteria but also demonstrated that similar mechanisms operate in human cells. This discovery had profound implications for our understanding of cancer, as defects in mismatch repair are known to be a major cause of certain types of cancer, including hereditary nonpolyposis colorectal cancer (HNPCC), also known as Lynch syndrome.

Aziz Sancar, a Turkish-American biochemist, was born on September 8, 1946, in the small town of Savur in southeastern Turkey. Growing up in a modest family, Sancar's early education was in local schools, but his academic potential quickly became evident. After earning his M.D. from Istanbul University in 1969, Sancar moved to the United States to pursue graduate studies in molecular biology at the University of Texas at Dallas, where he completed his Ph.D. in 1977. Sancar's scientific career took him to several prestigious institutions, including Yale University, where he conducted much of his groundbreaking research on DNA repair.

Sancar's contribution to the field of DNA repair focused on a process known as nucleotide excision repair (NER). This repair mechanism is critical for correcting a wide range of DNA lesions, particularly those caused by UV radiation. UV light can induce the formation of thymine dimers, a type of damage where two adjacent thymine bases on the DNA strand become covalently linked, distorting the DNA helix and blocking transcription and replication. If left unrepaired, these lesions can lead to mutations and contribute to the development of skin cancer.

Sancar's research provided a detailed understanding of how cells recognize and repair UV-induced DNA damage. He discovered that nucleotide excision repair operates through a multi-step process involving several key proteins. First, the damaged DNA is recognized by specific proteins that scan the genome for distortions in the DNA helix. Once a lesion is detected, the DNA is unwound, and a small section of the damaged strand is excised, or cut out, by specialized endonucleases. The resulting gap is then filled in by DNA polymerase, which synthesizes a new, correct sequence using the undamaged strand as a template, and the DNA is finally sealed by a ligase enzyme. Sancar's work also revealed that this repair process is conserved across many organisms, from bacteria to humans, highlighting its fundamental importance in maintaining genomic integrity.

Tomas Lindahl, a Swedish-born scientist, was born on January 28, 1938, in Stockholm, Sweden. Lindahl's interest in science was piqued during his early years, leading him to study chemistry and medicine at the Karolinska Institute in Stockholm, where he earned his M.D. and Ph.D. in the early 1960s. After completing his studies, Lindahl embarked on a research career that took him to the United States and then back to Europe, where he eventually became the director of the Clare Hall Laboratories at the Imperial Cancer Research Fund (now part of the Francis Crick Institute) in the United Kingdom.

Lindahl's Nobel-winning research focused on base excision repair (BER), another critical DNA repair mechanism that deals with the spontaneous damage that occurs to DNA under normal cellular conditions. Lindahl's work was motivated by a fundamental question: how is it possible for DNA, a molecule that is inherently unstable, to maintain its integrity over the lifespan of an organism? DNA is subject to constant chemical insults, such as the spontaneous deamination of cytosine to uracil or the oxidation of guanine to 8-oxoguanine, which can lead to mutations if not repaired.

Lindahl discovered that cells have evolved a sophisticated system to counteract this constant assault on their genetic material. Base excision repair involves the removal of damaged bases from the DNA. The process begins with a DNA glycosylase enzyme, which recognizes and removes the damaged base, leaving behind an abasic site (a site without a base). This site is then processed by an AP endonuclease, which cuts the DNA backbone at the abasic site, creating a nick. The resulting gap is filled in by DNA polymerase, which inserts the correct base, and the DNA strand is finally sealed by a ligase enzyme. Lindahl's work demonstrated that base excision repair is essential for preventing the accumulation of mutations that could otherwise lead to diseases such as cancer.

The collective work of Modrich, Sancar, and Lindahl provided a comprehensive understanding of the molecular mechanisms by which cells repair damaged DNA. Their discoveries revealed that the maintenance of genomic stability is a highly coordinated process involving multiple pathways, each tailored to address specific types of DNA damage. Mismatch repair, nucleotide excision repair, and base excision repair together form a robust defense system that protects cells from the potentially deleterious effects of DNA damage.

The implications of their research extend far beyond the basic understanding of DNA repair. Defects in these repair mechanisms are linked to a variety of diseases, most notably cancer. For example, individuals with inherited mutations in mismatch repair genes are at a significantly increased risk of developing certain types of cancer, particularly colorectal cancer. Understanding how these repair systems work has paved the way for the development of new diagnostic tools and targeted therapies aimed at exploiting the weaknesses in cancer cells' DNA repair machinery.

Moreover, the knowledge gained from their work has broader implications for our understanding of aging. DNA damage accumulates over time, and the efficiency of DNA repair mechanisms declines with age. This accumulation of damage is thought to contribute to the aging process and the onset of age-related diseases. By elucidating the molecular details of DNA repair, the research of Modrich, Sancar, and Lindahl has provided valuable insights into the mechanisms of aging and opened new avenues for potential interventions to slow the aging process and improve healthspan.

In addition to its impact on human health, the study of DNA repair has also influenced fields such as biotechnology and synthetic biology. The ability to manipulate and repair DNA with precision is crucial for genetic engineering, and the techniques developed from an understanding of DNA repair mechanisms have been instrumental in advancing these fields. The CRISPR-Cas9 gene-editing technology, for example, relies on the principles of DNA repair to introduce specific changes into the genome, offering the potential to correct genetic defects and treat a wide range of diseases.

The Nobel Prize in Chemistry awarded to Modrich, Sancar, and Lindahl in 2015 was a recognition of their monumental contributions to our understanding of one of the most fundamental processes in biology—the preservation of genetic information. Their work has had a lasting impact on science and medicine, providing a foundation for ongoing research in DNA repair and its applications in human health and disease. Their discoveries continue to inspire new generations of scientists to explore the molecular intricacies of life and to seek innovative solutions to some of the most pressing challenges in medicine and biotechnology.

Today, the legacy of Paul L. Modrich, Aziz Sancar, and Tomas Lindahl is evident in the ongoing research that builds upon their foundational discoveries. The field of DNA repair remains a vibrant and dynamic area of study, with new insights and applications emerging as scientists continue to unravel the complexities of the cellular machinery that safeguards our genetic code. Their work serves as a reminder of the importance of fundamental research in advancing our understanding of life at the molecular level and its potential to transform human health and well-being.

Chapter 15: Brian K. Kobilka & Robert J. Lefkowitz

Brian K. Kobilka and Robert J. Lefkowitz are two scientists whose groundbreaking research in the field of cell biology earned them the Nobel Prize in Chemistry in 2012. Their work focused on G-protein-coupled receptors (GPCRs), a large family of proteins that play a crucial role in how cells respond to external signals. The discovery and understanding of GPCRs have had far-reaching implications for biology and medicine, particularly in drug development, as these receptors are the target of a significant portion of all pharmaceuticals.

The story of their work begins with Robert J. Lefkowitz, an American physician-scientist born on April 15, 1943, in New York City. Lefkowitz initially trained as a physician, earning his medical degree from Columbia University in 1966. After completing his residency, he joined the National Institutes of Health (NIH) during a time when many young doctors were encouraged to engage in research as part of their training. It was at the NIH that Lefkowitz became interested in the mechanisms by which hormones exert their effects on cells.

Hormones are signaling molecules that regulate various physiological processes in the body, including metabolism, growth, and mood. They achieve these effects by binding to specific receptors on the surface of cells, initiating a cascade of events inside the cell that ultimately leads to a physiological response. However, in the 1960s and 1970s, the nature of these receptors was largely a mystery. Researchers knew that cells must have some kind of receptor to detect and respond to hormones, but these receptors had not yet been identified or characterized.

Lefkowitz's early work focused on understanding how adrenaline, a hormone that triggers the "fight or flight" response, interacts with cells. He used radioactively labeled hormones to trace their binding to receptors on the surface of cells. This technique allowed him to visualize and study these elusive receptors for the first time. Through this work, Lefkowitz identified and characterized the β-adrenergic receptor, a type of GPCR that binds adrenaline. This discovery was a significant breakthrough in the understanding of hormone action and laid the groundwork for future research on GPCRs.

Brian K. Kobilka, who would later join forces with Lefkowitz, was born on May 30, 1955, in Little Falls, Minnesota. Kobilka's path to scientific acclaim was somewhat unconventional. After earning a bachelor's degree in biology and chemistry from the University of Minnesota Duluth, he went on to study medicine at Yale University, where he received his M.D. in 1981. Rather than pursuing a traditional career in clinical medicine, Kobilka chose to focus on research, specifically in the area of molecular biology. After completing his residency, Kobilka joined Lefkowitz's laboratory at Duke University in 1984 as a postdoctoral fellow, where he began working on the challenging task of cloning the gene for the β-adrenergic receptor.

Cloning the gene for a GPCR was a monumental challenge in the 1980s. These receptors are embedded in the cell membrane, and their complex structure made them difficult to study using traditional biochemical techniques. However, Kobilka's determination and innovative approach led to success. By using a combination of molecular biology techniques, he was able to isolate and clone the gene for the β-adrenergic receptor, which was found to be similar to the visual pigment rhodopsin. This discovery revealed that GPCRs share a common structure, characterized by seven transmembrane helices, a feature that would become a hallmark of this receptor family.

The successful cloning of the β-adrenergic receptor not only confirmed the structural similarities between GPCRs but also opened the door to identifying and studying other members of this receptor family. It became clear that GPCRs are involved in a wide range of physiological processes, from sensing light and odors to regulating heart rate and immune responses. The importance of GPCRs in health and disease was further underscored by the realization that they are the target of a significant number of drugs, including beta-blockers, antihistamines, and many others.

One of the most significant contributions of Kobilka and Lefkowitz was their work on understanding how GPCRs function at a molecular level. GPCRs transmit signals from outside the cell to the inside by activating G-proteins, which are intracellular proteins that mediate various signaling pathways. When a ligand, such as a hormone or neurotransmitter, binds to a GPCR, the receptor undergoes a conformational change that activates the associated G-protein. The activated G-protein then interacts with other proteins inside the cell to trigger a specific response, such as the release of a second messenger molecule or the activation of an enzyme.

Kobilka and Lefkowitz's research provided critical insights into the structural changes that occur in GPCRs upon ligand binding. By using advanced techniques such as X-ray crystallography, Kobilka was able to capture high-resolution images of the β-adrenergic receptor in different states, revealing how the receptor's structure changes during activation. These structural studies were a major breakthrough, as they provided a detailed understanding of the receptor's function at the atomic level. This knowledge has been invaluable for the development of new drugs that target GPCRs, as it allows for the design of molecules that can specifically interact with the receptor in a desired way, either activating or inhibiting its function.

The work of Kobilka and Lefkowitz also had a profound impact on the broader field of cell signaling. Their discoveries helped to establish the concept of signal transduction, the process by which cells convert external signals into a response. This concept is fundamental to our understanding of how cells communicate with each other and respond to their environment. GPCRs are now recognized as one of the largest and most diverse families of proteins in the human genome, with over 800 different types identified, each playing a role in various physiological processes.

The implications of their research extend far beyond the basic understanding of cell signaling. GPCRs are involved in many diseases, including heart disease, cancer, and mental health disorders. As a result, they have become one of the most important targets for drug development. It is estimated that more than a third of all approved drugs act on GPCRs, highlighting the immense clinical significance of this receptor family. The detailed structural and functional insights provided by Kobilka and Lefkowitz have been instrumental in guiding the development of these drugs, leading to more effective and targeted therapies.

In addition to their scientific contributions, both Kobilka and Lefkowitz have had a significant impact on the training and mentoring of the next generation of scientists. Lefkowitz, in particular, is known for his dedication to mentoring young researchers, many of whom have gone on to make important contributions in their own right. Kobilka, after leaving Duke University, continued his research and mentoring work at Stanford University, where he has been a leader in the field of structural biology.

Their work also exemplifies the power of collaboration in science. The partnership between Kobilka and Lefkowitz, combining Lefkowitz's expertise in pharmacology and receptor biology with Kobilka's skills in molecular biology and structural biology, was crucial to the success of their research. Together, they pushed the boundaries of what was possible in the study of GPCRs, overcoming significant technical challenges and making discoveries that have had a lasting impact on both science and medicine.

The Nobel Prize in Chemistry awarded to Brian K. Kobilka and Robert J. Lefkowitz in 2012 was a recognition of their pioneering work on GPCRs and the profound implications of their discoveries. Their research has provided a detailed understanding of one of the most important mechanisms of cell signaling and has laid the foundation for the development of new therapies for a wide range of diseases. The legacy of their work continues to shape the field of molecular biology, as researchers build on their discoveries to explore new frontiers in cell signaling, drug development, and personalized medicine.

Today, the study of GPCRs remains a vibrant and rapidly evolving field, with ongoing research aimed at uncovering new functions of these receptors, understanding their role in disease, and developing innovative therapeutic strategies. The work of Kobilka and Lefkowitz serves as a testament to the importance of curiosity-driven research and the impact that fundamental discoveries can have on human health and well-being. Their achievements continue to inspire scientists around the world to explore the molecular mechanisms that underlie life and to seek new ways to harness this knowledge for the benefit of society.

Chapter 16: Barry Marshall & Robin Warren

Barry Marshall and Robin Warren are two Australian scientists whose pioneering research on the role of Helicobacter pylori bacteria in causing peptic ulcers revolutionized the understanding and treatment of gastrointestinal diseases. Their work, which defied the prevailing medical dogma of the time, ultimately earned them the Nobel Prize in Physiology or Medicine in 2005. This recognition was not only for their discovery but also for their perseverance in challenging established beliefs and demonstrating that a common bacterial infection, rather than stress or lifestyle factors, was responsible for most cases of peptic ulcers and gastritis.

In the late 19th and early 20th centuries, the prevailing belief in the medical community was that peptic ulcers, which are open sores that develop on the lining of the stomach, small intestine, or esophagus, were primarily caused by excess stomach acid, stress, and lifestyle factors such as diet, smoking, and alcohol consumption. These ulcers were thought to result from the corrosive effects of stomach acid on the delicate lining of the gastrointestinal tract, particularly when exacerbated by stress or an unhealthy lifestyle. Consequently, treatment focused on reducing stomach acid production using medications like antacids and, later, proton pump inhibitors, as well as recommending lifestyle changes.

Robin Warren, a pathologist at the Royal Perth Hospital in Western Australia, began challenging this conventional wisdom in the early 1970s. Warren, born on June 11, 1937, in Adelaide, South Australia, had a keen eye for detail and a passion for microscopy. He was known for his meticulous approach to examining tissue samples under the microscope. In 1979, Warren observed small, spiral-shaped bacteria in the stomach lining of patients suffering from gastritis, an inflammation of the stomach lining. These bacteria, which he later identified as Helicobacter pylori, were found in close proximity to inflamed areas of the stomach, leading Warren to suspect that they might play a role in causing the inflammation.

At the time, the idea that bacteria could survive in the highly acidic environment of the stomach was considered highly unlikely, if not impossible. The stomach's acidic pH, which is typically around 1.5 to 3.5, was thought to be too harsh for bacteria to survive, let alone thrive. As a result, Warren's observations were met with skepticism, and his initial findings were largely ignored by the broader medical community. Despite this, Warren continued to investigate the presence of these bacteria in patients with gastritis and peptic ulcers, believing that they could be a significant factor in the development of these conditions.

In 1981, Barry Marshall, a young and ambitious gastroenterologist, joined Warren at the Royal Perth Hospital. Marshall, born on September 30, 1951, in Kalgoorlie, Western Australia, had recently completed his medical training and was eager to make his mark in the field of gastroenterology. When he learned of Warren's findings, he became intrigued by the possibility that a bacterial infection could be responsible for peptic ulcers and gastritis. The two began collaborating on research to explore this hypothesis further.

Marshall and Warren conducted a series of studies to investigate the presence of Helicobacter pylori in patients with peptic ulcers and gastritis. They collected biopsy samples from patients undergoing endoscopy, a procedure that allows doctors to view the inside of the stomach and obtain tissue samples. Using special staining techniques, they were able to visualize the bacteria in the stomach lining. Their research showed that Helicobacter pylori was present in nearly all patients with duodenal ulcers (ulcers in the small intestine) and in a significant proportion of those with gastric ulcers (ulcers in the stomach). Moreover, they found that the bacteria were often found in areas of the stomach lining that were inflamed, suggesting a strong association between the presence of Helicobacter pylori and the development of gastritis and peptic ulcers.

Despite their compelling evidence, Marshall and Warren faced significant resistance from the medical community. The idea that a bacterial infection could cause peptic ulcers contradicted the long-held belief that these ulcers were primarily the result of lifestyle factors and stress. Many experts were reluctant to accept the notion that a simple bacterium could be responsible for such a common and serious condition. Additionally, there was skepticism about whether the bacteria could survive in the acidic environment of the stomach, and some researchers questioned the reliability of the staining techniques used to identify the bacteria.

Undeterred by the skepticism, Marshall and Warren continued to gather evidence to support their hypothesis. One of their key studies involved treating patients with peptic ulcers with antibiotics to eradicate the Helicobacter pylori infection. They found that patients who received antibiotic treatment had a significantly lower rate of ulcer recurrence compared to those who received only conventional acid-reducing therapy. This finding provided strong evidence that Helicobacter pylori was not only associated with peptic ulcers but was also directly involved in causing them.

In an effort to further prove the link between Helicobacter pylori and peptic ulcers, Marshall took an extraordinary step in 1984. Frustrated by the slow pace of acceptance within the medical community and the difficulties in obtaining funding for further research, Marshall decided to test the bacteria's effects on himself. He obtained a culture of Helicobacter pylori from a patient with gastritis and ingested it, hoping to develop symptoms that would demonstrate the bacteria's role in causing gastric inflammation.

Within days, Marshall began experiencing symptoms of gastritis, including nausea, vomiting, and abdominal pain. A subsequent endoscopy confirmed that he had developed gastritis, and biopsy samples revealed the presence of Helicobacter pylori in his stomach lining. Marshall then treated himself with antibiotics, which successfully eradicated the infection and resolved his symptoms. This self-experiment provided dramatic evidence of the bacteria's ability to cause gastritis and helped to convince many skeptics of the validity of Marshall and Warren's findings.

Following Marshall's self-experiment and the publication of their research, the medical community began to take notice. Over time, additional studies confirmed the link between Helicobacter pylori and peptic ulcers, leading to a paradigm shift in the understanding of these conditions. By the early 1990s, it was widely accepted that Helicobacter pylori infection was the primary cause of peptic ulcers, and treatment guidelines were updated to include antibiotics as a standard component of ulcer therapy.

The discovery of Helicobacter pylori's role in causing peptic ulcers had profound implications for the treatment and prevention of these conditions. Previously, peptic ulcers were often treated with long-term acid suppression therapy, which could provide relief from symptoms but did not address the underlying cause of the ulcers. As a result, many patients experienced recurrent episodes of ulcer disease. With the introduction of antibiotic therapy to eradicate Helicobacter pylori, patients could achieve a permanent cure for their ulcers, dramatically reducing the need for long-term medication and improving their quality of life.

The impact of Marshall and Warren's discovery extended beyond the treatment of peptic ulcers. Helicobacter pylori was also found to be associated with other gastrointestinal conditions, including chronic gastritis, gastric cancer, and mucosa-associated lymphoid tissue (MALT) lymphoma. The identification of this bacterium as a major risk factor for gastric cancer, one of the leading causes of cancer-related deaths worldwide, had significant public health implications. Efforts to screen for and treat Helicobacter pylori infection in populations at high risk for gastric cancer have become an important strategy for reducing the incidence of this deadly disease.

The recognition of Helicobacter pylori as a major cause of peptic ulcers and its role in other gastrointestinal diseases marked a turning point in the field of gastroenterology. It also highlighted the importance of questioning established medical dogma and remaining open to new ideas, even when they challenge long-held beliefs. Marshall and Warren's perseverance in the face of skepticism and their commitment to scientific inquiry serve as an inspiration to researchers and clinicians alike.

In 2005, Barry Marshall and Robin Warren were awarded the Nobel Prize in Physiology or Medicine for their discovery of Helicobacter pylori and its role in peptic ulcer disease. The Nobel Committee recognized the profound impact of their work on the understanding and treatment of gastrointestinal diseases, as well as the broader implications of their discovery for medical research and public health. The award also acknowledged the courage and determination of the two scientists in pursuing their research despite significant opposition and skepticism.

Today, the legacy of Marshall and Warren's discovery continues to influence the field of medicine. Helicobacter pylori remains one of the most extensively studied bacteria, with ongoing research exploring its mechanisms of infection, its interactions with the host immune system, and its role in various diseases. Advances in diagnostic techniques have made it easier to detect Helicobacter pylori infection, allowing for more accurate diagnosis and targeted treatment of peptic ulcers and other related conditions.

In addition to their scientific contributions, Marshall and Warren's story has become a powerful example of the importance of persistence and innovation in scientific research. Their willingness to challenge established beliefs and their commitment to finding the truth, even in the face of adversity, have inspired countless researchers to push the boundaries of knowledge and explore new frontiers in science and medicine.

As a result of their work, millions of people around the world have benefited from more effective treatment and prevention of peptic ulcers and related diseases. The discovery of Helicobacter pylori has not only transformed the management of these conditions but has also opened new avenues for research into the role of infectious agents in other chronic diseases. Marshall and Warren's achievements have had a lasting impact on the field of medicine and continue to shape the way we understand and treat gastrointestinal disorders.

Chapter 17: Arno Penzias & Robert Wilson

Arno Penzias and Robert Wilson are two American radio astronomers whose groundbreaking discovery of the cosmic microwave background radiation in 1964 provided one of the most significant pieces of evidence supporting the Big Bang theory of the origin of the universe. Their work earned them the Nobel Prize in Physics in 1978, and their discovery fundamentally changed the understanding of the universe, solidifying the Big Bang as the most widely accepted explanation for the beginning of the cosmos. This discovery was not only a scientific triumph but also a remarkable example of how serendipity, combined with meticulous scientific investigation, can lead to groundbreaking findings.

The story of Penzias and Wilson's discovery begins with the development of radio astronomy, a field that emerged in the early 20th century as scientists began to explore the universe using radio waves, which, unlike visible light, could penetrate Earth's atmosphere and reveal phenomena invisible to optical telescopes. In the post-World War II era, radio astronomy advanced rapidly, driven by technological innovations and a growing interest in understanding the universe beyond the capabilities of optical astronomy. By the 1960s, radio astronomy had become an essential tool for studying the cosmos, and researchers were exploring various ways to use radio waves to probe the mysteries of the universe.

Arno Penzias, born on April 26, 1933, in Munich, Germany, fled with his family to the United States in 1940 to escape the Nazi regime. He later pursued a career in physics, earning his Ph.D. from Columbia University. Penzias joined Bell Telephone Laboratories (later known as Bell Labs) in New Jersey, where he worked on various projects related to radio astronomy. At Bell Labs, he developed an interest in the nascent field of radio astronomy, which combined his expertise in physics with the cutting-edge technology of radio communication.

Robert Wilson, born on January 10, 1936, in Houston, Texas, also pursued a career in physics, earning his Ph.D. from the California Institute of Technology (Caltech). Like Penzias, Wilson joined Bell Labs, where he became involved in research related to radio astronomy. Bell Labs was known for its pioneering work in telecommunications and had a history of encouraging scientific research that could lead to technological innovations. It was in this environment that Penzias and Wilson began working together on a project that would ultimately lead to their historic discovery.

In the early 1960s, Penzias and Wilson were assigned to work on a large horn antenna at Bell Labs in Holmdel, New Jersey. The horn antenna, which was originally built for satellite communication experiments, was designed to detect faint radio signals from space. It was a highly sensitive instrument capable of picking up extremely weak signals, making it ideal for exploring the universe in the radio spectrum. Penzias and Wilson's initial goal was to use the antenna to study radio emissions from the Milky Way galaxy, particularly focusing on the radio waves emitted by hydrogen, the most abundant element in the universe.

As they began their observations, Penzias and Wilson encountered an unexpected problem. No matter where they pointed the antenna in the sky, they detected a persistent background noise that they could not explain. This noise, or "hiss," appeared as a faint but consistent signal that seemed to come from all directions, with no apparent source within the Milky Way or beyond. It was present day and night, and it did not vary with the position of the antenna or with changes in the environment. The noise was frustratingly consistent, and despite their efforts to eliminate it, Penzias and Wilson could not account for its origin.

The two scientists initially suspected that the noise might be due to interference from local sources, such as radio transmitters or ground-based electronics. They meticulously checked and rechecked their equipment, ruling out various potential sources of interference. They even considered the possibility that the noise was caused by pigeon droppings inside the horn antenna, which they referred to as "white dielectric material." After cleaning out the antenna and taking other precautions, the noise persisted, leaving Penzias and Wilson puzzled.

As they struggled to identify the source of the mysterious noise, Penzias and Wilson were unaware that a group of theoretical physicists at nearby Princeton University was working on a problem that would soon intersect with their own. The Princeton group, led by physicist Robert Dicke, was exploring the implications of the Big Bang theory, a cosmological model that proposed the universe began as a hot, dense point and expanded over billions of years to its current state. According to the Big Bang theory, the early universe would have been filled with intense radiation, which, as the universe expanded and cooled, would have stretched into longer wavelengths, becoming a faint, low-energy signal that permeated the entire cosmos.

Dicke and his colleagues, including physicists Jim Peebles, David Wilkinson, and Peter Roll, were searching for this remnant radiation, which they hypothesized would be detectable as a faint, uniform glow across the sky in the microwave region of the electromagnetic spectrum. They were in the process of designing an experiment to detect this "cosmic microwave background radiation" (CMB) when they learned of Penzias and Wilson's unexplained noise.

In a fortuitous turn of events, Penzias and Wilson were put in contact with the Princeton group through a mutual acquaintance. When Penzias described the characteristics of the noise to Dicke, the

Princeton physicist immediately recognized its significance. Dicke reportedly turned to his colleagues and said, "Boys, we've been scooped!" The noise that Penzias and Wilson had detected was, in fact, the cosmic microwave background radiation predicted by the Big Bang theory.

The discovery of the cosmic microwave background radiation was a monumental moment in the history of cosmology. It provided direct, observational evidence that the universe had indeed begun with a hot, dense state as described by the Big Bang theory. The CMB was the afterglow of the early universe, a snapshot of the cosmos when it was just 380,000 years old—long before stars and galaxies had formed. At this early stage, the universe was filled with a hot, ionized gas that scattered photons (particles of light) in all directions. As the universe expanded and cooled, these photons were released and began to travel freely through space, eventually stretching into the microwave region of the spectrum as the universe continued to expand.

The discovery of the CMB was a powerful confirmation of the Big Bang theory and marked the beginning of a new era in cosmology. It provided a "fossil" record of the early universe, offering scientists a way to study the conditions of the cosmos at a time when it was still in its infancy. The CMB also carried information about the universe's composition, structure, and evolution, making it an invaluable tool for understanding the fundamental properties of the universe.

For their discovery, Penzias and Wilson were awarded the Nobel Prize in Physics in 1978, sharing the prize with Soviet physicist Pyotr Kapitsa, who was recognized for his work in low-temperature physics. The Nobel Committee cited Penzias and Wilson's "discovery of cosmic microwave background radiation" as a critical piece of evidence supporting the Big Bang theory, noting its profound implications for the understanding of the universe's origin and evolution.

The impact of Penzias and Wilson's discovery cannot be overstated. The detection of the CMB provided a crucial piece of evidence that helped establish the Big Bang theory as the dominant model of cosmology. It also opened up new avenues of research, leading to a deeper understanding of the universe's structure, composition, and history. In the years following their discovery, scientists used the CMB to test various cosmological models, refine estimates of the universe's age and composition, and explore the processes that led to the formation of galaxies and other cosmic structures.

The study of the CMB has continued to yield important insights into the nature of the universe. In the 1990s and 2000s, experiments such as the Cosmic Background Explorer (COBE), the Wilkinson Microwave Anisotropy Probe (WMAP), and the Planck satellite provided increasingly detailed measurements of the CMB, revealing tiny fluctuations in temperature that corresponded to the seeds of galaxies and large-scale cosmic structures. These measurements allowed scientists to refine the parameters of the Big Bang model, leading to a more precise understanding of the universe's age, composition, and geometry.

Penzias and Wilson's discovery also had broader implications for the field of physics and the philosophy of science. It demonstrated the power of observational evidence in shaping scientific theories and highlighted the importance of serendipity in scientific discovery. The fact that Penzias and Wilson were not initially searching for the CMB, but rather stumbled upon it while investigating an unexplained noise, underscores the role of chance and curiosity in scientific advancement.

Moreover, the discovery of the CMB challenged the steady-state theory of the universe, which had been a competing model to the

Big Bang. The steady-state theory proposed that the universe had no beginning or end and that new matter was continuously created to maintain a constant density as the universe expanded. The detection of the CMB, which indicated a hot, dense origin for the universe, provided strong evidence against the steady-state theory and contributed to its decline as a viable cosmological model.

In addition to its impact on cosmology, Penzias and Wilson's work influenced other areas of science and technology. The development of sensitive radio and microwave detection equipment, which was critical to their discovery, has had applications in fields ranging from telecommunications to remote sensing. Their work also highlighted the importance of interdisciplinary collaboration, as their discovery was the result of a confluence of advances in physics, engineering, and astronomy.

Today, Penzias and Wilson's discovery of the cosmic microwave background radiation is regarded as one of the most significant achievements in the history of science. It provided a window into the early universe and laid the foundation for much of modern cosmology. Their work continues to inspire scientists and researchers, demonstrating the value of curiosity, perseverance, and the willingness to explore the unknown in the pursuit of knowledge.

In conclusion, Arno Penzias and Robert Wilson's discovery of the cosmic microwave background radiation stands as a testament to the power of scientific inquiry and the impact of observational evidence on our understanding of the universe. Their work not only confirmed the Big Bang theory but also opened up new frontiers in cosmology, allowing scientists to explore the origins and evolution of the cosmos in unprecedented detail. Their legacy endures in the ongoing study of the CMB and its role in shaping our understanding of the universe.

Chapter 18: Gertrude B. Elion & George H. Hitchings

Gertrude B. Elion and George H. Hitchings are two remarkable figures in the field of medicinal chemistry, whose groundbreaking work has had a profound and lasting impact on the development of pharmaceutical drugs. Their collaboration, which began in the late 1940s and spanned several decades, led to the creation of numerous life-saving medications that have transformed the treatment of various diseases, including cancer, autoimmune disorders, and infectious diseases. Their work was pioneering not just because of the drugs they developed but also because of the innovative approach they took towards drug discovery, an approach that departed from the traditional trial-and-error method and instead focused on a more rational design of drugs based on an understanding of the biochemical processes underlying diseases.

Gertrude B. Elion was born on January 23, 1918, in New York City. From a young age, she was deeply interested in science, particularly chemistry, and she was determined to pursue a career in this field despite the limited opportunities available to women at the time. She earned her bachelor's degree in chemistry from Hunter College in 1937 and went on to pursue graduate studies at New York University, where she obtained her master's degree in 1941. However, due to financial constraints and the lack of opportunities for women in scientific research, she was unable to continue her education at the doctoral level. Nevertheless, she persisted in her quest for a career in chemistry, working in a variety of jobs before eventually joining the research team at Burroughs Wellcome (now part of GlaxoSmithKline) in 1944.

George H. Hitchings was born on April 18, 1905, in Hoquiam, Washington. He developed an early interest in science, particularly biology and chemistry, and went on to earn his bachelor's degree in chemistry from the University of Washington in 1927. He continued his studies at Harvard University, where he earned his master's degree in 1928 and his Ph.D. in 1933. After completing his doctoral studies, Hitchings began his career in academia, holding various teaching and research positions before joining Burroughs Wellcome in 1942.

The partnership between Elion and Hitchings began when Elion joined Burroughs Wellcome and started working in Hitchings' laboratory. At the time, the field of drug development was dominated by the trial-and-error approach, where scientists would randomly test thousands of compounds in the hope of finding one that worked as a drug. This approach was not only time-consuming and costly but also had a low success rate. Hitchings, however, had a different vision. He believed that it was possible to design drugs in a more rational and targeted way by understanding the biochemical processes that underlie diseases. This idea was revolutionary at the time and would form the basis of the work that Elion and Hitchings would carry out together.

One of the key concepts that guided their work was the idea that certain diseases are caused by disruptions in specific biochemical pathways, such as the synthesis of nucleic acids (the building blocks of DNA and RNA). Hitchings theorized that by targeting these pathways, it would be possible to develop drugs that could selectively inhibit the growth of harmful cells, such as cancer cells or bacteria, without harming normal cells. To achieve this, they focused on designing molecules that could interfere with the enzymes involved in these pathways, effectively "starving" the diseased cells of the materials they needed to survive and reproduce.

Their first major breakthrough came with the development of the drug 6-mercaptopurine (6-MP), which was introduced in the early 1950s. 6-MP was the first drug specifically designed to treat leukemia, a type of cancer that affects the blood and bone marrow. At the time, leukemia was considered a death sentence, with very few treatment options available. However, 6-MP proved to be highly effective in inducing remission in patients with leukemia, and it quickly became a standard treatment for the disease. This was a major achievement, not only because it provided a new hope for leukemia patients but also because it validated the rational drug design approach that Elion and Hitchings had pioneered.

Following the success of 6-MP, Elion and Hitchings continued to apply their approach to the development of other drugs. One of their most significant contributions was the development of azathioprine, an immunosuppressive drug that is widely used to prevent organ rejection in transplant patients. Before the advent of azathioprine, organ transplants were extremely risky procedures, as the body's immune system would often attack and destroy the transplanted organ. Azathioprine, however, was able to suppress the immune response, allowing the transplanted organ to survive and function in the recipient's body. This drug has had a profound impact on the field of organ transplantation, making it possible for thousands of patients to receive life-saving transplants.

Another major achievement of Elion and Hitchings was the development of allopurinol, a drug used to treat gout, a painful condition caused by the buildup of uric acid in the joints. Allopurinol works by inhibiting the enzyme xanthine oxidase, which is involved in the production of uric acid. By reducing the levels of uric acid in the body, allopurinol helps to prevent the formation of the painful crystals that cause gout attacks. This drug has become a mainstay of gout treatment and is still widely used today.

In addition to these drugs, Elion and Hitchings also developed a number of other important medications, including pyrimethamine, used to treat malaria; trimethoprim, an antibiotic used to treat bacterial infections; and acyclovir, an antiviral drug used to treat herpes infections. Each of these drugs was developed using the same rational drug design approach, and each has had a significant impact on the treatment of their respective diseases.

One of the remarkable aspects of the work of Elion and Hitchings is the breadth of their contributions. Unlike many researchers who focus on a single disease or a single class of drugs, Elion and Hitchings worked on a wide range of diseases, including cancer, infectious diseases, autoimmune disorders, and metabolic disorders. This versatility is a testament to the power of their approach, which was based on fundamental principles of biochemistry rather than on the specifics of any one disease.

The work of Elion and Hitchings was recognized with numerous awards and honors. In 1988, they were jointly awarded the Nobel Prize in Physiology or Medicine, along with Sir James Black, for their contributions to the development of drugs that have had a major impact on human health. The Nobel Committee cited their work as having "opened new fields of study and led to the development of important new drugs" and praised their "imaginative and pioneering work" in the field of medicinal chemistry.

The legacy of Gertrude B. Elion and George H. Hitchings extends far beyond the drugs they developed. Their work laid the foundation for modern drug discovery, which is now based on a rational design approach rather than on random screening. This approach has led to the development of many other life-saving drugs and has transformed the pharmaceutical industry. Moreover, their work demonstrated the importance of collaboration and interdisciplinary research, as their success was due in large part to their ability to integrate knowledge from different fields, including chemistry, biology, and medicine.

Elion and Hitchings also left a lasting impact on the field of education and mentorship. Throughout their careers, they were deeply committed to training the next generation of scientists, and they mentored many young researchers who went on to make their own significant contributions to the field. Elion, in particular, was known for her dedication to mentoring women in science, and she played a key role in encouraging and supporting women to pursue careers in chemistry and medicine at a time when such opportunities were limited.

In conclusion, the partnership between Gertrude B. Elion and George H. Hitchings represents one of the most successful and influential collaborations in the history of medicinal chemistry. Their innovative approach to drug discovery, based on an understanding of the biochemical mechanisms underlying diseases, led to the development of numerous life-saving drugs and transformed the way that new medications are developed. Their work has had a profound and lasting impact on the treatment of many diseases, and their legacy continues to inspire scientists and researchers around the world. Their story is a testament to the power of collaboration, perseverance, and the pursuit of knowledge, and it serves as an enduring example of the impact that science can have on improving human health and well-being.

Chapter 19: Charles K. Kao

Charles K. Kao, widely known as the "Father of Fiber Optics," is a figure of monumental importance in the history of telecommunications and modern technology. His pioneering work in the field of fiber optics revolutionized the way information is transmitted across the globe, laying the groundwork for the internet and many other forms of modern communication that we now take for granted. Kao's groundbreaking contributions have had a lasting impact on various fields, including telecommunications, computer networking, medical imaging, and even entertainment, as his work made possible the rapid transmission of data through optical fibers, a technology that underpins everything from high-speed internet to cable television.

Born on November 4, 1933, in Shanghai, China, Charles Kuen Kao showed an early aptitude for science and engineering. His family valued education, and Kao was encouraged to pursue his interests in these areas from a young age. In 1948, amidst the Chinese Civil War, Kao's family moved to Hong Kong, where he completed his secondary education. He then went on to study electrical engineering at the University of London, graduating with a Bachelor of Science degree in 1957. Afterward, he continued his studies at the same institution, earning a Ph.D. in electrical engineering in 1965.

Kao's journey into the world of fiber optics began when he joined Standard Telecommunication Laboratories (STL) in Harlow, England, in 1960. At the time, STL was a research division of ITT Corporation, a major telecommunications company. It was here that Kao first encountered the idea of using light to transmit information. While the concept of optical communication had been around for some time, it was largely dismissed as impractical due to the significant loss of signal strength, or attenuation, that occurred when light traveled through glass. This attenuation, caused by impurities in the glass, was so severe that optical communication was thought to be unfeasible for long-distance transmission.

However, Kao was not deterred by the prevailing skepticism. He believed that the problem of attenuation could be overcome and that fiber optics could become a viable medium for transmitting information over long distances. Along with his colleague, George Hockham, Kao began investigating the properties of glass fibers and exploring ways to reduce attenuation. In 1966, they published a groundbreaking paper that would change the course of telecommunications history.

In their paper, Kao and Hockham proposed that the attenuation in glass fibers was not an inherent property of the material itself, but rather a result of impurities in the glass. They theorized that if these impurities could be removed, it would be possible to create glass fibers with significantly lower attenuation, making them suitable for long-distance communication. Furthermore, they calculated that a glass fiber with an attenuation of less than 20 decibels per kilometer (dB/km) would be capable of transmitting light over distances of several kilometers without significant loss of signal. This was a bold assertion, as the best glass fibers at the time had attenuations of around 1,000 dB/km.

Kao's work marked a turning point in the field of optical communications. His theoretical insights and rigorous analysis challenged the prevailing assumptions about the limitations of glass fibers and opened up new possibilities for their use in telecommunications. Following the publication of his paper, Kao embarked on a mission to find a material that could meet the stringent requirements he had outlined. He collaborated with glass manufacturers and materials scientists in an effort to develop ultra-pure glass fibers that would have the low attenuation necessary for practical use in telecommunications.

The breakthrough came in 1970 when researchers at Corning Glass Works, inspired by Kao's work, succeeded in producing a glass fiber with an attenuation of just 17 dB/km. This achievement, which was a direct result of Kao's theoretical work, validated his predictions and demonstrated that fiber optics could indeed be used for long-distance communication. With this discovery, the field of telecommunications was on the cusp of a revolution.

The development of low-attenuation optical fibers paved the way for the commercialization of fiber optic technology. By the late 1970s and early 1980s, fiber optic communication systems were being deployed around the world, replacing traditional copper wire systems in many applications. Fiber optics offered numerous advantages over copper wires, including higher bandwidth, lower signal loss, and immunity to electromagnetic interference. These benefits made fiber optics the preferred choice for high-speed data transmission, leading to the rapid expansion of global telecommunications networks.

Kao's contributions to fiber optics did not end with the development of low-attenuation fibers. He continued to be an active and influential figure in the field, advocating for the widespread adoption of fiber optic technology and contributing to its ongoing development. In 1970, Kao joined the Chinese University of Hong Kong (CUHK) as the founding chairman of the Department of Electronics, where he played a key role in establishing the university's reputation as a leading center for research in telecommunications and electronics. He also served as the university's vice-chancellor from 1987 to 1996, during which time he oversaw significant expansion and modernization efforts.

Kao's work had far-reaching implications beyond telecommunications. The principles of fiber optic communication have been applied in various fields, leading to advancements in medical technology, scientific research, and entertainment. For example, in the medical field, fiber optics have been used to develop endoscopic devices that allow doctors to view inside the human body with minimal invasiveness. In scientific research, fiber optics are used in a variety of instruments, including spectrometers and sensors, to measure and analyze light in various contexts. In the entertainment industry, fiber optics have enabled the high-speed transmission of data necessary for streaming video, online gaming, and other digital media services.

One of the most significant impacts of Kao's work has been on the development of the internet. The high bandwidth and low attenuation of fiber optic cables have made them the backbone of the global internet infrastructure. Today, the vast majority of internet data is transmitted through fiber optic cables, enabling the rapid exchange of information across the globe. Without Kao's pioneering work, the internet as we know it today would not exist. The ability to transmit large amounts of data quickly and efficiently has transformed nearly every aspect of modern life, from business and education to entertainment and social interaction.

Kao's achievements have been widely recognized and celebrated. In 2009, he was awarded the Nobel Prize in Physics for his "groundbreaking achievements concerning the transmission of light in fibers for optical communication." The Nobel Committee praised Kao for "laying the foundation of modern optical communication technology" and noted that his work had "enabled the development of the broadband networks that we use today." The Nobel Prize was just one of many honors Kao received during his lifetime. He was also awarded the Marconi Prize in 1985, the IEEE Alexander Graham Bell Medal in 1989, and the Charles Stark Draper Prize in 1999, among many other accolades.

Despite his many achievements, Kao remained humble and focused on his work throughout his life. He was known for his dedication to science and his commitment to advancing knowledge in the field of telecommunications. He was also deeply committed to education and mentoring, and he inspired countless students and young researchers to pursue careers in science and engineering. Kao's influence extended far beyond the laboratory, as he played a key role in shaping the future of telecommunications and ensuring that the benefits of fiber optic technology were realized on a global scale.

In his later years, Kao was diagnosed with Alzheimer's disease, a condition that gradually robbed him of his ability to communicate and recognize the world around him. Despite this, he continued to be a symbol of inspiration for many in the scientific community, and his legacy lives on in the countless technologies and innovations that were made possible by his work. Kao passed away on September 23, 2018, at the age of 84, leaving behind a legacy that continues to shape the world in profound ways.

In conclusion, Charles K. Kao's contributions to the field of telecommunications and fiber optics represent one of the most significant advancements in modern technology. His groundbreaking work on the transmission of light through glass fibers revolutionized the way information is transmitted and laid the foundation for the development of the internet and other modern communication systems. Kao's legacy extends far beyond the field of telecommunications, as his work has had a profound impact on many other areas of science and technology. His dedication to science, education, and innovation serves as an enduring example of the power of human curiosity and the potential for scientific discoveries to change the world.

Chapter 20: Emmanuelle Charpentier & Jennifer Doudna

Emmanuelle Charpentier and Jennifer Doudna are two of the most influential scientists of the 21st century, celebrated for their pioneering work on CRISPR-Cas9, a revolutionary technology that has transformed the field of genetics and molecular biology. Their discovery of the CRISPR-Cas9 gene-editing tool has opened up new avenues in medicine, agriculture, and biotechnology, offering unprecedented possibilities for understanding and manipulating the genetic code. The profound implications of their work, both in terms of its scientific impact and its ethical considerations, have sparked a global conversation about the future of genetic engineering and its potential to reshape humanity.

Emmanuelle Charpentier was born on December 11, 1968, in Juvisy-sur-Orge, France. From an early age, she exhibited a strong interest in science, particularly in biology and the natural world. She pursued her studies in microbiology and biochemistry, earning a degree in biochemistry from Pierre and Marie Curie University in Paris, followed by a Ph.D. in microbiology from the Pasteur Institute in 1995. Charpentier's research career took her across several prestigious institutions in Europe and the United States, where she focused on bacterial pathogens and the mechanisms of RNA regulation.

Jennifer Doudna was born on February 19, 1964, in Washington, D.C., but she spent much of her childhood in Hilo, Hawaii. Growing up in the diverse and natural environment of Hawaii, Doudna developed a fascination with the natural sciences. She earned her bachelor's degree in biochemistry from Pomona College in California and went on to obtain her Ph.D. in biological chemistry and molecular pharmacology from Harvard Medical

School in 1989. Doudna's early research focused on RNA, a molecule that plays a crucial role in the expression of genetic information. Her work on the structure and function of RNA led her to become one of the leading experts in the field.

The paths of Charpentier and Doudna converged through their shared interest in RNA and its role in bacterial immunity. In 2011, Charpentier, who was then working at the University of Vienna, was studying the bacterium *Streptococcus pyogenes*, a pathogen known for causing various infections in humans. During her research, she discovered an RNA molecule that was part of a previously unknown bacterial immune system, which bacteria use to protect themselves from viruses. This immune system, known as CRISPR (Clustered Regularly Interspaced Short Palindromic Repeats), allowed bacteria to recognize and cut viral DNA, preventing the viruses from replicating and spreading.

Charpentier's discovery of the CRISPR system was groundbreaking, but it was only the beginning. She realized that the CRISPR system could potentially be harnessed as a tool for editing genes in other organisms, including humans. To explore this possibility, she sought out the expertise of Jennifer Doudna, who was then a professor at the University of California, Berkeley. Doudna's extensive experience with RNA and her background in structural biology made her the perfect collaborator for Charpentier's ambitious project.

The collaboration between Charpentier and Doudna was highly productive, and in 2012, they published a landmark paper that would change the course of genetics forever. In their paper, they described how the CRISPR-Cas9 system could be engineered to precisely cut DNA at specific locations, allowing for the targeted modification of genes. The CRISPR-Cas9 system works by using a guide RNA to direct the Cas9 enzyme to a specific sequence of DNA, where it makes a precise cut. Once the DNA is cut, the cell's natural repair mechanisms can be harnessed to either disable a gene or introduce new genetic material at the site of the cut.

The simplicity, precision, and versatility of the CRISPR-Cas9 system quickly made it the most powerful tool in the field of genetics. Unlike previous gene-editing technologies, which were often complex, time-consuming, and expensive, CRISPR-Cas9 allowed scientists to edit genes with unprecedented ease and accuracy. The implications of this technology were vast, offering the potential to correct genetic defects, treat diseases, enhance agricultural crops, and even alter the genetic makeup of entire species.

One of the most immediate applications of CRISPR-Cas9 has been in the field of medicine, where it has been used to develop new therapies for genetic diseases. For example, researchers have used CRISPR-Cas9 to correct mutations that cause sickle cell anemia, a debilitating blood disorder that affects millions of people worldwide. By editing the defective gene in stem cells taken from a patient's bone marrow, scientists have been able to produce healthy blood cells that can be transplanted back into the patient, potentially curing the disease. Similar approaches are being explored for other genetic disorders, such as cystic fibrosis, muscular dystrophy, and Huntington's disease.

In addition to treating genetic diseases, CRISPR-Cas9 has also shown promise in the fight against cancer. By editing the genes of immune cells, researchers have been able to create "supercharged" immune cells that are more effective at recognizing and attacking cancer cells. This approach, known as CAR-T cell therapy, has already shown success in treating certain types of leukemia and lymphoma, and it holds the potential to be applied to other forms of cancer as well.

The impact of CRISPR-Cas9 extends beyond medicine. In agriculture, the technology has been used to develop crops that are more resistant to pests, diseases, and environmental stresses. For example, scientists have used CRISPR-Cas9 to create rice varieties that are resistant to bacterial blight, a devastating disease that can wipe out entire crops. Similarly, CRISPR-Cas9 has been used to enhance the nutritional content of crops, such as by increasing the levels of essential vitamins and minerals in staple foods like wheat and maize. These advancements have the potential to improve food security and nutrition for millions of people around the world.

CRISPR-Cas9 has also opened up new possibilities in the field of synthetic biology, where scientists are using the technology to engineer organisms with entirely new functions. For example, researchers have used CRISPR-Cas9 to create bacteria that can produce biofuels, biodegradable plastics, and other valuable chemicals. In another example, scientists have engineered yeast cells to produce the active ingredients in certain drugs, offering a more sustainable and cost-effective way to manufacture pharmaceuticals.

Despite the many potential benefits of CRISPR-Cas9, the technology has also raised significant ethical concerns, particularly when it comes to its use in humans. One of the most contentious issues is the possibility of using CRISPR-Cas9 to edit the human germline, meaning the genetic material that is passed on to future generations. Editing the germline would allow for the permanent alteration of the human gene pool, raising concerns about the potential for unintended consequences, such as the creation of new genetic diseases or the exacerbation of social inequalities.

The ethical debate surrounding CRISPR-Cas9 came to a head in 2018 when a Chinese scientist, He Jiankui, announced that he had used the technology to create the world's first genetically edited babies. He claimed to have edited the embryos of twin girls to make them resistant to HIV, but his actions were widely condemned by the scientific community and led to calls for stricter regulation of gene-editing technologies. The incident underscored the need for a global consensus on the ethical use of CRISPR-Cas9 and highlighted the importance of responsible research and oversight.

Both Charpentier and Doudna have been vocal advocates for the responsible use of CRISPR-Cas9 and have called for careful consideration of the ethical implications of their work. They have emphasized the need for transparent and inclusive discussions about the potential risks and benefits of gene editing, as well as the importance of establishing clear guidelines and regulations to govern its use. In 2015, Doudna co-organized the first international summit on human gene editing, bringing together scientists, ethicists, and policymakers to discuss the future of the technology and its implications for society.

In recognition of their groundbreaking contributions to science, Emmanuelle Charpentier and Jennifer Doudna have received numerous awards and honors. In 2020, they were jointly awarded the Nobel Prize in Chemistry for the development of CRISPR-Cas9, making them the first two women to share the prize in the field of chemistry. The Nobel Committee praised their work as "a tool for rewriting the code of life" and highlighted its potential to "bring the greatest benefit to humankind." The Nobel Prize was just one of many accolades they have received, including the Breakthrough Prize in Life Sciences, the Kavli Prize in Nanoscience, and the Japan Prize.

The work of Charpentier and Doudna has not only revolutionized the field of genetics but has also inspired a new generation of scientists and researchers. Their story is a testament to the power of curiosity, collaboration, and perseverance in the pursuit of scientific discovery. It also serves as a reminder of the profound impact that science can have on society and the importance of using that power responsibly.

Looking to the future, the potential applications of CRISPR-Cas9 are vast and continue to expand. Researchers are exploring new ways to improve the precision and efficiency of the technology, as well as developing new tools and techniques for editing the genome. For example, recent advances in "base editing" and "prime editing" have allowed scientists to make even more precise changes to the DNA sequence, further expanding the possibilities of gene editing. These advancements hold the promise of even greater breakthroughs in medicine, agriculture, and beyond.

At the same time, the ethical and societal implications of CRISPR-Cas9 continue to be a topic of intense debate. As the technology becomes more accessible and widespread, there is an urgent need to address the challenges it presents, including issues related to equity, consent, and the potential for misuse. Ensuring that the benefits of CRISPR-Cas9 are shared widely and that its risks are managed responsibly will require ongoing dialogue and collaboration among scientists, ethicists, policymakers, and the public.

In conclusion, the discovery of CRISPR-Cas9 by Emmanuelle Charpentier and Jennifer Doudna represents one of the most significant scientific achievements of the modern era. Their work has transformed our understanding of the genetic code and has opened up new possibilities for treating diseases, improving agriculture, and advancing biotechnology. At the same time, it has raised important ethical questions about the future of genetic engineering and the responsibilities that come with such powerful tools. As we continue to explore the potential of CRISPR-Cas9, the legacy of Charpentier and Doudna will undoubtedly shape the direction of science and society for generations to come. Their story is a powerful reminder of the impact that science can have on the world and the importance of pursuing knowledge with both curiosity and care.

Chapter 21: Wieschaus, Nüsslein-Volhard, & B. Lewis

The collaborative work of Eric Wieschaus, Christiane Nüsslein-Volhard, and Edward B. Lewis represents a landmark achievement in the field of developmental biology. Their groundbreaking research on the genetic control of embryonic development, particularly in the fruit fly *Drosophila melanogaster*, revolutionized our understanding of how genes regulate the formation of complex organisms. This trio of scientists unveiled the intricate genetic networks that dictate body plan development, revealing how a single fertilized egg can give rise to a fully formed organism with distinct body segments, tissues, and organs. Their discoveries have had profound implications, not only for developmental biology but also for genetics, evolutionary biology, and medicine. For their pioneering work, they were awarded the Nobel Prize in Physiology or Medicine in 1995, an honor that underscored the significance of their contributions to science.

The story of their collaboration begins with Edward B. Lewis, an American geneticist born on May 20, 1918, in Wilkes-Barre, Pennsylvania. Lewis had a deep interest in genetics from an early age, and he went on to study biology at the University of Minnesota, where he earned his bachelor's degree in 1939. He then pursued his Ph.D. at the California Institute of Technology (Caltech), where he studied under the legendary geneticist Alfred Sturtevant, a student of Thomas Hunt Morgan, the founder of modern genetics. Lewis's early work focused on the genetic regulation of development, particularly in *Drosophila melanogaster*, a model organism that had already proven invaluable in genetic research.

Lewis's research centered on a group of genes known as the "homeotic genes," which are responsible for determining the identity of body segments in *Drosophila*. These genes are part of a larger gene complex known as the "Hox genes," which play a crucial role in patterning the body plan of all bilaterian organisms, including humans. In the 1940s and 1950s, Lewis conducted a series of meticulous genetic experiments that revealed how mutations in homeotic genes could cause dramatic transformations in the body plan of the fly. For example, he showed that a mutation in the *Ultrabithorax* gene could cause a segment that would normally develop into a haltere (a small balancing organ) to instead develop into a second pair of wings. Similarly, mutations in the *Antennapedia* gene could cause legs to grow in place of antennae on the fly's head.

Lewis's work demonstrated that homeotic genes are responsible for specifying the identity of each body segment, effectively instructing cells on what structures they should form. He also discovered that these genes are arranged in a specific order on the chromosome, with the sequence of genes corresponding to the sequence of body segments they regulate. This phenomenon, known as "colinearity," was a striking example of how the genetic information is organized in a way that directly reflects the organism's body plan. Lewis's research laid the foundation for our understanding of how genes control the development of complex body structures and provided the first glimpse into the genetic basis of body plan organization.

While Lewis was making his groundbreaking discoveries in the United States, Christiane Nüsslein-Volhard and Eric Wieschaus were conducting their own pioneering research in Europe. Nüsslein-Volhard, born on October 20, 1942, in Magdeburg, Germany, developed an early interest in biology and pursued her studies at the University of Tübingen, where she completed her Ph.D. in 1973. After working as a postdoctoral researcher at the University of Basel in Switzerland, she returned to Tübingen to work at the Max Planck Institute for Developmental Biology, where she began her seminal research on *Drosophila*.

Eric Wieschaus, born on June 8, 1947, in South Bend, Indiana, also developed a passion for biology at a young age. He studied biology at the University of Notre Dame, earning his bachelor's degree in 1969, and then pursued his Ph.D. at Yale University, where he studied under the renowned developmental biologist Donald Poulson. After completing his Ph.D. in 1974, Wieschaus moved to Europe to work as a postdoctoral researcher at the University of Zurich, where he collaborated with Walter Gehring, a leading figure in the field of developmental genetics. It was during this time that Wieschaus and Nüsslein-Volhard met and began their collaboration, which would lead to some of the most significant discoveries in developmental biology.

In the late 1970s, Nüsslein-Volhard and Wieschaus embarked on an ambitious project to systematically identify the genes involved in early embryonic development in *Drosophila*. At the time, it was known that the development of an organism from a single fertilized egg into a complex, multicellular entity was governed by a series of genetic instructions. However, the identity of these genes and how they functioned was largely unknown. Nüsslein-Volhard and Wieschaus sought to answer these fundamental questions by using a genetic screen to identify mutations that disrupted normal embryonic development in the fly.

Their approach was both simple and elegant. They exposed *Drosophila* embryos to a chemical mutagen that induced random mutations in the fly's genome. They then screened thousands of mutant embryos for those that exhibited defects in their body plan, such as missing segments, duplicated segments, or incorrect segment identities. By identifying and characterizing these mutations, Nüsslein-Volhard and Wieschaus were able to pinpoint the genes responsible for controlling different aspects of embryonic development.

The results of their screen were nothing short of astonishing. They identified a total of 139 genes that were essential for the proper development of the fly embryo, many of which had never been described before. These genes fell into three broad categories, each corresponding to a different stage of development: "gap genes," which define broad regions of the embryo; "pair-rule genes," which establish the periodic pattern of segments; and "segment polarity genes," which determine the anterior-posterior polarity of each segment. Together, these genes formed a genetic hierarchy that controlled the step-by-step process of segment formation in the embryo.

One of the most significant findings from their work was the discovery of the "bicoid" gene, a maternal-effect gene that plays a crucial role in establishing the anterior-posterior axis of the embryo. The bicoid gene is expressed in the mother fly and its mRNA is deposited in the anterior region of the egg. After fertilization, the bicoid mRNA is translated into a protein that forms a concentration gradient along the length of the embryo, with the highest levels at the anterior end. This gradient acts as a positional cue for the developing embryo, instructing cells at different positions along the axis to adopt specific identities. The discovery of the bicoid gene provided the first molecular explanation for how positional information is established in the early embryo and demonstrated the importance of maternal gene products in controlling embryonic development.

The work of Nüsslein-Volhard and Wieschaus also revealed that the genetic mechanisms controlling development in *Drosophila* are highly conserved across species. Many of the genes they identified in the fly have homologs in other organisms, including vertebrates, where they play similar roles in regulating development. This conservation of developmental pathways underscores the universality of the genetic code and the evolutionary significance of the genes that control body plan formation. It also highlights the power of *Drosophila* as a model organism for studying the fundamental principles of development.

The research of Lewis, Nüsslein-Volhard, and Wieschaus has had far-reaching implications beyond developmental biology. Their discoveries have provided key insights into the genetic basis of congenital disorders, cancer, and other diseases that result from the misregulation of developmental processes. For example, mutations in human homologs of the Hox genes have been linked to a variety of congenital malformations, such as limb deformities and spinal defects. Similarly, the misexpression of genes involved in segment polarity and cell signaling pathways has been implicated in the development of cancer, as these genes play critical roles in controlling cell proliferation, differentiation, and apoptosis.

The impact of their work is also evident in the field of evolutionary biology, where their findings have shed light on the genetic mechanisms underlying the evolution of body plans. The discovery that the same set of genes controls segment formation in a wide range of organisms suggests that the basic genetic framework for body plan development was established early in evolution and has been conserved across diverse lineages. This insight has led to the concept of "evolutionary developmental biology," or "evo-devo," which seeks to understand how changes in the regulation of developmental genes can lead to the evolution of new body plans and species.

The Nobel Prize in Physiology or Medicine in 1995 was a fitting recognition of the transformative impact of the work of Lewis, Nüsslein-Volhard, and Wieschaus. Their discoveries have fundamentally changed our understanding of the genetic control of development and have provided a framework for exploring the complex interactions between genes, cells, and tissues during the formation of an organism. The knowledge they generated continues to drive research in genetics, developmental biology, and medicine, and it serves as a testament to the power of curiosity, creativity, and collaboration in the pursuit of scientific discovery.

In addition to their scientific achievements, Lewis, Nüsslein-Volhard, and Wieschaus have also made significant contributions to the training and mentoring of the next generation of scientists. Their work has inspired countless researchers to pursue careers in developmental biology and genetics, and they have played a key role in shaping the direction of these fields. Nüsslein-Volhard, in particular, has been a strong advocate for the advancement of women in science, and she has established a foundation to support young female scientists in Germany. Wieschaus, meanwhile, has continued to teach and mentor students at Princeton University, where he has been a professor since 1981.

The legacy of their work is also reflected in the ongoing research that builds on their discoveries. Scientists are continuing to explore the genetic networks that control development, using new technologies such as CRISPR-Cas9 gene editing and single-cell RNA sequencing to probe the functions of genes with unprecedented precision. These advances are providing new insights into the molecular mechanisms that underlie development and are opening up new possibilities for treating diseases and understanding the evolutionary origins of diversity in the natural world.

In conclusion, the work of Eric Wieschaus, Christiane Nüsslein-Volhard, and Edward B. Lewis represents one of the most significant achievements in the history of biology. Their discoveries have transformed our understanding of the genetic control of development and have provided a foundation for a wide range of research in genetics, medicine, and evolutionary biology. Their work has not only expanded our knowledge of the fundamental processes that shape life but has also inspired future generations of scientists to continue exploring the mysteries of development and evolution. The impact of their research will continue to be felt for many years to come, as new discoveries build on the foundation they established and as we continue to uncover the secrets of the genetic code that governs the development of all living organisms.

Chapter 22: Ernest Rutherford

Ernest Rutherford, often referred to as the father of nuclear physics, was a pioneering scientist whose contributions to our understanding of atomic structure laid the groundwork for modern physics. Born on August 30, 1871, in the small rural town of Brightwater near Nelson, New Zealand, Rutherford's journey from a humble upbringing to becoming one of the most influential physicists in history is a testament to his intellect, curiosity, and relentless pursuit of knowledge. His groundbreaking work not only revolutionized the field of atomic physics but also paved the way for the development of quantum mechanics and nuclear physics, disciplines that have profoundly shaped our understanding of the natural world.

Rutherford's early life was marked by a strong emphasis on education, despite the modest means of his family. His parents, James Rutherford, a Scottish wheelwright, and Martha Thompson, an English schoolteacher, instilled in him the importance of learning and hard work. Rutherford excelled in school, displaying a keen interest in science and mathematics from a young age. His academic abilities earned him a scholarship to attend Nelson College, a prestigious secondary school in New Zealand, where he continued to thrive academically. It was here that Rutherford first began to develop the skills and knowledge that would later define his scientific career.

In 1890, Rutherford was awarded a scholarship to attend Canterbury College in Christchurch, New Zealand, which is now known as the University of Canterbury. At Canterbury College, Rutherford pursued a Bachelor of Arts degree in mathematics and physical sciences, graduating with first-class honors in 1893. During his time at university, Rutherford conducted his first research project on the properties of high-frequency electrical waves, which sparked his lifelong interest in experimental physics. His exceptional performance earned him the prestigious 1851 Exhibition Science Scholarship, which provided him with the opportunity to further his studies in England, a turning point in his life that would set him on the path to becoming one of the most celebrated scientists of his time.

In 1895, Rutherford traveled to England to study at the University of Cambridge's Cavendish Laboratory, one of the leading centers for experimental physics in the world. At the Cavendish, Rutherford worked under the supervision of J.J. Thomson, a prominent physicist who would later become known for his discovery of the electron. Under Thomson's guidance, Rutherford conducted experiments on the conductivity of gases, leading to his first major scientific breakthrough: the discovery of the concept of "ionization," the process by which atoms or molecules acquire a charge by gaining or losing electrons. This work earned Rutherford his first major recognition in the scientific community and established his reputation as a brilliant experimental physicist.

In 1898, Rutherford was appointed to a professorship at McGill University in Montreal, Canada, where he continued his research on radioactivity. It was at McGill that Rutherford made some of his most significant contributions to the field of atomic physics. Working alongside Frederick Soddy, a young chemist who would later win the Nobel Prize in Chemistry, Rutherford conducted a series of experiments that led to the discovery of the phenomenon of radioactive decay, the process by which unstable atomic nuclei lose energy by emitting radiation. Rutherford and Soddy demonstrated that radioactive elements, such as uranium and thorium, undergo spontaneous decay into other elements over time, a process that releases energy in the form of alpha, beta, and gamma radiation. This work provided the first empirical evidence for the existence of atomic nuclei and laid the foundation for the modern understanding of nuclear reactions.

One of Rutherford's most famous experiments, often referred to as the "gold foil experiment," was conducted in 1909 at the University of Manchester, where he had taken up a new position as a professor of physics. In collaboration with his students Hans Geiger and Ernest Marsden, Rutherford aimed to investigate the structure of the atom by observing the scattering of alpha particles, which are helium nuclei, as they passed through a thin sheet of gold foil. According to the prevailing model of the atom at the time, known as the "plum pudding model" proposed by J.J. Thomson, the atom was thought to consist of a diffuse cloud of positive charge with negatively charged electrons embedded within it, like raisins in a pudding. This model predicted that alpha particles would pass through the atom with only slight deflections, as the positive charge was thought to be spread out evenly across the atom.

However, the results of Rutherford's experiment were shocking and unexpected. While most of the alpha particles did pass through the gold foil with little or no deflection, a small fraction of them were deflected at large angles, with some even bouncing back in the direction they came from. Rutherford famously described this result as being "as if you fired a 15-inch shell at a piece of tissue paper and it came back and hit you." The only explanation for these observations was that the positive charge in the atom was not spread out evenly, but rather concentrated in a very small, dense region at the center of the atom. This led Rutherford to propose a new model of the atom, known as the "nuclear model," in which the atom consists of a tiny, dense nucleus containing all of the positive charge and most of the mass, surrounded by a cloud of electrons.

The nuclear model of the atom was a revolutionary concept that fundamentally changed our understanding of atomic structure. Rutherford's discovery of the nucleus provided the first evidence that atoms have a complex internal structure, rather than being indivisible particles as had been previously thought. This discovery also explained the phenomenon of radioactive decay, as the unstable nuclei of radioactive elements were found to be responsible for emitting radiation. Rutherford's work on the nuclear model of the atom earned him widespread acclaim and established him as one of the leading physicists of his time.

In 1911, Rutherford published his findings in a paper titled "The Scattering of Alpha and Beta Particles by Matter and the Structure of the Atom," which is considered one of the most important papers in the history of physics. This work laid the groundwork for the development of quantum mechanics, a new branch of physics that would emerge in the early 20th century to explain the behavior of subatomic particles. Rutherford's nuclear model of the atom also provided the basis for Niels Bohr's model of the hydrogen atom, which introduced the concept of quantized energy levels and explained the spectral lines of hydrogen. Bohr's model, in turn, led to the development of quantum theory, which has become the foundation of modern physics.

Rutherford's contributions to science extended beyond his work on atomic structure. During World War I, he applied his expertise in physics to the development of new technologies for the war effort. He was involved in research on submarine detection, using sound waves to locate enemy submarines, and he also contributed to the development of the first practical method for detecting and measuring radioactivity, known as the Geiger counter. After the war, Rutherford returned to his research on nuclear physics, where he made another groundbreaking discovery: the artificial transmutation of elements.

In 1917, Rutherford conducted an experiment in which he bombarded nitrogen gas with alpha particles and observed the production of oxygen and a proton. This experiment demonstrated that it was possible to change one element into another by altering the structure of its atomic nucleus, a process that became known as "nuclear transmutation." Rutherford's work on nuclear transmutation marked the first time that an artificial nuclear reaction had been achieved, and it provided the first direct evidence for the existence of protons, the positively charged particles found in the nucleus. This discovery further solidified Rutherford's reputation as a pioneer in the field of nuclear physics and opened up new possibilities for research into the nature of atomic nuclei.

In recognition of his numerous contributions to science, Rutherford was awarded the Nobel Prize in Chemistry in 1908 for his investigations into the disintegration of the elements and the chemistry of radioactive substances. While Rutherford considered himself primarily a physicist, his work had a profound impact on both chemistry and physics, blurring the lines between the two disciplines. The Nobel Prize was just one of many honors Rutherford received during his lifetime, including being knighted in 1914 and being named a Fellow of the Royal Society, one of the most prestigious scientific organizations in the world.

In 1919, Rutherford was appointed as the director of the Cavendish Laboratory at the University of Cambridge, succeeding his former mentor, J.J. Thomson. Under Rutherford's leadership, the Cavendish Laboratory became a world center for research in nuclear physics, attracting some of the brightest minds of the time, including future Nobel laureates such as James Chadwick, who discovered the neutron, and John Cockcroft and Ernest Walton, who built the first particle accelerator and achieved the first artificial nuclear disintegration. Rutherford's influence as a mentor and leader helped shape the direction of nuclear physics for decades to come, and his legacy as a teacher is reflected in the many groundbreaking discoveries made by his students and colleagues.

Rutherford's later years were marked by continued research and public service. He was a strong advocate for the peaceful use of atomic energy and played a key role in the establishment of the

Cavendish Professorship of Physics at the University of Cambridge, a position that continues to be one of the most prestigious academic posts in physics. He also served as president of the Royal Society from 1925 to 1930, where he worked to promote scientific research and education.

Ernest Rutherford passed away on October 19, 1937, at the age of 66, leaving behind a legacy that has had a lasting impact on the field of physics and beyond. His contributions to our understanding of atomic structure, radioactivity, and nuclear reactions laid the foundation for many of the technological advancements of the 20th century, including nuclear power and medical imaging technologies such as X-rays and PET scans. Rutherford's work also paved the way for the development of quantum mechanics and the discovery of the neutron, which ultimately led to the development of nuclear weapons and the exploration of nuclear energy.

Rutherford's legacy extends beyond his scientific achievements to his role as a mentor, educator, and leader in the scientific community. His commitment to rigorous experimentation, critical thinking, and the pursuit of knowledge has inspired generations of scientists to push the boundaries of what is known and to explore the mysteries of the natural world. His work continues to be celebrated and studied by physicists, chemists, and historians of science, and his name remains synonymous with the pioneering spirit of discovery that drives scientific progress.

In conclusion, Ernest Rutherford's contributions to science were nothing short of transformative. His discoveries fundamentally changed our understanding of the atom and the nature of matter, and his work laid the groundwork for many of the most important scientific advancements of the 20th century. Rutherford's legacy is one of curiosity, perseverance, and a deep commitment to the pursuit of knowledge. He remains a towering figure in the history of science, and his work continues to inspire and inform the ongoing quest to understand the fundamental principles that govern the universe.

Chapter 23: Shockley, Bardeen, & Brattain

The collaborative work of William Shockley, John Bardeen, and Walter Brattain at Bell Laboratories in the mid-20th century marks one of the most significant turning points in modern technology, laying the foundation for the electronic age through their invention of the transistor. This achievement not only revolutionized the field of electronics but also catalyzed the development of computers, telecommunications, and countless other technologies that define the modern world. Their work on the transistor, for which they were awarded the Nobel Prize in Physics in 1956, represents a cornerstone in the history of science and technology, encapsulating the transformative power of human ingenuity and collaboration.

The story of the transistor's invention is rooted in the scientific exploration of semiconductors, materials that possess electrical conductivity properties between those of a conductor and an insulator. The understanding of semiconductors, particularly their behavior at the atomic level, was essential for the development of solid-state electronics. Before the transistor, the primary device used to amplify electrical signals was the vacuum tube, which, despite its effectiveness, was bulky, consumed a lot of power, and was prone to frequent failure. The scientific community and the burgeoning electronics industry were in dire need of a more reliable, efficient, and compact alternative.

William Shockley, born on February 13, 1910, in London, England, was a physicist and inventor who played a central role in the conceptualization and eventual invention of the transistor. Shockley's early life was marked by a strong interest in science, and he pursued his education at the California Institute of Technology, where he earned a bachelor's degree in physics. He later obtained his Ph.D. from the Massachusetts Institute of Technology (MIT) in 1936. After completing his studies, Shockley joined Bell Telephone Laboratories, where he became involved in research on solid-state physics, particularly the behavior of semiconductors.

At Bell Labs, Shockley was joined by John Bardeen and Walter Brattain, who would become his collaborators in the quest to develop a solid-state amplifier. John Bardeen, born on May 23, 1908, in Madison, Wisconsin, was an exceptionally gifted physicist and engineer. He completed his undergraduate studies in electrical engineering at the University of Wisconsin-Madison before pursuing a Ph.D. in mathematical physics at Princeton University. Bardeen's keen interest in the behavior of electrons in solids made him an ideal candidate for the research team at Bell Labs. Walter Brattain, born on February 10, 1902, in Amoy, China, where his father was a teacher, was another brilliant physicist who specialized in surface physics and solid-state research. He completed his undergraduate studies at Whitman College and earned his Ph.D. in physics from the University of Minnesota.

The collaboration between Shockley, Bardeen, and Brattain began in the late 1940s when they were tasked with finding a solution to the limitations of vacuum tubes. They focused on understanding how semiconductors, particularly silicon and germanium, could be used to control electrical signals. Semiconductors were known to exhibit unique properties, such as the ability to conduct electricity under certain conditions while acting as insulators under others. This dual nature made them prime candidates for developing a new type of electronic device that could amplify signals.

The trio's research initially centered on the idea of creating a "field-effect" transistor, a device that would use an electric field to control the flow of current through a semiconductor. However, their early attempts were unsuccessful, and they struggled to achieve the desired amplification. Despite these setbacks, the team persisted, experimenting with different materials, configurations, and approaches. The turning point came when Bardeen proposed that surface states at the interface between the semiconductor and the surrounding materials might be interfering with the flow of electrons. This insight led to a series of experiments that culminated in the invention of the point-contact transistor in December 1947.

The point-contact transistor was a small, simple device consisting of a piece of germanium with two closely spaced gold contacts pressed against it. When a small current was applied to one contact (the emitter), it caused a much larger current to flow through the germanium and out of the second contact (the collector). This amplification of the current was the key to the transistor's operation, allowing it to function as a switch or amplifier in electronic circuits. The point-contact transistor was the first successful implementation of a solid-state amplifier, and it demonstrated that semiconductors could be used to control electrical signals in a way that was far more efficient and reliable than vacuum tubes.

The significance of the point-contact transistor cannot be overstated. It marked the beginning of the transition from bulky, power-hungry vacuum tubes to compact, energy-efficient solid-state devices. The transistor's small size, low power consumption, and durability made it ideal for a wide range of applications, from radios and televisions to computers and telecommunications equipment. The invention of the transistor ushered in a new era of electronics, enabling the development of smaller, faster, and more reliable electronic devices that could be mass-produced at a lower cost.

Following the success of the point-contact transistor, Shockley continued to refine and improve the design. He was driven by the desire to create a more robust and manufacturable version of the transistor, which led him to conceive the junction transistor in 1948. The junction transistor was based on a different principle than the point-contact transistor, using layers of semiconductor material with different electrical properties (known as p-type and n-type semiconductors) to control the flow of current. Shockley's junction transistor was more reliable and easier to manufacture than the point-contact transistor, and it quickly became the standard for solid-state electronics.

While the junction transistor was a significant advancement, it was not without its challenges. Shockley's intense focus on developing the junction transistor and his determination to take full credit for the invention led to tensions between him and his collaborators, particularly Bardeen and Brattain. The strain on their working relationship grew as Shockley sought to assert his leadership over the project, often sidelining the contributions of his colleagues. Despite these interpersonal conflicts, the trio's collective efforts had already set in motion a revolution in electronics that would reshape the world.

The impact of the transistor was immediate and far-reaching. In the 1950s, transistor radios became one of the first consumer products to benefit from this new technology. These portable radios were smaller, lighter, and more energy-efficient than their vacuum tube predecessors, and they quickly gained popularity around the world. The success of transistor radios demonstrated the practical advantages of solid-state electronics and helped to fuel further research and development in the field.

As the technology matured, transistors became the building blocks of more complex electronic systems, including computers. The development of the integrated circuit, which combined multiple transistors and other electronic components onto a single piece of semiconductor material, was a direct outgrowth of the transistor's invention. Integrated circuits made it possible to build powerful computers that were far smaller and more efficient than earlier machines, leading to the development of personal computers, smartphones, and other digital devices that have become integral to modern life.

The invention of the transistor also had profound implications for telecommunications. Transistors enabled the development of more reliable and efficient communication systems, from telephone networks to satellite communications. The miniaturization of electronic components made possible by transistors allowed for the creation of sophisticated communication devices, such as cell phones, that have revolutionized the way people connect with one another across the globe.

The transistor's influence extended beyond consumer electronics and telecommunications to virtually every aspect of modern society. In medicine, transistors have enabled the development of advanced diagnostic and therapeutic equipment, such as MRI machines and pacemakers. In transportation, transistors have contributed to the development of electronic control systems that improve the safety and efficiency of vehicles. In energy, transistors are integral to the operation of renewable energy systems, such as solar panels and wind turbines, which rely on electronic controls to optimize power generation.

The broader scientific and technological impact of the transistor is reflected in the numerous accolades and honors received by its inventors. In 1956, William Shockley, John Bardeen, and Walter Brattain were awarded the Nobel Prize in Physics for their "researches on semiconductors and their discovery of the transistor effect." The Nobel Committee recognized that their work had not only advanced the understanding of solid-state physics but had also laid the foundation for an entire industry that would transform the world.

Despite the recognition and acclaim, the personal dynamics between the three inventors were complex and often strained. Shockley, who had a reputation for being difficult to work with, eventually left Bell Labs to start his own company, Shockley Semiconductor Laboratory, in 1956. However, his management style and interpersonal conflicts led to the departure of key employees, who went on to form Fairchild Semiconductor, a company that would play a central role in the development of the Silicon Valley tech industry.

John Bardeen, who was known for his modesty and collaborative spirit, continued to make significant contributions to science after the invention of the transistor. He returned to academia, where he became a professor at the University of Illinois at Urbana-Champaign. In 1972, Bardeen achieved the rare distinction of winning a second Nobel Prize in Physics, this time for his role in developing the theory of superconductivity, known as the BCS theory, alongside Leon Cooper and Robert Schrieffer. Bardeen remains one of only four individuals to have won the Nobel Prize in Physics twice, underscoring his extraordinary contributions to science.

Walter Brattain, who had focused on the experimental aspects of the transistor's development, also continued his research in solid-state physics after leaving Bell Labs. He returned to academia, joining the faculty of Whitman College, where he continued to teach and conduct research until his retirement. Brattain was known for his dedication to mentoring students and his commitment to advancing scientific knowledge.

The legacy of Shockley, Bardeen, and Brattain is evident in the ubiquitous presence of transistors in the modern world. Today, billions of transistors are manufactured every day, and they are found in nearly every electronic device, from smartphones and laptops to automobiles and industrial machinery. The miniaturization of transistors has enabled the development of microprocessors, the "brains" of computers, which have revolutionized industries, economies, and societies.

The invention of the transistor also played a crucial role in the rise of Silicon Valley as the global center of technology and innovation. The region's growth was fueled by the semiconductor industry, which was built on the foundation laid by the work of Shockley, Bardeen, and Brattain. Companies like Intel, AMD, and many others trace their origins back to the early pioneers of transistor technology, and the principles of innovation, collaboration, and entrepreneurship that defined the transistor's development continue to drive the tech industry today.

In conclusion, the work of William Shockley, John Bardeen, and Walter Brattain in inventing the transistor stands as one of the most significant achievements in the history of science and technology. Their collaborative efforts not only transformed the field of electronics but also laid the groundwork for the digital revolution that has reshaped the world. The transistor's impact is felt in every corner of modern life, from the devices we use every day to the global networks that connect us. The legacy of these three scientists is a testament to the power of human ingenuity and the profound impact that scientific discovery can have on the world.

Chapter 24: Tu Youyou

Tu Youyou, born on December 30, 1930, in Ningbo, Zhejiang province, China, is a remarkable figure in the history of science and medicine. Her work has saved millions of lives and fundamentally altered the course of global public health, particularly in the fight against malaria, one of the deadliest diseases in human history. Tu's groundbreaking discovery of artemisinin, a powerful antimalarial drug, not only earned her international recognition but also highlighted the importance of traditional medicine in modern scientific research. She became the first Chinese woman to receive the Nobel Prize in Physiology or Medicine in 2015, an honor that was a testament to her perseverance, ingenuity, and dedication to improving global health.

Tu's journey to becoming a Nobel laureate is a story of resilience and determination. Growing up in China during a time of great political and social upheaval, Tu was inspired by her father's encouragement to pursue education and by her own passion for medicine. She enrolled in the Peking University School of Medicine, where she studied pharmacology, a field that blends the knowledge of traditional herbal remedies with modern medical science. This interdisciplinary approach would later prove crucial in her groundbreaking research.

After completing her studies in 1955, Tu joined the China Academy of Traditional Chinese Medicine (now the China Academy of Chinese Medical Sciences) in Beijing. Her early career was marked by extensive research into the medicinal properties of traditional Chinese herbs. This period of her life was a time of intense learning and exploration, as Tu immersed herself in the rich history of Chinese herbal medicine, which had been developed and refined over thousands of years. She became particularly interested in the potential of these ancient remedies to treat modern diseases, a focus that would guide her work in the years to come.

Tu's expertise in traditional Chinese medicine set the stage for her involvement in what would become one of the most important scientific endeavors of the 20th century. In the 1960s, during the Vietnam War, malaria was a major health crisis, particularly in Southeast Asia. The disease, caused by Plasmodium parasites and transmitted by Anopheles mosquitoes, was responsible for millions of deaths worldwide. The existing treatments for malaria, primarily chloroquine and quinine, were becoming increasingly ineffective due to the rapid development of drug-resistant strains of the parasite. This growing resistance posed a serious threat to global health, and the search for new antimalarial drugs became an urgent priority.

In 1967, as part of China's Cultural Revolution, the Chinese government launched Project 523, a secret military program aimed at finding a cure for malaria. The project was named after its starting date, May 23rd (5/23), and was a response to a request from North Vietnamese leader Ho Chi Minh, who sought assistance from China in combating the malaria epidemic that was devastating his troops. Tu Youyou was appointed as the head of a research team within this project, tasked with identifying and developing new antimalarial compounds.

Tu's approach to this challenge was both innovative and rooted in tradition. Recognizing the limitations of modern synthetic drugs, she turned to ancient Chinese medical texts, searching for herbal remedies that had been used for centuries to treat fever and other symptoms associated with malaria. This decision was not without risks, as the Cultural Revolution was a time of significant political turmoil, and traditional medicine was often dismissed or undervalued by the ruling authorities. Nevertheless, Tu persisted, driven by her belief in the potential of these ancient remedies.

Her team meticulously reviewed over 2,000 traditional Chinese herbal prescriptions, ultimately focusing on 640 different plants that had been used to treat malaria-like symptoms. They conducted hundreds of experiments to extract and test the active compounds from these plants, but progress was slow and results were often disappointing. Many of the extracts they tested showed little to no efficacy against malaria, and the pressure to deliver results was mounting.

One of the turning points in Tu's research came when she revisited a 1,600-year-old text, the "Handbook of Prescriptions for Emergencies," written by Ge Hong during the Jin Dynasty. This ancient medical treatise described the use of a plant called qinghao (Artemisia annua, or sweet wormwood) to treat intermittent fevers, a symptom commonly associated with malaria. Inspired by this reference, Tu decided to focus her efforts on Artemisia annua, hoping that it might hold the key to a new antimalarial drug.

Tu's initial attempts to extract the active compound from Artemisia annua using traditional methods were unsuccessful, as the extracts showed only weak activity against the malaria parasite. Undeterred, she revisited the ancient texts and made a crucial observation: the traditional preparation involved soaking the plant in cold water rather than boiling it. This insight led her to modify her extraction process, using a low-temperature method with ether as the solvent. The result was a much more potent extract, which she later identified as containing the active compound artemisinin.

The discovery of artemisinin was a monumental breakthrough. Artemisinin proved to be highly effective against Plasmodium falciparum, the deadliest of the malaria parasites, and it worked by rapidly reducing the parasite burden in the blood. The compound's unique mechanism of action, which involves the generation of free radicals that damage the parasite's proteins, made it particularly effective against drug-resistant strains of malaria. Tu's team conducted extensive testing in animal models and later in human trials, where artemisinin showed remarkable efficacy in treating malaria.

Despite the success of her research, Tu faced significant challenges in bringing her discovery to the world. The political climate in China during the Cultural Revolution was hostile to scientific innovation, particularly when it involved traditional medicine. Furthermore, the secrecy surrounding Project 523 meant that Tu's work could not be published or shared with the international scientific community for several years. Nevertheless, she persisted, driven by the knowledge that artemisinin had the potential to save millions of lives.

In the years following her discovery, Tu continued to work tirelessly to ensure that artemisinin would be developed into a widely available treatment for malaria. Her efforts eventually paid off, as artemisinin-based combination therapies (ACTs) became the standard treatment for malaria worldwide. ACTs, which combine artemisinin with other antimalarial drugs to prevent the development of resistance, have been credited with significantly reducing malaria-related deaths, particularly in sub-Saharan Africa and Southeast Asia, where the disease is most prevalent.

The global impact of Tu Youyou's work cannot be overstated. Artemisinin-based therapies have saved millions of lives and continue to be a critical tool in the fight against malaria. The World Health Organization (WHO) has endorsed artemisinin as an essential medicine, and it remains one of the most effective treatments for malaria today. Tu's discovery has not only had a profound impact on public health but has also inspired a renewed interest in the potential of traditional medicine to contribute to modern scientific advancements.

In recognition of her extraordinary contributions to science and medicine, Tu Youyou has received numerous awards and honors.

In 2011, she was awarded the Lasker-DeBakey Clinical Medical Research Award, one of the most prestigious medical awards in the United States, often referred to as "America's Nobel Prize." The Lasker Foundation recognized her for the discovery of artemisinin and its significant impact on the treatment of malaria.

Tu's most significant recognition came in 2015 when she was awarded the Nobel Prize in Physiology or Medicine. The Nobel Committee honored her for her discovery of artemisinin, which they described as having "revolutionized the treatment of malaria." Tu's Nobel Prize was particularly noteworthy as she was the first Chinese woman to receive a Nobel Prize in any scientific field, and she did so without a medical degree, a doctorate, or experience working in a Western research institution. Her achievement was celebrated as a triumph not only for her personally but also for the global scientific community, demonstrating that groundbreaking discoveries can come from any part of the world.

Tu Youyou's legacy extends beyond her discovery of artemisinin. She has become a symbol of the power of interdisciplinary research, combining traditional knowledge with modern science to achieve breakthroughs that were previously thought impossible. Her work has inspired a new generation of scientists to explore the potential of natural products in drug discovery, a field that continues to yield important new treatments for a variety of diseases.

Tu's life and career also highlight the importance of perseverance and dedication in the face of adversity. Her journey was marked by numerous challenges, including political obstacles, limited resources, and the skepticism of her peers. Yet, she remained committed to her work, driven by the belief that her research could make a difference in the lives of millions of people. Her success is a testament to the idea that great science often requires not only brilliance and innovation but also determination and resilience.

In the years since her Nobel Prize, Tu Youyou has continued to be an active voice in the scientific community, advocating for the integration of traditional medicine with modern research methods. She has emphasized the importance of preserving traditional knowledge while subjecting it to rigorous scientific scrutiny to identify and develop new treatments. Her work has also underscored the importance of international collaboration in addressing global health challenges, as the fight against malaria and other infectious diseases requires the combined efforts of scientists, governments, and organizations around the world.

Tu Youyou's story is one of inspiration and hope. It is a reminder that even in the most challenging circumstances, one person's dedication and passion for science can lead to discoveries that change the world. Her work has had a profound impact on global health, saving millions of lives and providing a model for how traditional knowledge can be harnessed to solve modern problems. As the world continues to face new and emerging health challenges, Tu's legacy serves as a beacon of what is possible when science, tradition, and determination come together in the pursuit of a better future for all.

Chapter 25: François Englert & Peter Higgs

François Englert and Peter Higgs are two towering figures in the field of theoretical physics, whose work has fundamentally reshaped our understanding of the universe. Their pioneering contributions to the theory of the Higgs mechanism and the prediction of the Higgs boson, often referred to as the "God particle," represent one of the most significant achievements in modern science. The discovery of the Higgs boson in 2012 at the Large Hadron Collider (LHC) at CERN not only confirmed a critical aspect of the Standard Model of particle physics but also marked the culmination of nearly five decades of theoretical and experimental work. In recognition of their groundbreaking contributions, Englert and Higgs were jointly awarded the Nobel Prize in Physics in 2013, an honor that underscored the profound impact of their ideas on the scientific community and our understanding of the fundamental forces that govern the universe.

François Englert was born on November 6, 1932, in Etterbeek, Belgium. His early life was marked by the turmoil of World War II, during which he and his family, who were Jewish, faced persecution under the Nazi occupation of Belgium. Despite these hardships, Englert showed an early aptitude for science and mathematics, which he pursued with determination after the war. He studied engineering at the Free University of Brussels, where he received his Ph.D. in 1959. Englert's scientific career took off when he began collaborating with Robert Brout, an American physicist who had also moved to Belgium. This partnership would prove to be highly productive, leading to their joint work on spontaneous symmetry breaking in quantum field theory, a key concept in the development of the Higgs mechanism.

Peter Higgs, born on May 29, 1929, in Newcastle upon Tyne, England, also demonstrated a strong interest in science from an early age. Higgs was particularly influenced by the work of Paul Dirac, a pioneering theoretical physicist who made significant contributions to quantum mechanics and quantum field theory. Higgs studied physics at King's College London, where he earned his doctorate in 1954. After completing his Ph.D., Higgs held several academic positions in the United Kingdom, where he continued his research in theoretical physics. His work in the early 1960s focused on the role of symmetries in particle physics, an area of study that would eventually lead him to propose the existence of a new fundamental particle, now known as the Higgs boson.

The Higgs mechanism, the theoretical framework that Higgs, Englert, and Brout helped to develop, addresses one of the most fundamental questions in physics: how particles acquire mass. In the early 20th century, physicists had developed quantum field theory, a powerful mathematical framework that describes the interactions of subatomic particles. However, despite its successes, quantum field theory could not fully explain why some particles, such as the W and Z bosons (which mediate the weak nuclear force), have mass, while others, like the photon (which mediates the electromagnetic force), are massless. This discrepancy posed a significant challenge to the development of a unified theory of the fundamental forces.

The solution to this problem emerged in the 1960s, when several physicists, including Higgs, Englert, Brout, Gerald Guralnik, C.R. Hagen, and Tom Kibble, independently proposed a mechanism by which particles could acquire mass through the process of spontaneous symmetry breaking. In essence, the Higgs mechanism suggests that a scalar field, now known as the Higgs field, permeates all of space. Particles acquire mass by interacting with this field; the more strongly a particle interacts with the Higgs field, the more massive it becomes. The Higgs boson is the quantum excitation of the Higgs field, and its discovery was critical to confirming the validity of the Higgs mechanism.

In 1964, François Englert and Robert Brout were the first to publish a paper on the spontaneous breaking of gauge symmetry, a key concept underlying the Higgs mechanism. They demonstrated that the presence of a scalar field could break the symmetry of the underlying physical laws, leading to the emergence of massive gauge bosons. Shortly thereafter, Peter Higgs published two papers, in which he independently arrived at similar conclusions. In his second paper, Higgs explicitly predicted the existence of a new particle, the Higgs boson, which would be a byproduct of the symmetry-breaking process. This prediction marked a significant milestone in theoretical physics, as it provided a testable hypothesis that could be explored through experimentation.

The idea of the Higgs boson and the Higgs mechanism was met with skepticism initially, as the particle's existence seemed almost impossible to verify with the technology available at the time. The Higgs boson was expected to be extremely massive, and detecting it would require an unprecedented level of energy in particle collisions. Nonetheless, the concept gradually gained acceptance as it became clear that the Higgs mechanism was an essential component of the Standard Model, the prevailing theory that describes the fundamental particles and forces in the universe.

The Standard Model, developed throughout the 1970s, is one of the most successful theories in the history of science. It describes the electromagnetic, weak, and strong nuclear forces, as well as the particles that mediate these forces, with extraordinary precision. However, the Higgs boson remained the missing piece of the puzzle. Without experimental confirmation of the Higgs boson, the Standard Model would be incomplete, as the Higgs mechanism is responsible for giving mass to the W and Z bosons and, by extension, to other elementary particles.

The search for the Higgs boson became one of the primary goals of particle physics in the latter half of the 20th century. Experiments at particle accelerators around the world, including those at CERN in Switzerland and Fermilab in the United States, were designed to probe the high-energy regimes where the Higgs boson was expected to be found. However, despite decades of effort, the elusive particle remained undetected, leading some to question whether it existed at all.

The breakthrough came with the construction of the Large Hadron Collider (LHC) at CERN, the most powerful particle accelerator ever built. The LHC, which began operation in 2008, was designed specifically to search for new particles, including the Higgs boson, by smashing protons together at nearly the speed of light. These high-energy collisions create conditions similar to those that existed just moments after the Big Bang, allowing physicists to study the fundamental building blocks of the universe.

On July 4, 2012, after years of painstaking research and data analysis, scientists at CERN announced that they had discovered a new particle consistent with the Higgs boson. The discovery was made independently by two research teams, ATLAS and CMS, which had been analyzing the vast amounts of data generated by the LHC. The new particle had a mass of about 125 gigaelectronvolts (GeV), which was within the range predicted by the Standard Model. The statistical significance of the discovery was so high that it left little doubt that the long-sought Higgs boson had finally been found.

The discovery of the Higgs boson was hailed as one of the greatest scientific achievements of the 21st century. It provided the final piece of evidence needed to confirm the validity of the Standard Model, cementing our understanding of the fundamental forces that govern the universe. The Higgs boson also opened up new avenues of research in particle physics, as scientists began to explore its properties in greater detail and to investigate potential connections to other areas of physics, such as dark matter and the origins of the universe.

In recognition of their pioneering work, François Englert and Peter Higgs were awarded the Nobel Prize in Physics in 2013. The Nobel Committee honored them "for the theoretical discovery of a mechanism that contributes to our understanding of the origin of mass of subatomic particles, and which recently was confirmed through the discovery of the predicted fundamental particle, by the ATLAS and CMS experiments at CERN's Large Hadron Collider." This prestigious award acknowledged the profound impact of their contributions on the field of physics and highlighted the importance of theoretical predictions in guiding experimental discoveries.

The legacy of Englert and Higgs extends far beyond the discovery of the Higgs boson. Their work has inspired generations of physicists to explore the deepest questions about the nature of the universe, from the origins of mass to the fundamental forces that shape reality. The Higgs mechanism, in particular, has become a cornerstone of modern physics, influencing research in a wide range of areas, including cosmology, particle physics, and even condensed matter physics.

Moreover, the discovery of the Higgs boson has had significant implications for our understanding of the universe. The Higgs field, which gives particles their mass, is thought to play a crucial role in the evolution of the early universe, particularly during the period known as cosmic inflation. During this period, the universe expanded rapidly from a tiny, hot, and dense state to the vast, cool cosmos we observe today. The Higgs field may have been responsible for driving this inflationary expansion, making it a key player in the history of the universe.

The discovery of the Higgs boson has also raised new questions about the nature of reality and the limits of our current understanding. For example, the mass of the Higgs boson, as measured by the LHC, suggests that the universe may exist in a precarious state, known as a "metastable" vacuum. In this scenario, the universe could eventually transition to a lower-energy state, leading to a catastrophic event known as vacuum decay. While this possibility is purely theoretical and would likely occur on timescales far longer than the current age of the universe, it highlights the profound implications of the Higgs field for the ultimate fate of the cosmos.

The work of François Englert and Peter Higgs has also had a lasting impact on the broader scientific community. Their discovery has demonstrated the power of collaboration between theorists and experimentalists, showing how theoretical ideas can guide experimental searches for new phenomena, and how experimental discoveries can, in turn, validate and refine theoretical models. The story of the Higgs boson is a testament to the importance of perseverance and creativity in science, as well as to the value of international cooperation in tackling the most challenging questions in physics.

Today, research on the Higgs boson continues, as physicists seek to understand its properties more fully and to explore its potential connections to other areas of physics. The LHC has entered a new phase of operation, with upgraded detectors and higher collision energies, allowing for even more precise measurements of the Higgs boson and the search for new particles and forces beyond the Standard Model. The discovery of the Higgs boson has opened the door to a new era of particle physics, with the potential to reveal deeper insights into the nature of the universe and the fundamental laws that govern it.

In conclusion, the work of François Englert and Peter Higgs represents one of the most significant achievements in the history of science. Their theoretical insights into the origin of mass and the prediction of the Higgs boson have fundamentally changed our understanding of the universe, providing a critical piece of the puzzle that is the Standard Model of particle physics. The discovery of the Higgs boson at the Large Hadron Collider stands as a triumph of human ingenuity and collaboration, a testament to the power of theoretical physics to unlock the deepest mysteries of the cosmos. The legacy of Englert and Higgs will continue to inspire future generations of scientists as they seek to unravel the remaining mysteries of the universe and to explore the uncharted territories of the subatomic world.

Chapter 26: Goodenough, Whittingham, & Yoshino

The story of John B. Goodenough, M. Stanley Whittingham, and Akira Yoshino is one of remarkable scientific achievement and innovation, culminating in the development of the lithium-ion battery, a technology that has revolutionized the way we live and work. Their contributions to the creation of this rechargeable power source have had a profound impact on modern society, enabling the widespread use of portable electronic devices, advancing the field of renewable energy, and laying the foundation for the electric vehicle industry. In recognition of their groundbreaking work, the trio was awarded the Nobel Prize in Chemistry in 2019, a testament to the transformative power of their discoveries and their lasting influence on technology and the environment.

The journey to the lithium-ion battery began in the 1970s during a time of global energy crisis and rising interest in alternative energy sources. M. Stanley Whittingham, a British-American chemist, was at the forefront of this movement. Born in 1941 in Nottingham, England, Whittingham pursued his education at the University of Oxford, where he earned his bachelor's, master's, and doctoral degrees in chemistry. After completing his studies, Whittingham moved to the United States, where he began working for ExxonMobil in the early 1970s. At that time, Exxon was exploring new energy technologies as a response to the oil crisis, which had underscored the vulnerability of relying solely on fossil fuels.

Whittingham's research focused on the development of new materials for energy storage, specifically batteries. He was interested in finding a way to store and release energy efficiently in a rechargeable form. In 1976, Whittingham made a critical breakthrough when he discovered that titanium disulfide (TiS2) could serve as a cathode material in a battery. Titanium disulfide has a layered structure that allows lithium ions to intercalate, or insert themselves, between the layers during the discharge process, and to be removed during charging. This process of intercalation was key to the development of rechargeable batteries, as it enabled the movement of lithium ions without causing significant structural damage to the material.

Whittingham paired the titanium disulfide cathode with a lithium metal anode, creating the first working lithium battery. This battery had a significantly higher energy density than previous batteries, meaning it could store more energy in a smaller and lighter package. However, there was a major drawback: the use of lithium metal in the anode posed serious safety risks. Lithium is highly reactive, and the battery was prone to short-circuiting and catching fire. Despite its promise, the technology was deemed too dangerous for commercial use, and further development stalled.

While Whittingham's lithium battery was not yet ready for widespread adoption, his work laid the groundwork for future advancements. His discovery of the intercalation process was particularly important, as it provided a new way of thinking about energy storage materials and inspired other scientists to explore similar ideas. Among those who took up the challenge was John B. Goodenough, an American physicist whose contributions would prove to be decisive in overcoming the limitations of Whittingham's design.

John B. Goodenough was born on July 25, 1922, in Jena, Germany, to American parents. He grew up in the United States and pursued a career in physics, earning his doctorate from the University of Chicago in 1952. Goodenough's early work focused on the study of magnetism and the electronic properties of materials, areas in which he made significant contributions. In the 1950s and

1960s, he was involved in research on the magnetic properties of transition metal oxides, a topic that would later inform his work on batteries.

In 1976, the same year Whittingham developed his lithium battery, Goodenough was appointed professor and head of the Inorganic Chemistry Laboratory at the University of Oxford. It was here that he began to explore ways to improve upon Whittingham's design. Goodenough recognized that the key to developing a safer and more efficient lithium battery lay in finding a suitable cathode material that could operate at a higher voltage, thereby increasing the energy density of the battery.

Through his research, Goodenough identified a class of materials known as layered oxides, which had similar properties to titanium disulfide but could operate at a higher voltage. In 1980, he made a breakthrough when he discovered that lithium cobalt oxide ($LiCoO_2$) could serve as an effective cathode material. Lithium cobalt oxide has a layered structure similar to titanium disulfide, allowing lithium ions to move in and out during the charging and discharging process. However, unlike titanium disulfide, lithium cobalt oxide could operate at a voltage of around 4 volts, which significantly increased the energy density of the battery.

Goodenough's discovery of lithium cobalt oxide as a cathode material was a game-changer. It allowed for the development of lithium-ion batteries that were not only more efficient but also safer, as they did not require the use of highly reactive lithium metal in the anode. Instead, the anode could be made from a variety of other materials, including carbon-based materials like graphite. The combination of a lithium cobalt oxide cathode and a graphite anode became the basis for the first commercial lithium-ion batteries.

The next major step in the development of lithium-ion batteries came from Japan, where Akira Yoshino, a Japanese chemist and engineer, made critical contributions. Born on January 30, 1948, in

Suita, Osaka, Yoshino pursued his studies in chemistry at Kyoto University, where he earned his bachelor's and master's degrees. He later joined the Asahi Kasei Corporation, a Japanese chemical company, where he began working on battery technology in the early 1980s.

Yoshino was inspired by Goodenough's work on lithium cobalt oxide and saw the potential for developing a rechargeable battery that could be used in portable electronic devices. However, he recognized that the use of lithium metal in the anode remained a major obstacle to commercialization. Yoshino set out to find an alternative anode material that would be safer and more stable.

In 1985, Yoshino succeeded in creating the first practical lithium-ion battery by using petroleum coke, a carbon material, as the anode. Petroleum coke, like graphite, could intercalate lithium ions without the risk of forming dangerous dendrites that could cause short circuits. Yoshino paired this anode with Goodenough's lithium cobalt oxide cathode, creating a battery that was not only rechargeable and high in energy density but also much safer than previous designs.

Yoshino's lithium-ion battery was the first to be truly practical for widespread commercial use. It was lightweight, had a high energy density, and could be recharged hundreds of times without significant loss of capacity. These characteristics made it ideal for use in portable electronic devices, such as laptops, cell phones, and eventually, electric vehicles. Recognizing the potential of this technology, Sony Corporation, in collaboration with Asahi Kasei, began mass-producing lithium-ion batteries in 1991, marking the beginning of a new era in consumer electronics.

The impact of the lithium-ion battery on society has been profound. It enabled the development of portable electronic devices that have become ubiquitous in modern life, from smartphones and laptops to tablets and wearable technology. The high energy density and rechargeable nature of lithium-ion batteries also made them essential for the advancement of renewable energy technologies. Solar panels and wind turbines, which generate electricity intermittently, require efficient energy storage solutions to provide a stable supply of power. Lithium-ion batteries have become a key component of energy storage systems, allowing for the integration of renewable energy into the electrical grid and reducing reliance on fossil fuels.

In addition to their use in consumer electronics and renewable energy, lithium-ion batteries have played a critical role in the development of electric vehicles (EVs). The high energy density of lithium-ion batteries makes them ideal for powering electric cars, which require lightweight, efficient, and long-lasting energy storage to achieve practical driving ranges. The widespread adoption of EVs, driven in large part by advances in lithium-ion battery technology, is helping to reduce greenhouse gas emissions and combat climate change.

The work of Goodenough, Whittingham, and Yoshino has not only transformed technology but also has had significant environmental and economic impacts. The proliferation of portable electronics and electric vehicles has driven demand for lithium-ion batteries, leading to advancements in battery manufacturing and recycling processes. This, in turn, has created new industries and jobs, while also contributing to efforts to reduce the environmental footprint of energy production and consumption.

In recognition of their contributions to the development of lithium-ion batteries, John B. Goodenough, M. Stanley Whittingham, and Akira Yoshino were awarded the Nobel Prize in Chemistry in 2019. The Nobel Committee honored them "for the development of lithium-ion batteries," emphasizing the global significance of their work. The award was particularly notable for Goodenough, who became the oldest Nobel laureate in history at the age of 97, a testament to the enduring impact of his contributions to science and technology.

The legacy of Goodenough, Whittingham, and Yoshino extends far beyond their individual achievements. Their work has inspired a new generation of researchers and engineers to explore further advancements in battery technology, including the development of next-generation batteries with even higher energy densities, faster charging times, and greater safety. Research into solid-state batteries, which use a solid electrolyte instead of a liquid one, holds the promise of further improving the performance and safety of energy storage systems, potentially leading to new applications in transportation, renewable energy, and beyond.

The story of lithium-ion batteries is also a story of international collaboration and the importance of interdisciplinary research. The contributions of Goodenough, Whittingham, and Yoshino spanned continents, with each building on the work of the others to achieve a common goal. Their success underscores the value of collaboration in scientific research, as well as the importance of bringing together diverse perspectives and expertise to solve complex problems.

Today, lithium-ion batteries are an integral part of the global economy and a critical technology in the fight against climate change. As the world continues to grapple with the challenges of energy sustainability and environmental protection, the importance of efficient and reliable energy storage cannot be overstated. The work of Goodenough, Whittingham, and Yoshino has provided the foundation for a future in which clean, renewable energy can be harnessed to meet the growing demand for power, while reducing the environmental impact of energy production and consumption.

In conclusion, the development of lithium-ion batteries by John B. Goodenough, M. Stanley Whittingham, and Akira Yoshino represents one of the most significant technological advancements of the 20th and 21st centuries. Their contributions have fundamentally changed the way we live, work, and interact with the world around us, enabling the proliferation of portable electronic devices, advancing renewable energy technologies, and driving the growth of the electric vehicle industry. The impact of their work will continue to be felt for generations to come, as lithium-ion batteries remain a cornerstone of modern technology and a key tool in the global effort to build a more sustainable future. The Nobel Prize in Chemistry awarded to these three scientists in 2019 is a fitting recognition of their groundbreaking achievements and a celebration of the power of science and innovation to change the world.

Chapter 27: Arber, Nathans, & Smith

The story of Werner Arber, Daniel Nathans, and Hamilton O. Smith is one of groundbreaking scientific discovery that has had a profound and lasting impact on the field of molecular biology. Their work, which centers around the discovery and application of restriction enzymes, has revolutionized our understanding of genetics, opened the door to the development of recombinant DNA technology, and laid the foundation for modern biotechnology. The contributions of these three scientists, recognized with the Nobel Prize in Physiology or Medicine in 1978, have not only transformed scientific research but have also had far-reaching implications for medicine, agriculture, and industry.

To appreciate the significance of their achievements, it is essential to understand the scientific context in which they were working. In the mid-20th century, the field of molecular biology was rapidly advancing, driven by the discovery of the structure of DNA by James Watson and Francis Crick in 1953. This breakthrough revealed that DNA was the hereditary material in living organisms and provided the blueprint for the transmission of genetic information from one generation to the next. However, while the structure of DNA was known, the mechanisms by which genetic material was manipulated and regulated within cells were still largely mysterious.

One of the central challenges in molecular biology was understanding how organisms protect themselves from foreign genetic material, such as viruses. Bacteria, for example, are frequently attacked by bacteriophages, which are viruses that infect and replicate within bacterial cells. It was known that some bacteria possessed a natural defense mechanism that allowed them to resist infection by certain bacteriophages, but the molecular basis of this resistance was not yet understood.

Werner Arber, a Swiss microbiologist, was one of the first scientists to investigate this phenomenon. Born on June 3, 1929, in Gränichen, Switzerland, Arber pursued his education in the natural sciences, eventually earning his Ph.D. from the University of Geneva in 1958. His early research focused on bacterial genetics, and he became interested in the mechanisms by which bacteria defended themselves against bacteriophage infections. In the 1960s, Arber and his colleagues made a groundbreaking discovery: they found that bacteria produced specific enzymes that could recognize and cut foreign DNA at certain sequences, thereby inactivating the invading genetic material. These enzymes, which Arber called "restriction enzymes," provided bacteria with a molecular "immune system" that allowed them to protect themselves from viral attacks.

Arber's discovery of restriction enzymes was a major breakthrough in molecular biology. It revealed that DNA could be precisely cut at specific locations, a capability that had significant implications for genetic research. The ability to cut DNA at defined sites meant that scientists could now isolate and study individual genes, a task that had previously been impossible. However, while Arber had identified the existence of restriction enzymes, much work remained to be done to fully understand their properties and potential applications.

It was at this point that two American scientists, Daniel Nathans and Hamilton O. Smith, made crucial contributions to the field. Daniel Nathans was born on October 30, 1928, in Wilmington, Delaware, and pursued his education in chemistry and medicine, earning his M.D. from Washington University in St. Louis in 1954. Nathans developed a keen interest in molecular biology and joined the faculty at Johns Hopkins University in 1962, where he began working on the genetics of viruses. His work focused on understanding how viral genes were expressed and regulated within host cells, a topic that was closely related to the mechanisms of restriction enzymes.

Hamilton O. Smith, born on August 23, 1931, in New York City, also pursued a career in medicine and molecular biology. After earning his M.D. from Johns Hopkins University in 1956, Smith became interested in bacterial genetics and the molecular mechanisms that governed DNA replication and repair. In the late 1960s, Smith was investigating the bacterium *Haemophilus influenzae* when he discovered that it produced a restriction enzyme that specifically recognized a particular sequence of DNA and cut it in a precise manner. This enzyme, which Smith named HindII, was the first restriction enzyme to be characterized in detail, and its discovery marked a turning point in molecular biology.

Smith's work on HindII provided critical insights into the nature of restriction enzymes. He demonstrated that these enzymes could be used as precise molecular "scissors" to cut DNA at specific sites, creating fragments that could be analyzed, manipulated, and recombined in the laboratory. Smith's discovery was significant not only because it confirmed Arber's earlier findings but also because it opened up new possibilities for genetic research. With the ability to cut and splice DNA, scientists could now study the structure and function of individual genes in unprecedented detail.

Daniel Nathans quickly recognized the potential of restriction enzymes for genetic research. He realized that these enzymes could be used to map the genomes of viruses, bacteria, and other organisms by cutting their DNA into smaller, manageable pieces. Nathans applied this approach to the study of simian virus 40 (SV40), a small DNA virus that had been implicated in cancer research. By using restriction enzymes to cut the SV40 genome into specific fragments, Nathans was able to create a physical map of the virus's genetic material. This map provided valuable information about the organization of the viral genome and the locations of key genes involved in viral replication and oncogenesis.

Nathans' work on SV40 demonstrated the power of restriction enzymes as tools for molecular biology. His experiments showed that these enzymes could be used not only to map genomes but also to clone and manipulate individual genes, laying the foundation for the emerging field of genetic engineering. The ability to cut, splice, and recombine DNA fragments allowed scientists to create recombinant DNA molecules, which could be inserted into host cells to produce new genetic combinations. This technology opened up new possibilities for research, medicine, and biotechnology, including the development of genetically modified organisms, the production of recombinant proteins, and the creation of gene therapies for inherited diseases.

The contributions of Arber, Smith, and Nathans to the discovery and application of restriction enzymes had a profound impact on the field of molecular biology and beyond. Their work laid the groundwork for the development of recombinant DNA technology, which has become a cornerstone of modern biotechnology. The ability to manipulate DNA at the molecular level has enabled scientists to explore the genetic basis of life in unprecedented detail, leading to new insights into the mechanisms of heredity, development, and evolution.

In addition to their impact on basic research, restriction enzymes have had significant practical applications in medicine, agriculture, and industry. For example, the production of recombinant proteins, such as insulin and growth hormones, has revolutionized the treatment of various diseases, providing safe and effective therapies for millions of patients worldwide. In agriculture, genetic engineering has led to the development of crops with improved resistance to pests, diseases, and environmental stress, contributing to increased food production and sustainability. In industry, restriction enzymes have been used in the production of biofuels, biodegradable plastics, and other environmentally friendly products, helping to reduce the reliance on fossil fuels and minimize the environmental impact of human activities.

The work of Arber, Smith, and Nathans also had important ethical and social implications. The development of recombinant DNA technology raised new questions about the potential risks and benefits of genetic engineering, as well as the ethical considerations surrounding the manipulation of genetic material. In response to these concerns, the scientific community organized the Asilomar Conference on Recombinant DNA in 1975, where researchers, policymakers, and ethicists came together to discuss the safety and regulation of genetic engineering. The guidelines developed at the conference helped to establish a framework for the responsible conduct of research in this rapidly evolving field.

The legacy of Werner Arber, Hamilton O. Smith, and Daniel Nathans is one of innovation, discovery, and collaboration. Their work has had a lasting impact on the field of molecular biology, transforming our understanding of genetics and paving the way for countless advances in science and technology. Their contributions have not only expanded the frontiers of knowledge but have also led to practical applications that have improved human health, agriculture, and industry.

In recognition of their pioneering work, Arber, Smith, and Nathans were awarded the Nobel Prize in Physiology or Medicine in 1978. The Nobel Committee honored them "for the discovery of restriction enzymes and their application to problems of molecular genetics," highlighting the global significance of their achievements. The award was a fitting tribute to three scientists whose curiosity, creativity, and dedication have had a profound impact on the world.

Today, the work of Arber, Smith, and Nathans continues to inspire new generations of scientists as they explore the possibilities of genetic research and biotechnology. The discovery of restriction enzymes and the development of recombinant DNA technology have opened up new avenues of investigation, leading to breakthroughs in genomics, personalized medicine, synthetic biology, and more. As we continue to unravel the complexities of the genetic code and harness the power of molecular biology, the contributions of these three scientists will remain at the heart of our understanding of life itself.

In conclusion, the discoveries of Werner Arber, Hamilton O. Smith, and Daniel Nathans represent a milestone in the history of science. Their work on restriction enzymes has transformed the field of molecular biology, enabling the precise manipulation of genetic material and paving the way for the development of recombinant DNA technology. The impact of their discoveries has been felt across multiple disciplines, from medicine and agriculture to industry and environmental science. Their legacy is one of innovation, collaboration, and the relentless pursuit of knowledge, and it continues to shape the future of science and technology in ways that are both profound and far-reaching. The Nobel Prize awarded to these three scientists in 1978 is a testament to the enduring significance of their contributions and a celebration of the transformative power of scientific discovery.

Chapter 28: Peter Agre & Roderick MacKinnon

The story of Peter Agre and Roderick MacKinnon is a tale of pioneering scientific discoveries that have fundamentally deepened our understanding of the biological processes that govern cellular function. Their work, which earned them the Nobel Prize in Chemistry in 2003, centers on elucidating the mechanisms by which water and ions move across cell membranes—a process that is critical for the survival and function of all living cells. Agre's discovery of aquaporins, the specialized proteins that facilitate the transport of water across cell membranes, and MacKinnon's detailed structural analysis of ion channels, which regulate the flow of ions across cell membranes, have had profound implications for biology, medicine, and our understanding of life at the molecular level.

Peter Agre's journey to his groundbreaking discovery began with a deep interest in the intricacies of cellular processes. Born on January 30, 1949, in Northfield, Minnesota, Agre was drawn to the natural sciences from an early age. He pursued his undergraduate studies in chemistry at Augsburg College and later earned his medical degree from Johns Hopkins University School of Medicine in 1974. Agre's early career was marked by a focus on hematology, the study of blood, but it was his curiosity about how cells manage the flow of water that led him to his most significant scientific contribution.

The movement of water into and out of cells is a fundamental process that is vital for maintaining cellular homeostasis—the balance of fluid and electrolytes that allows cells to function properly. For decades, scientists understood that water could pass through cell membranes via osmosis, a process driven by differences in concentration across the membrane. However, the precise mechanism by which water molecules traversed the lipid bilayer of the cell membrane remained unclear. The lipid bilayer is hydrophobic, meaning it repels water, so the idea that water could move freely across it without assistance seemed paradoxical.

In the early 1990s, while working at Johns Hopkins University, Agre and his colleagues were studying the Rh protein in red blood cells when they stumbled upon a protein of unknown function. Through a series of experiments, Agre's team identified this protein as a channel that allowed water molecules to pass through the cell membrane at an extraordinarily fast rate—far faster than could be explained by simple diffusion through the lipid bilayer. This protein, which Agre later named "aquaporin," was the first member of what would become known as a family of water channels.

Aquaporins are integral membrane proteins that form pores in the cell membrane, allowing water molecules to pass through while blocking the movement of ions and other solutes. These channels are selective, meaning they only permit water molecules to pass through, and they do so in a single file, allowing for rapid and efficient water transport. Agre's discovery was groundbreaking because it provided a molecular explanation for how cells manage water flow, a process that is essential for numerous physiological functions, including kidney filtration, the maintenance of blood pressure, and the regulation of body temperature.

The identification of aquaporins opened up a new field of research, with scientists around the world investigating the roles of these proteins in various tissues and organisms. It was soon discovered that aquaporins are ubiquitous, found in all forms of life, from bacteria to humans. In humans, aquaporins play critical roles in the kidneys, where they are involved in concentrating urine and conserving water; in the brain, where they help maintain the balance of cerebrospinal fluid; and in the eyes, where they are essential for the production of aqueous humor. Mutations in aquaporin genes have been linked to a variety of medical conditions, including nephrogenic diabetes insipidus, a disorder characterized by excessive thirst and urination due to the kidneys' inability to concentrate urine, and brain edema, a potentially life-threatening accumulation of fluid in the brain.

Agre's discovery of aquaporins has had far-reaching implications for both basic science and medicine. It has provided new insights into the molecular mechanisms underlying water balance in the body and has led to the development of new diagnostic tools and potential therapies for diseases related to water imbalance. The significance of this discovery was recognized with the Nobel Prize in Chemistry in 2003, which Agre shared with Roderick MacKinnon, another scientist whose work on ion channels has similarly transformed our understanding of cellular physiology.

Roderick MacKinnon's contribution to science centers on his groundbreaking research into the structure and function of ion channels—proteins that control the flow of ions, such as sodium, potassium, calcium, and chloride, across cell membranes. Ion channels are crucial for a wide range of physiological processes, including the generation of electrical signals in nerve and muscle cells, the regulation of heartbeats, and the release of hormones. The precise control of ion flow is essential for the proper functioning of cells, and any disruption in this process can lead to serious diseases, including epilepsy, cardiac arrhythmias, and cystic fibrosis.

Born on February 19, 1956, in Burlington, Massachusetts, Roderick MacKinnon initially pursued a career in medicine, earning his M.D. from Tufts University School of Medicine in 1982. However, his interest in the fundamental mechanisms of biology led him to shift his focus to research. After completing a residency in internal medicine, MacKinnon joined the laboratory of Christopher Miller at Brandeis University, where he began studying the biophysics of ion channels. This decision would set the stage for his later discoveries.

In the 1990s, MacKinnon embarked on a quest to solve one of the most challenging problems in molecular biology: determining the structure of ion channels at the atomic level. At the time, the molecular structure of ion channels was poorly understood, largely because these proteins are embedded in the cell membrane, making them difficult to isolate and study using traditional biochemical methods. MacKinnon was determined to overcome these challenges, recognizing that understanding the structure of ion channels was key to unraveling how they functioned.

MacKinnon's breakthrough came in 1998 when he and his team at Rockefeller University successfully determined the high-resolution crystal structure of a potassium channel from the bacterium *Streptomyces lividans*. This achievement was a tour de force of molecular biology and structural biology, as it provided the first detailed view of how an ion channel is constructed at the atomic level. The potassium channel, known as KcsA, was shown to be a tetramer, consisting of four identical subunits that form a central pore through which potassium ions pass.

One of the most striking features of the KcsA channel structure was the selectivity filter—a narrow region near the entrance of the pore that allows potassium ions to pass through while excluding other ions, such as sodium. The selectivity filter is lined with carbonyl oxygen atoms that interact with the potassium ions, stabilizing them as they move through the channel. The structure of the filter explained the high selectivity of potassium channels for potassium ions over sodium ions, despite the fact that sodium ions are smaller and might be expected to pass through more easily. The filter is precisely tuned to the size and charge of potassium ions, allowing them to shed their hydration shell and move through the channel in a dehydrated state, while sodium ions, which are too small to interact with the filter in the same way, are excluded.

MacKinnon's work on potassium channels provided critical insights into how ion channels achieve their remarkable selectivity and how they open and close in response to changes in voltage across the cell membrane—a process known as gating. The discovery of the structure of the KcsA channel also had broader implications for understanding the function of other types of ion channels, including sodium and calcium channels, which play essential roles in nerve signal transmission and muscle contraction.

The implications of MacKinnon's research extended beyond basic science, influencing the development of new drugs and treatments for diseases related to ion channel dysfunction. For example, understanding the structure and function of potassium channels has informed the design of drugs that target these channels to treat conditions such as epilepsy, cardiac arrhythmias, and chronic pain. MacKinnon's work has also contributed to our understanding of the molecular basis of neurological diseases caused by mutations in ion channel genes, known as channelopathies.

The discovery of the structure of potassium channels was recognized as a monumental achievement in molecular biology and was celebrated with the awarding of the Nobel Prize in Chemistry in 2003, which MacKinnon shared with Peter Agre. The Nobel Committee honored them "for discoveries concerning channels in cell membranes," highlighting the fundamental importance of their work in understanding the mechanisms of life at the molecular level.

The combined achievements of Agre and MacKinnon have had a transformative impact on the field of biochemistry and molecular biology. Their discoveries have not only provided key insights into the fundamental processes that govern cellular function but have also opened up new avenues of research and therapeutic development. Aquaporins and ion channels are now recognized as critical components of cellular physiology, and their study continues to yield new insights into health and disease.

In the years since their Nobel-winning discoveries, the work of Agre and MacKinnon has inspired further research into the roles of aquaporins and ion channels in various physiological and pathological processes. For example, ongoing studies are exploring the role of aquaporins in cancer, where they are thought to play a role in tumor growth and metastasis by regulating water flow and cell migration. Similarly, research on ion channels continues to uncover their involvement in a wide range of diseases, from neurodegenerative disorders to hypertension.

The legacy of Peter Agre and Roderick MacKinnon is one of scientific curiosity, perseverance, and a commitment to understanding the fundamental principles of biology. Their work has not only advanced our knowledge of how cells function but has also provided new tools and approaches for studying complex biological systems. The discoveries of aquaporins and ion channels have become foundational knowledge in biochemistry and molecular biology, and their impact will continue to be felt for generations to come.

In conclusion, the contributions of Peter Agre and Roderick MacKinnon to our understanding of membrane transport mechanisms represent a major milestone in the history of science. Their discoveries of aquaporins and the detailed structure of potassium channels have revolutionized our understanding of how water and ions move across cell membranes, processes that are essential for life. The implications of their work extend far beyond basic science, influencing the development of new medical therapies and providing insights into a wide range of diseases. The Nobel Prize awarded to Agre and MacKinnon in 2003 is a testament to the significance of their discoveries and a celebration of the power of scientific inquiry to unravel the mysteries of life.

Chapter 29: Enrico Fermi

Enrico Fermi, one of the most significant figures in the history of modern science, made profound contributions that shaped the course of nuclear physics, quantum mechanics, and our understanding of the fundamental forces of nature. Fermi's work laid the groundwork for the development of quantum theory and nuclear energy, leading to his recognition as one of the architects of the atomic age. His scientific achievements, spanning from theoretical insights to experimental breakthroughs, are marked by a combination of intellectual rigor, creativity, and an uncanny ability to bridge the gap between theory and practice. Fermi's legacy extends beyond his individual contributions, influencing generations of physicists and altering the trajectory of scientific research in the 20th century.

Born on September 29, 1901, in Rome, Italy, Enrico Fermi showed an early aptitude for mathematics and science. His fascination with the physical world led him to the University of Pisa, where he studied physics and completed his doctorate in 1922. Fermi's early work focused on statistical mechanics, a branch of physics that deals with the behavior of systems with a large number of particles. This interest in the statistical properties of matter would later play a crucial role in his formulation of quantum theory.

In the 1920s, quantum mechanics was a rapidly developing field, revolutionizing our understanding of the atomic and subatomic world. Fermi quickly established himself as a leading figure in this new scientific landscape. One of his most important contributions during this period was the development of Fermi-Dirac statistics, a quantum statistical model that describes the distribution of particles known as fermions. Fermions, named after Fermi, are particles that obey the Pauli exclusion principle, which states that no two fermions can occupy the same quantum state simultaneously. This principle is fundamental to the structure of atoms and the behavior of electrons in solids, making Fermi-Dirac statistics a cornerstone of modern physics.

Fermi's work on quantum statistics had far-reaching implications for a wide range of physical phenomena, from the behavior of electrons in metals to the properties of white dwarf stars. His insights into the statistical behavior of particles were critical for the development of quantum theory and provided a framework for understanding the complex behavior of matter at the atomic level. This theoretical foundation was crucial for the subsequent development of quantum mechanics, solid-state physics, and other areas of modern science.

In the 1930s, Fermi turned his attention to nuclear physics, a field that was still in its infancy. At the time, the atom was understood to be composed of a dense nucleus surrounded by a cloud of electrons, but the nature of the forces holding the nucleus together was not well understood. Fermi's interest in the nucleus led him to explore the newly discovered phenomenon of beta decay, a type of radioactive decay in which a neutron in the nucleus is transformed into a proton, an electron, and a neutrino. This process puzzled physicists because it appeared to violate the conservation of energy, a fundamental principle of physics.

To resolve this issue, Fermi proposed a groundbreaking theory of beta decay in 1934, which introduced the concept of the weak force, one of the four fundamental forces of nature. Fermi's theory suggested that beta decay was mediated by the weak force, which allowed a neutron to transform into a proton while emitting an electron and a neutrino. This was the first theoretical framework to describe the weak interaction, and it provided a foundation for our understanding of subatomic processes. Fermi's work on beta decay was a monumental achievement, marking the birth of weak interaction theory and laying the groundwork for later discoveries in particle physics.

Fermi's theory of beta decay also introduced the concept of the neutrino, a nearly massless and electrically neutral particle that interacts only weakly with matter. Although the neutrino was initially hypothetical, Fermi's theory predicted its existence, and it was later confirmed experimentally. The discovery of the neutrino was a major milestone in particle physics, and it has since become a central focus of research in the field, leading to important discoveries about the nature of the universe and the fundamental forces that govern it.

In addition to his theoretical work, Fermi was an exceptional experimentalist, known for his ability to design and conduct experiments that provided crucial evidence for his theoretical ideas. In 1934, Fermi began a series of experiments in Rome aimed at exploring the behavior of neutrons when they were used to bombard various elements. At the time, neutrons were a relatively new discovery, and their properties were not well understood. Fermi's experiments involved slowing down neutrons by passing them through a substance like paraffin wax, which increased their likelihood of being captured by atomic nuclei.

Fermi's experiments with neutron bombardment led to a series of discoveries that would have profound implications for the future of nuclear physics. He found that when neutrons were slowed down, they were more easily captured by atomic nuclei, leading to the formation of new, often radioactive, isotopes. This discovery of the enhanced capture of slow neutrons was pivotal because it provided a method for artificially inducing radioactivity in a wide range of elements, opening up new possibilities for research in nuclear physics and chemistry.

One of the most significant outcomes of Fermi's experiments was the discovery of nuclear fission, although Fermi himself did not immediately recognize the full implications of his findings. In 1938, while bombarding uranium with neutrons, Fermi observed the production of several radioactive isotopes, but it was not until later that it was understood that he had actually split the uranium nucleus into lighter elements, a process that releases a tremendous amount of energy. This discovery of nuclear fission, later clarified by Otto Hahn and Lise Meitner, would become the basis for the development of nuclear energy and atomic weapons.

Fermi's work on neutron bombardment earned him the Nobel Prize in Physics in 1938 "for his demonstrations of the existence of new radioactive elements produced by neutron irradiation, and for his related discovery of nuclear reactions brought about by slow neutrons." This recognition solidified Fermi's reputation as one of the leading physicists of his time and underscored the significance of his contributions to nuclear physics.

In the late 1930s, the rise of fascism in Italy and the increasing threat of war in Europe prompted Fermi, who was married to a Jewish woman, to leave Italy for the United States. He accepted a position at Columbia University in New York, where he continued his research in nuclear physics. As the world moved closer to war, Fermi's work took on a new urgency, as the potential for harnessing nuclear fission for both energy production and weaponry became increasingly apparent.

Fermi's move to the United States marked the beginning of a new phase in his career, one that would have a profound impact on the world. In 1942, Fermi joined the Manhattan Project, the secret U.S. government program aimed at developing an atomic bomb. As one of the project's leading scientists, Fermi played a central role in the construction and operation of the first nuclear reactor, known as the Chicago Pile-1. On December 2, 1942, Fermi and his team achieved the first controlled nuclear chain reaction, a critical milestone in the development of nuclear energy and weapons.

The successful demonstration of a controlled nuclear chain reaction was a monumental achievement that confirmed the feasibility of using nuclear fission as a source of energy. This breakthrough paved the way for the development of both nuclear power and atomic weapons, fundamentally altering the course of history. Fermi's work on the Manhattan Project culminated in the successful testing of the first atomic bomb in July 1945, followed by the bombing of Hiroshima and Nagasaki in August 1945. The use of atomic weapons brought an end to World War II but also ushered in the nuclear age, with all its associated ethical, political, and environmental challenges.

After the war, Fermi continued his research in nuclear physics, becoming a professor at the University of Chicago, where he played a key role in establishing the university's Institute for Nuclear Studies. His post-war research focused on high-energy physics and the study of subatomic particles, including neutrinos and pions. Fermi's work in this area led to the development of the Fermi theory of weak interactions, which provided a framework for understanding the interactions of subatomic particles via the weak force.

Fermi's later years were marked by continued contributions to both theoretical and experimental physics. He made important contributions to the understanding of cosmic rays, the high-energy particles that bombard the Earth from space, and developed what is now known as Fermi acceleration, a mechanism by which particles gain energy as they interact with magnetic fields in space. Fermi's work in this area laid the groundwork for modern astrophysics and our understanding of high-energy phenomena in the universe.

Throughout his career, Fermi was known for his exceptional ability to bridge the gap between theory and experiment. He was a master of what is often referred to as "Fermi questions" or "Fermi problems," which are problems that require rough, order-of-magnitude estimates rather than precise calculations.

Fermi's talent for making quick, insightful estimates allowed him to make rapid progress in his research and to identify the most promising directions for further investigation. This approach to problem-solving became a hallmark of his scientific style and has influenced the way physicists think about complex problems to this day.

Fermi was also an inspiring teacher and mentor, known for his ability to communicate complex ideas in a clear and accessible manner. His influence extended to a generation of physicists who went on to make their own significant contributions to science, including several who would later win Nobel Prizes. Fermi's legacy as an educator is reflected in the many students and colleagues who were shaped by his guidance and who continued to push the boundaries of knowledge in the years after his death.

Enrico Fermi passed away on November 28, 1954, at the age of 53, from stomach cancer. His death marked the loss of one of the most brilliant and versatile physicists of the 20th century. Fermi's contributions to science were vast and varied, spanning multiple fields and leaving a lasting impact on the development of modern physics. His work on quantum mechanics, nuclear physics, and particle physics has shaped our understanding of the fundamental forces of nature and has had profound implications for both science and society.

Fermi's legacy lives on in the many scientific concepts, theories, and discoveries that bear his name, including Fermi-Dirac statistics, the Fermi paradox (which questions the apparent contradiction between the high probability of extraterrestrial life and the lack of evidence for it), and the Fermi energy (the energy level at which the probability of finding an electron is 50%). The Fermi National Accelerator Laboratory (Fermilab), one of the leading centers for particle physics research in the world, is named in his honor, reflecting his enduring influence on the field of high-energy physics.

In conclusion, Enrico Fermi's contributions to science were nothing short of revolutionary. His work laid the foundations for our understanding of quantum mechanics, nuclear physics, and the weak interaction, and his discoveries have had a profound impact on both theoretical and experimental physics. Fermi's ability to move seamlessly between theory and experiment, combined with his intellectual rigor and creativity, made him one of the most influential scientists of the 20th century. His legacy continues to inspire scientists and researchers around the world, and his contributions will remain a cornerstone of modern physics for generations to come.

Chapter 30: Frederick Sanger

Frederick Sanger stands as one of the most distinguished scientists of the 20th century, with a career marked by groundbreaking discoveries that have fundamentally reshaped our understanding of biochemistry and genetics. His work, characterized by a meticulous approach to scientific inquiry and an unparalleled dedication to solving some of the most complex problems in molecular biology, earned him the rare distinction of being awarded the Nobel Prize in Chemistry twice, an honor shared by only a few individuals in history. Sanger's contributions to the field of biochemistry, particularly his pioneering methods for sequencing proteins and nucleic acids, have left an indelible mark on science, paving the way for the rapid advancements in genomics and molecular biology that we witness today.

Born on August 13, 1918, in Rendcomb, Gloucestershire, England, Frederick Sanger was the second son of a general practitioner. His upbringing in a Quaker household, which emphasized values such as simplicity, humility, and hard work, profoundly influenced his character and approach to life. Sanger's early education at the Downs School and later at Bryanston School exposed him to a broad curriculum, but it was his interest in science, particularly chemistry and biology, that began to take precedence. Encouraged by his father, Sanger developed a strong foundation in these subjects, setting the stage for his future career as a scientist.

In 1936, Sanger entered St. John's College, Cambridge, where he initially studied natural sciences with a focus on physics, chemistry, and biochemistry. It was during his time at Cambridge that Sanger became increasingly interested in the chemical basis of life, particularly the role of proteins and enzymes in biological processes. This interest led him to pursue a research project on the metabolism of the amino acid lysine, under the supervision of Albert Neuberger.

Sanger's early research in this area provided him with valuable experience in biochemical techniques and introduced him to the challenges of studying complex biological molecules.

After completing his undergraduate degree in 1939, Sanger remained at Cambridge to pursue a Ph.D. under the guidance of A.C. Chibnall, a prominent biochemist who specialized in the study of proteins. It was under Chibnall's mentorship that Sanger began his groundbreaking work on the structure of proteins, focusing initially on the amino acid composition of insulin. At the time, little was known about the precise structure of proteins, and many scientists believed that proteins were composed of amino acids arranged in random sequences. Sanger, however, hypothesized that proteins, like other biological molecules, had a defined structure that was crucial to their function.

Sanger's work on insulin marked the beginning of a long and arduous journey that would ultimately lead to one of the most significant discoveries in the history of biochemistry. Insulin, a hormone produced by the pancreas, plays a critical role in regulating blood sugar levels, and its structure was of great interest to scientists studying diabetes and other metabolic disorders. To determine the structure of insulin, Sanger developed a novel method for sequencing proteins, which involved the stepwise degradation of the protein into smaller fragments, followed by the identification of the amino acids in each fragment.

This method, which came to be known as the Sanger method of protein sequencing, was a major breakthrough in biochemistry. It allowed Sanger to determine the precise order of amino acids in a protein, providing the first evidence that proteins were composed of specific sequences of amino acids arranged in a linear chain. Sanger's work on insulin, which was completed in 1955 after nearly a decade of painstaking research, revealed that insulin consisted of two polypeptide chains, each with a unique sequence of amino acids. This discovery was a monumental achievement, as it provided the first complete sequence of a protein and demonstrated that proteins had a defined, reproducible structure.

The implications of Sanger's work on insulin were profound, as it established the principle that the sequence of amino acids in a protein determined its structure and function. This insight laid the foundation for the field of molecular biology, as it suggested that the information required to produce a functional protein was encoded in its amino acid sequence. Sanger's discovery also had significant implications for medicine, as it provided a deeper understanding of how proteins function in the body and how alterations in protein structure could lead to disease.

In recognition of his groundbreaking work on the structure of proteins, Frederick Sanger was awarded the Nobel Prize in Chemistry in 1958. The award was a testament to the significance of his contributions to biochemistry and his role in advancing our understanding of the molecular basis of life. Sanger's work on protein sequencing not only provided a powerful tool for studying the structure of proteins but also paved the way for future research on the genetic code and the relationship between genes and proteins.

Following his success with protein sequencing, Sanger turned his attention to the study of nucleic acids, the molecules that carry genetic information in all living organisms. In the early 1960s, the structure of DNA had been elucidated by James Watson and Francis Crick, but the sequence of nucleotides in DNA and RNA remained largely unknown. Sanger recognized that understanding the sequence of nucleotides in nucleic acids was essential for deciphering the genetic code and understanding how genetic information is stored and transmitted.

To tackle the challenge of sequencing nucleic acids, Sanger once again developed a novel method, building on his previous work with proteins. His approach, known as the Sanger method of DNA sequencing, involved the use of chain-terminating nucleotides, which halted the synthesis of DNA at specific points, allowing for the determination of the sequence of nucleotides. This method, which was first described in 1977, revolutionized the field of genetics by providing a reliable and efficient way to sequence DNA.

The Sanger method of DNA sequencing was a monumental achievement, as it allowed scientists to determine the precise sequence of nucleotides in a DNA molecule. This breakthrough opened the door to a wide range of research in molecular biology, including the identification of genes, the study of genetic mutations, and the exploration of evolutionary relationships among species. The Sanger method became the standard technique for DNA sequencing for nearly three decades and was instrumental in the success of the Human Genome Project, an international effort to sequence the entire human genome.

In recognition of his pioneering work on DNA sequencing, Frederick Sanger was awarded his second Nobel Prize in Chemistry in 1980, shared with Paul Berg and Walter Gilbert, who were also recognized for their contributions to the field of nucleic acid research. Sanger's achievement of receiving two Nobel Prizes in Chemistry is a rare and remarkable accomplishment, highlighting the profound impact of his work on the field of molecular biology.

Sanger's contributions to science extended beyond his groundbreaking discoveries in protein and DNA sequencing. Throughout his career, he was known for his modesty, humility, and dedication to the pursuit of knowledge. Despite his significant achievements, Sanger remained committed to the principles of rigorous scientific inquiry and was always willing to share his knowledge and expertise with others. His work has had a lasting impact on the field of biochemistry and genetics, and his methods continue to be used by researchers around the world.

Sanger's legacy is reflected in the many scientific advances that have been made possible by his work. The ability to sequence proteins and nucleic acids has revolutionized our understanding of the molecular basis of life, leading to important discoveries in fields such as genomics, evolutionary biology, and medicine. The techniques developed by Sanger have been used to identify the genetic basis of numerous diseases, to study the evolution of species, and to develop new therapies for treating genetic disorders.

In addition to his scientific achievements, Sanger was also a dedicated educator and mentor, known for his willingness to guide and support young scientists. His approach to research, characterized by careful experimentation and a deep respect for the complexity of biological systems, has influenced generations of scientists and continues to inspire researchers today.

Frederick Sanger passed away on November 19, 2013, at the age of 95. His death marked the end of an era in molecular biology, but his legacy lives on in the countless discoveries and innovations that have been made possible by his work. Sanger's contributions to science have had a profound and lasting impact, and his methods continue to be used by researchers around the world as they seek to unravel the mysteries of life at the molecular level.

In conclusion, Frederick Sanger's work has left an indelible mark on the field of biochemistry and molecular biology. His pioneering methods for sequencing proteins and nucleic acids have transformed our understanding of the molecular basis of life and have paved the way for many of the scientific advances of the past century. Sanger's legacy as a scientist, educator, and mentor continues to inspire researchers around the world, and his contributions will remain a cornerstone of modern science for generations to come.

Chapter 31: Subrahmanyan Chandrasekhar

Subrahmanyan Chandrasekhar was one of the most brilliant astrophysicists of the 20th century, whose work significantly advanced our understanding of stellar evolution, black holes, and the fundamental processes that govern the universe. His contributions to science were not only profound in their theoretical insights but also remarkable for their breadth, covering a wide range of topics from the physics of white dwarf stars to the theory of black holes, the dynamics of star clusters, and the hydrodynamics of fluid systems. Chandrasekhar's work, characterized by its mathematical rigor and deep conceptual clarity, earned him the Nobel Prize in Physics in 1983, shared with William A. Fowler for their contributions to the understanding of the later evolutionary stages of massive stars. Chandrasekhar's legacy extends far beyond his individual discoveries, as he played a crucial role in shaping modern astrophysics and mentoring a generation of scientists who continued to build on his foundational work.

Born on October 19, 1910, in Lahore, British India (now in Pakistan), Subrahmanyan Chandrasekhar was the son of C. Subrahmanyan Ayyar, a government worker, and Sitalakshmi Ayyar, who had a strong influence on his early intellectual development. Chandrasekhar belonged to a prominent Tamil family, and his uncle, the renowned physicist C. V. Raman, had won the Nobel Prize in Physics in 1930 for his work on the scattering of light, known as the Raman Effect. Growing up in an environment that valued education and intellectual achievement, Chandrasekhar showed early signs of exceptional talent in mathematics and science.

Chandrasekhar's early education took place in Madras (now Chennai), where he attended the Hindu High School and later the

Presidency College. His exceptional abilities in mathematics and physics were evident from an early age, and he quickly outpaced his peers. At the age of 18, Chandrasekhar published his first scientific paper, which was a critique of the statistical theory of atoms, demonstrating his precociousness and deep understanding of advanced scientific concepts.

In 1930, Chandrasekhar was awarded a scholarship to study at the University of Cambridge in England, where he joined Trinity College to pursue a degree in physics. It was during his time at Cambridge that Chandrasekhar made the discovery that would define his early career and later earn him widespread recognition in the scientific community. While on a voyage to England, Chandrasekhar began to contemplate the fate of stars at the end of their life cycles. This line of thinking led him to explore the question of what happens to a star after it has exhausted its nuclear fuel and can no longer sustain the pressure needed to counteract gravitational collapse.

Chandrasekhar's investigations into this problem led to the formulation of what is now known as the Chandrasekhar limit, a theoretical upper limit to the mass of a white dwarf star. White dwarfs are the remnants of stars that have exhausted their nuclear fuel and have collapsed under their own gravity, with the pressure of electron degeneracy providing the force to counterbalance gravitational collapse. However, Chandrasekhar discovered that if a white dwarf's mass exceeds approximately 1.4 times the mass of the Sun (now called the Chandrasekhar limit), electron degeneracy pressure would no longer be sufficient to halt the collapse, leading to the star's further contraction into a more compact object such as a neutron star or black hole.

Chandrasekhar's work on the Chandrasekhar limit was initially met with skepticism and resistance from some of the most prominent physicists of the time, including Sir Arthur Eddington, a leading authority in astrophysics. Eddington, who held considerable influence in the field, disagreed with Chandrasekhar's conclusions, arguing that they implied the existence of black holes, which he considered absurd. Despite this opposition, Chandrasekhar remained steadfast in his calculations and theoretical framework, which were based on the principles of quantum mechanics and relativity.

The controversy surrounding the Chandrasekhar limit and Eddington's public criticism of Chandrasekhar's work had a profound impact on the young scientist. Although deeply disappointed by the lack of acceptance of his theory, Chandrasekhar continued to pursue his research with unwavering dedication. His work on the structure and stability of stars laid the foundation for the modern understanding of stellar evolution and the eventual fate of massive stars. The Chandrasekhar limit is now recognized as one of the most important results in astrophysics, and it plays a central role in the theory of white dwarfs, neutron stars, and black holes.

After completing his Ph.D. at Cambridge in 1933, Chandrasekhar spent some time at the University of Copenhagen, where he worked with the great physicist Niels Bohr. During this period, Chandrasekhar continued to refine his ideas on stellar structure and evolution, developing a deeper understanding of the physical processes that govern the life cycles of stars. In 1937, Chandrasekhar accepted a position as a faculty member at the University of Chicago, where he would spend the rest of his career.

At the University of Chicago, Chandrasekhar's research interests expanded to encompass a wide range of topics in theoretical astrophysics, fluid dynamics, and radiative transfer. One of his significant contributions during this period was his work on the stability of rotating fluid masses, which has applications in both astrophysics and geophysics. Chandrasekhar's work in this area led to the publication of his influential book *Hydrodynamic and*

Hydromagnetic Stability in 1961, which remains a foundational text in the field of fluid dynamics.

In addition to his research on fluid dynamics, Chandrasekhar made important contributions to the study of star clusters, galaxy dynamics, and the theory of black holes. His work on the dynamics of star clusters provided insights into the processes of relaxation and energy exchange in these systems, leading to a better understanding of their long-term evolution. Chandrasekhar's studies of galaxy dynamics helped elucidate the role of dynamical friction in the formation and evolution of galaxies.

One of Chandrasekhar's most significant contributions to astrophysics was his work on the theory of black holes, which he pursued with great intensity in the later stages of his career. Building on the general theory of relativity, Chandrasekhar developed a mathematical framework for describing the structure and properties of black holes, particularly those with rotating or charged characteristics. His work on the Kerr metric, which describes the geometry of spacetime around a rotating black hole, was a major advance in the field and helped to establish black holes as a fundamental aspect of astrophysical theory.

Chandrasekhar's contributions to the theory of black holes were recognized as some of the most important developments in the field, providing the mathematical tools needed to understand these enigmatic objects. His work laid the groundwork for subsequent research on black hole thermodynamics, quantum gravity, and the study of gravitational waves. The significance of Chandrasekhar's contributions to black hole theory was further highlighted when he was awarded the Nobel Prize in Physics in 1983.

Throughout his career, Chandrasekhar was known not only for his scientific achievements but also for his dedication to teaching and mentoring young scientists. He supervised more than 50 Ph.D. students during his time at the University of Chicago, many of whom went on to become leading figures in astrophysics and related fields. Chandrasekhar was deeply committed to the idea of scientific rigor and excellence, and he was known for his insistence on clarity, precision, and mathematical elegance in scientific research.

Chandrasekhar was also a prolific writer, authoring several influential books and over 400 research papers on a wide range of topics in astrophysics, physics, and applied mathematics. His books, such as *Introduction to the Study of Stellar Structure* (1939), *Principles of Stellar Dynamics* (1942), *Radiative Transfer* (1950), and *The Mathematical Theory of Black Holes* (1983), have become classics in their respective fields and continue to be used by students and researchers around the world.

Chandrasekhar's approach to science was characterized by a deep respect for the mathematical foundations of physics and a belief in the power of abstract reasoning to uncover the underlying principles of the natural world. He was a firm believer in the unity of science, often drawing connections between seemingly disparate areas of research and emphasizing the importance of interdisciplinary approaches to solving complex problems.

Despite his many achievements, Chandrasekhar remained humble and modest throughout his life. He was known for his quiet demeanor, his meticulous attention to detail, and his unwavering commitment to scientific truth. Chandrasekhar's humility was perhaps most evident in his refusal to engage in public disputes or self-promotion, even when his work was met with resistance or criticism. He believed that the pursuit of knowledge was its own reward and that scientific progress depended on the collective efforts of the entire scientific community.

Chandrasekhar's contributions to science were recognized with numerous awards and honors, including the Royal Medal of the Royal Society (1962), the National Medal of Science (1966), and the Copley Medal (1984). In addition to the Nobel Prize, these accolades reflected the profound impact of his work on the field of astrophysics and his role in advancing our understanding of the universe.

Subrahmanyan Chandrasekhar passed away on August 21, 1995, at the age of 84. His death marked the loss of one of the greatest minds in the history of science, but his legacy continues to inspire and guide researchers in the field of astrophysics. Chandrasekhar's work has left an indelible mark on the study of stellar evolution, black holes, and the fundamental processes that govern the cosmos. His contributions to science have not only expanded our knowledge of the universe but have also provided the tools and frameworks necessary for future discoveries.

In conclusion, Subrahmanyan Chandrasekhar's life and work represent a pinnacle of scientific achievement. His discovery of the Chandrasekhar limit fundamentally changed our understanding of stellar evolution and laid the groundwork for the modern theory of black holes. His contributions to the study of fluid dynamics, star clusters, galaxy dynamics, and black hole physics have had a lasting impact on the field of astrophysics. Chandrasekhar's legacy is not only one of profound scientific insight but also of a deep commitment to the principles of rigor, precision, and intellectual honesty. His work continues to influence and inspire scientists around the world, ensuring that his contributions to science will be remembered for generations to come.

Chapter 32: Betzig, W. Hell, & E. Moerner

The Nobel Prize in Chemistry for 2014 was awarded to three pioneering scientists—Eric Betzig, Stefan W. Hell, and William E. Moerner—for the development of super-resolved fluorescence microscopy, a revolutionary technique that has profoundly transformed the field of microscopy and has had a significant impact on biological and medical research. The work of Betzig, Hell, and Moerner represents a major breakthrough in the ability to observe and study the molecular and cellular processes that are fundamental to life, providing researchers with a powerful tool to visualize structures and dynamics at the nanoscale. This achievement broke the so-called "diffraction limit," a longstanding barrier that had restricted the resolution of optical microscopy for over a century, thereby enabling scientists to see details at a scale that was previously thought to be impossible.

To appreciate the significance of their work, it is essential to understand the historical context in which these discoveries were made. Optical microscopy, since its inception in the 17th century, had been constrained by the diffraction limit, a physical phenomenon first described by Ernst Abbe in 1873. According to Abbe's theory, the resolution of a conventional light microscope was limited to about half the wavelength of light used for imaging, typically around 200-250 nanometers for visible light. This meant that objects or structures smaller than this threshold could not be resolved as separate entities using traditional optical microscopy. While this resolution was sufficient for many biological studies, it was inadequate for observing the finer details of cellular structures, proteins, and other biomolecules, which often measure only a few nanometers in size.

The diffraction limit posed a significant challenge to researchers, especially in the field of cell biology, where understanding the intricate details of cellular architecture and the dynamics of molecular interactions was crucial. For many years, scientists believed that this barrier was insurmountable, and the quest to see beyond it seemed like a distant dream. However, the determination and ingenuity of Eric Betzig, Stefan W. Hell, and William E. Moerner led to the development of techniques that circumvented the diffraction limit, giving rise to super-resolution microscopy—a set of methods that have revolutionized our ability to visualize the nanoworld.

William E. Moerner, often referred to as W.E. Moerner, played a crucial role in the foundation of super-resolution microscopy through his work on single-molecule spectroscopy. Born on June 24, 1953, in Pleasanton, California, Moerner displayed an early aptitude for science and went on to pursue a Ph.D. in physics from Cornell University. His groundbreaking work began in the late 1980s when he succeeded in detecting the fluorescence of a single molecule at cryogenic temperatures. This achievement marked the first time that individual molecules could be observed directly, rather than as part of an ensemble, where the behavior of many molecules is averaged out. Moerner's work opened up a new field of single-molecule spectroscopy, allowing researchers to study the behavior and properties of individual molecules in unprecedented detail.

Moerner's contributions were pivotal in demonstrating that the fluorescence from a single molecule could be switched on and off, a concept that would later become integral to the development of super-resolution techniques. By controlling the fluorescence of individual molecules, it became possible to differentiate between molecules that were spatially close to each other, thus overcoming the diffraction limit. Moerner's work laid the groundwork for the techniques that Betzig and Hell would later develop, and it established the principle that individual molecules could be used as probes to achieve resolutions far beyond the limits imposed by diffraction.

Stefan W. Hell, born on December 23, 1962, in Arad, Romania, and later moving to Germany, made his seminal contribution to super-resolution microscopy through the development of stimulated emission depletion (STED) microscopy. Hell's journey to this discovery was marked by his determination to challenge the prevailing assumptions in the field of optical microscopy. After completing his Ph.D. at the University of Heidelberg, Hell became increasingly interested in overcoming the diffraction limit and achieving higher resolution in light microscopy. His work led him to explore the principles of stimulated emission, a process that had been well understood in the context of lasers but had not been applied to microscopy.

In 1994, Hell proposed the concept of STED microscopy, which involved using a second laser to selectively deactivate fluorescence in a controlled manner, effectively sharpening the image and allowing for higher resolution. The basic idea behind STED is to use a pair of lasers: one to excite the fluorescent molecules, and another to deplete the fluorescence from the surrounding area, leaving only a small region that emits light. By scanning this small region across the sample, it becomes possible to build up an image with a resolution far beyond the diffraction limit. STED microscopy was a radical departure from traditional methods and provided a powerful new tool for imaging biological structures at the nanoscale. Hell's work demonstrated that it was possible to achieve resolutions as small as 20-30 nanometers, which was a significant improvement over conventional optical microscopy.

Eric Betzig, born on January 13, 1960, in Ann Arbor, Michigan, made his mark in the field of super-resolution microscopy through the development of photoactivated localization microscopy

(PALM). Betzig's career trajectory was somewhat unconventional. After earning his Ph.D. in applied physics from Cornell University, he worked at Bell Laboratories, where he conducted research on near-field optical microscopy, a technique that aimed to surpass the diffraction limit by using a sharp tip to scan very close to the sample surface. However, after a series of frustrations with the limitations of this approach, Betzig left scientific research in the late 1990s to work in his father's machine tool company. Despite his departure from academia, Betzig remained intrigued by the idea of achieving super-resolution and continued to think about the problem.

Betzig returned to research in the early 2000s, inspired by the work of Moerner and others in the field of single-molecule fluorescence. He recognized that by using fluorescent molecules that could be activated and deactivated at will, it would be possible to localize individual molecules with high precision and then reconstruct a super-resolved image by combining the positions of many such molecules. This insight led to the development of PALM, a technique that involves photoactivating a sparse subset of fluorescent molecules in a sample, recording their positions, and then repeating the process until a high-resolution image is built up. PALM allowed for imaging with a resolution of about 20 nanometers, which was a dramatic improvement over traditional microscopy methods.

The work of Betzig, Hell, and Moerner converged to create a new era in optical microscopy, one that allowed scientists to see the molecular machinery of life in unprecedented detail. The impact of their discoveries has been profound, with super-resolution microscopy being applied to a wide range of biological and medical research areas. For example, these techniques have been used to study the structure and function of cellular components such as the cytoskeleton, synaptic vesicles, and membrane proteins. They have also been instrumental in understanding the mechanisms of diseases, including cancer, neurodegenerative disorders, and infectious diseases, by allowing researchers to visualize the interactions between biomolecules in their native environments.

Super-resolution microscopy has also spurred the development of new fluorescent probes and labeling techniques, further expanding the possibilities for studying complex biological systems. The ability to observe individual molecules and their interactions in living cells has provided insights into processes such as signal transduction, gene expression, and protein trafficking, which were previously inaccessible to direct observation. Moreover, the principles underlying super-resolution microscopy have inspired the development of other imaging techniques, such as single-molecule tracking and super-resolved fluorescence correlation spectroscopy, which have opened up new avenues for exploring the dynamics of biomolecular processes.

The significance of the work by Betzig, Hell, and Moerner cannot be overstated. Their contributions have transformed microscopy from a tool that was limited by the diffraction of light to one that can now reveal the intricate details of the molecular world. This transformation has not only advanced our understanding of fundamental biological processes but has also had practical implications in fields such as drug discovery, where super-resolution microscopy is being used to study the mechanisms of drug action and to identify potential therapeutic targets. In addition, the ability to visualize and manipulate biological structures at the nanoscale has important implications for nanotechnology and materials science, where the precise control of molecular interactions is critical.

The story of Betzig, Hell, and Moerner is also a testament to the power of perseverance and creativity in scientific research. Each of these scientists faced significant challenges and setbacks in their careers, but their determination to push the boundaries of what was thought possible led to breakthroughs that have had a lasting impact on science and medicine. Their work exemplifies the importance of interdisciplinary collaboration, as their discoveries were made possible by combining insights from physics, chemistry, and biology.

In recognition of their groundbreaking contributions to super-resolution microscopy, Betzig, Hell, and Moerner were awarded the Nobel Prize in Chemistry in 2014. The Nobel Committee acknowledged their role in "bringing optical microscopy into the nanodimension," highlighting the transformative nature of their work. The award also underscored the significance of their contributions to the broader scientific community, as super-resolution microscopy has become an indispensable tool for researchers around the world.

The legacy of Betzig, Hell, and Moerner continues to inspire new generations of scientists, who are building on their work to develop even more advanced imaging techniques. As super-resolution microscopy continues to evolve, it promises to provide even deeper insights into the molecular mechanisms that underlie life and to drive new discoveries that will shape the future of biology and medicine.

In conclusion, the work of Eric Betzig, Stefan W. Hell, and William E. Moerner represents a monumental achievement in the field of microscopy, one that has fundamentally changed the way we observe and understand the biological world. Their development of super-resolution microscopy has broken through the diffraction limit, allowing scientists to visualize structures and processes at the nanoscale with unprecedented clarity. This breakthrough has had a profound impact on biological research, enabling new discoveries in cell biology, neuroscience, and medicine. The contributions of Betzig, Hell, and Moerner have not only expanded the frontiers of science but have also demonstrated the power of innovation and perseverance in overcoming seemingly insurmountable challenges. Their work has opened up new possibilities for exploring the mysteries of life at the molecular level, ensuring that their legacy will continue to influence scientific progress for years to come.

Chapter 33: Stanley Cohen & Rita Levi-Montalcini

The story of Stanley Cohen and Rita Levi-Montalcini is one of profound scientific discovery that has significantly influenced our understanding of cellular growth and development. Their work, which culminated in the discovery of nerve growth factor (NGF), laid the groundwork for the modern field of neurobiology and has had far-reaching implications in medicine, particularly in understanding and treating neurodegenerative diseases and cancers. The journey to this discovery is rich with perseverance, ingenuity, and collaboration, embodying the spirit of scientific inquiry that pushes the boundaries of human knowledge.

Rita Levi-Montalcini was born in 1909 in Turin, Italy, to a well-educated Jewish family. Despite facing significant obstacles due to the oppressive societal norms of the time, which discouraged women from pursuing higher education, Levi-Montalcini was determined to follow her passion for science. She enrolled in the University of Turin's medical school, where she studied under the guidance of Giuseppe Levi, an influential professor of histology. Her early work focused on the development of the nervous system, a subject that would remain central to her research throughout her career.

During World War II, Levi-Montalcini faced additional challenges due to the Fascist regime's anti-Semitic laws, which barred her from academic positions. However, her determination and resourcefulness led her to set up a makeshift laboratory in her bedroom, where she continued her research on nerve cells using chicken embryos. Despite the dire conditions, she managed to produce significant work that would later contribute to her groundbreaking discoveries. Her research during this period demonstrated her resilience and unwavering commitment to scientific inquiry, even in the face of persecution and adversity.

Stanley Cohen, born in 1922 in Brooklyn, New York, came from a different background but shared a similar passion for science. After earning his Ph.D. in biochemistry from the University of Michigan, Cohen embarked on a career that would eventually intersect with Levi-Montalcini's. Cohen's early work focused on enzymes and nucleic acids, providing him with a strong foundation in molecular biology. His curiosity about how biological molecules influenced cellular behavior would become a driving force in his later research.

The collaboration between Levi-Montalcini and Cohen began in the early 1950s when Levi-Montalcini accepted an invitation to join Viktor Hamburger's laboratory at Washington University in St. Louis. There, she continued her research on the nervous system, specifically focusing on the mechanisms that controlled the growth of nerve cells. It was during this time that she made the serendipitous discovery of NGF, a protein that plays a crucial role in the growth, maintenance, and survival of nerve cells.

The discovery of NGF was a milestone in the field of neurobiology. While studying the development of the nervous system in chick embryos, Levi-Montalcini noticed that certain tumors, when transplanted into the embryos, stimulated the growth of nerve fibers. This observation led her to hypothesize that the tumors were releasing a substance that promoted nerve growth. To investigate this further, she conducted a series of experiments that involved isolating the substance responsible for this effect. With the help of Cohen, who was skilled in biochemistry and molecular biology, they were able to isolate and characterize NGF.

Cohen's expertise was instrumental in identifying the molecular structure of NGF. He was able to purify the protein and determine that it was a signaling molecule, a discovery that helped to explain how cells communicate and coordinate their activities during development. Cohen also discovered that NGF was not limited to nerve cells but had broader implications for understanding cellular growth in general. His work demonstrated that NGF was one of the first growth factors to be identified, a finding that would pave the way for the discovery of other growth factors, such as epidermal growth factor (EGF), which Cohen also later discovered.

The discovery of NGF had profound implications for understanding the development of the nervous system. It provided a new framework for understanding how neurons grow, differentiate, and establish connections during embryonic development. NGF was shown to be essential for the survival of certain types of neurons, particularly sensory and sympathetic neurons. The discovery also shed light on the mechanisms of programmed cell death, or apoptosis, as it became clear that neurons required NGF to avoid undergoing apoptosis during development.

Moreover, NGF's role in neurodevelopment opened up new avenues of research into neurodegenerative diseases. Scientists began to explore the possibility that deficits in NGF or its signaling pathways might contribute to conditions such as Alzheimer's disease, where the death of neurons leads to cognitive decline. The therapeutic potential of NGF became an area of intense interest, leading to research on how NGF could be used to promote nerve regeneration and repair in various neurological conditions.

In addition to its impact on neurobiology, the discovery of NGF had broader implications for understanding the regulation of cell growth and differentiation in other tissues. Growth factors like NGF were found to play critical roles in many biological processes, including wound healing, immune responses, and the regulation of cell proliferation. Cohen's later discovery of EGF, which stimulates the growth of epidermal cells, further expanded the understanding of how growth factors influence cellular behavior. EGF and its receptor were found to be involved in the regulation of cell division, and abnormalities in EGF signaling were linked to the development of cancers. This connection between growth factors and cancer biology opened up new research avenues for developing targeted therapies that could inhibit abnormal growth factor signaling in tumors.

The groundbreaking work of Levi-Montalcini and Cohen was recognized with the Nobel Prize in Physiology or Medicine in 1986. Their discovery of NGF not only advanced the understanding of neurobiology but also highlighted the importance of interdisciplinary collaboration in scientific research. Their partnership combined Levi-Montalcini's expertise in neuroanatomy and developmental biology with Cohen's skills in biochemistry and molecular biology, demonstrating how different scientific disciplines can come together to achieve transformative breakthroughs.

Rita Levi-Montalcini's later years were marked by continued contributions to science and society. She became an advocate for science education and women's rights, using her influence to promote the importance of research and education. Her legacy extends beyond her scientific achievements, as she became a role model for perseverance, intellectual curiosity, and dedication to the pursuit of knowledge. Levi-Montalcini's work has inspired generations of scientists, particularly women, to pursue careers in science despite societal barriers.

Stanley Cohen, after receiving the Nobel Prize, continued his research on growth factors and their role in cellular processes. His work has had a lasting impact on the fields of cell biology and cancer research, as the principles he helped to uncover have informed the development of targeted cancer therapies. Growth factor research, which Cohen helped to pioneer, remains a vital area of study with implications for understanding and treating a wide range of diseases.

The discovery of NGF also had a profound impact on the broader field of developmental biology. It provided a model for understanding how signaling molecules guide the development of complex biological systems, from the nervous system to the immune system. The concept of growth factors as key regulators of cellular communication and development has become a central theme in biology, influencing research in areas ranging from stem cell biology to tissue engineering.

In summary, the work of Stanley Cohen and Rita Levi-Montalcini represents a landmark achievement in the history of science. Their discovery of nerve growth factor revolutionized the understanding of how the nervous system develops and functions, and it opened up new possibilities for treating neurodegenerative diseases and cancers. Their collaboration exemplifies the power of interdisciplinary research and the importance of combining different scientific perspectives to solve complex biological problems. The legacy of Cohen and Levi-Montalcini continues to resonate in the scientific community, as their discoveries have laid the foundation for ongoing research into the molecular mechanisms that govern cellular growth, development, and disease. Their contributions have not only advanced the field of neurobiology but have also had a lasting impact on medicine, providing new insights into the treatment of some of the most challenging diseases of our time. Their work is a testament to the enduring value of curiosity-driven research and the profound impact that basic scientific discoveries can have on human health and well-being.

Chapter 34: Sidney Altman & Thomas Cech

The discovery of catalytic RNA, an achievement that earned Sidney Altman and Thomas Cech the Nobel Prize in Chemistry in 1989, is one of the most remarkable milestones in molecular biology. Their work fundamentally altered our understanding of RNA, a molecule that had long been considered merely a passive intermediary in the flow of genetic information. Altman and Cech's discoveries revealed that RNA could not only carry genetic information but also catalyze chemical reactions, a role that had previously been thought to be the exclusive domain of proteins. This discovery reshaped the way scientists think about the origin of life, the evolution of biological molecules, and the basic principles of molecular biology.

To fully appreciate the significance of Altman and Cech's work, it's essential to understand the scientific context in which their discoveries were made. By the mid-20th century, the central dogma of molecular biology was well established: DNA serves as the template for RNA, which in turn is translated into proteins. Proteins, in turn, were understood to be the workhorses of the cell, performing a vast array of functions, including serving as enzymes to catalyze biochemical reactions. RNA was thought to have a more limited role as a messenger that conveyed genetic information from DNA to the protein-synthesizing machinery of the cell. This view of RNA as a passive intermediary was so entrenched that few researchers considered the possibility that RNA might have catalytic functions.

Sidney Altman, born in 1939 in Montreal, Canada, began his scientific career with an interest in biophysics and eventually moved into the study of molecular biology. After earning his Ph.D. in biophysics from the University of Colorado, Boulder, he conducted postdoctoral research at Harvard University, where he worked under the guidance of Matthew Meselson, a prominent molecular biologist. Altman's early work focused on the replication of bacteriophage DNA, but his research interests soon shifted towards the mechanisms of RNA processing.

Altman's groundbreaking work on catalytic RNA began during his tenure at Yale University, where he was investigating the processing of precursor tRNA (transfer RNA) molecules in the bacterium *Escherichia coli*. It was known that tRNA, which plays a critical role in translating genetic information into proteins, is initially synthesized as a longer precursor molecule that must be processed into its mature form before it can function properly. Altman was interested in understanding how this processing occurred, specifically focusing on an enzyme known as RNase P, which was responsible for cleaving the precursor tRNA at a specific site to produce the mature tRNA.

During his research, Altman made a surprising observation: RNase P, which was believed to be a protein enzyme, contained an RNA component that was essential for its catalytic activity. This RNA component, known as M1 RNA, was not merely a structural component but was actually responsible for the catalytic function of RNase P. This was a radical departure from the accepted view that all enzymes were proteins. Altman's discovery showed that RNA itself could act as a catalyst, challenging the long-held belief that only proteins could have enzymatic activity.

Altman's work on RNase P was meticulous and involved a series of carefully designed experiments to demonstrate that the RNA component alone could catalyze the cleavage of precursor tRNA in vitro. This finding was met with skepticism at first, as it contradicted the prevailing dogma, but Altman's results were reproducible and eventually led to the recognition that RNA could have catalytic functions. His work opened up new avenues of research into the roles of RNA in cellular processes and suggested that RNA might have played a much more central role in the early evolution of life than previously thought.

Around the same time that Altman was making his discoveries, Thomas Cech, born in 1947 in Chicago, Illinois, was conducting research that would lead to a similar groundbreaking conclusion. Cech completed his Ph.D. in chemistry at the University of California, Berkeley, and took up a faculty position at the University of Colorado, Boulder, where he began studying the transcription and splicing of RNA in the single-celled organism *Tetrahymena thermophila*. His focus was on understanding how certain RNA molecules are processed after being transcribed from DNA.

Cech and his colleagues were investigating the splicing of precursor ribosomal RNA (rRNA) in *Tetrahymena*. Ribosomal RNA is a key component of ribosomes, the cellular machines that synthesize proteins. Like tRNA, rRNA is initially synthesized as a longer precursor molecule that must be processed to produce the mature, functional form. In particular, Cech's group was studying a specific intron—a non-coding sequence—that had to be removed from the precursor rRNA to produce mature rRNA.

Cech's research led to an unexpected and revolutionary discovery: the intron in the precursor rRNA was capable of catalyzing its own excision from the RNA molecule. This meant that the RNA itself was acting as an enzyme to remove the intron, without the need for any protein enzymes. Cech termed this type of RNA a "ribozyme," a portmanteau of "ribonucleic acid" and "enzyme." This finding was astonishing because it demonstrated that RNA could not only store and transmit genetic information but could also perform complex biochemical reactions—a function that had been thought to be the exclusive domain of proteins.

The implications of Cech's discovery were profound. It provided strong evidence that RNA could have been the original molecule of life, capable of both storing genetic information and catalyzing the chemical reactions necessary for life's origin. This idea, known as the "RNA world" hypothesis, suggests that early life forms may have relied on RNA for both genetic information and catalysis before the evolution of DNA and proteins. The RNA world hypothesis has since become a central concept in the study of the origin of life, and it has guided much research in evolutionary biology, biochemistry, and molecular biology.

The work of Altman and Cech not only revolutionized our understanding of RNA but also had far-reaching implications for the study of molecular biology. Their discoveries led to the identification of many other ribozymes in nature, further demonstrating the versatility and catalytic potential of RNA. These discoveries also spurred the development of new experimental techniques and technologies, including the use of ribozymes as tools for genetic engineering and biotechnology. Ribozymes have been explored as potential therapeutic agents, capable of targeting and cleaving specific RNA sequences in the treatment of diseases such as viral infections and cancer.

The discovery of catalytic RNA also had a significant impact on the field of biochemistry, particularly in the study of enzyme mechanisms. It prompted scientists to reconsider the basic principles of catalysis and to explore the possibility that other types of molecules, beyond proteins, could serve as catalysts. This broadened the scope of enzymology and led to a more comprehensive understanding of the diversity of catalytic mechanisms in nature.

The recognition of RNA's catalytic abilities also had implications for the understanding of RNA processing and gene regulation. It became clear that RNA molecules were not merely passive intermediaries but played active roles in controlling gene expression and cellular processes. This understanding has been crucial in the study of RNA interference (RNAi) and other RNA-based regulatory mechanisms, which are now known to be involved in a wide range of biological processes, from development to disease.

In recognition of their groundbreaking discoveries, Sidney Altman and Thomas Cech were jointly awarded the Nobel Prize in Chemistry in 1989. The Nobel Committee praised their work for its fundamental contribution to our understanding of the role of RNA in biology and its implications for the origin of life. The award highlighted the significance of their discoveries and cemented their place in the history of molecular biology.

Sidney Altman's work on RNase P and its catalytic RNA component has continued to influence research on RNA processing and the evolution of RNA-based enzymes. His discoveries have shed light on the mechanisms by which RNA molecules are processed and matured in cells, and they have provided important insights into the evolution of complex biological systems. Altman's research has also contributed to the development of RNA-based technologies, including the design of artificial ribozymes for use in biotechnology and medicine.

Thomas Cech's discovery of self-splicing RNA introns has had a lasting impact on the study of gene expression and RNA processing. His work has inspired research into the mechanisms of RNA splicing and the role of introns in regulating gene expression. Cech's contributions have also been instrumental in advancing our understanding of the evolution of RNA-based life and the transition from RNA to DNA and protein-based life forms. His research has continued to explore the functions of non-coding RNA and its role in cellular processes, further expanding our knowledge of the diverse roles that RNA plays in biology.

The legacy of Altman and Cech's discoveries extends beyond their immediate impact on molecular biology. Their work has inspired a new generation of scientists to explore the many functions of RNA and to investigate the potential of RNA-based technologies for addressing some of the most pressing challenges in medicine and biotechnology. The discovery of catalytic RNA has also deepened our understanding of the fundamental principles of life and has provided new perspectives on the origins and evolution of biological molecules.

In conclusion, the discoveries of Sidney Altman and Thomas Cech have fundamentally transformed our understanding of RNA and its role in biology. Their work revealed that RNA is not merely a passive carrier of genetic information but also a versatile catalyst capable of driving essential biochemical reactions. This breakthrough has had profound implications for the study of molecular biology, biochemistry, and the origin of life. The recognition of catalytic RNA has opened up new avenues of research and has inspired the development of novel technologies and therapeutic approaches. The legacy of Altman and Cech's discoveries continues to shape the future of science, ensuring that their contributions will be remembered as a pivotal moment in the history of molecular biology.

Chapter 35: Alexander Fleming

Alexander Fleming, a name synonymous with one of the most significant medical discoveries of the 20th century, was born on August 6, 1881, in Lochfield, Scotland. He grew up on a farm, where he developed an early appreciation for the natural world, a fascination that would later play a crucial role in his groundbreaking work. Fleming's academic journey began at Kilmarnock Academy and later at St. Mary's Hospital Medical School in London. Initially, his interest was more inclined towards surgery, but fate had other plans. After serving in the London Scottish Regiment of the Territorial Army and witnessing the horrors of war during World War I, where he saw countless soldiers die from infections, his focus shifted towards bacteriology and finding ways to combat infectious diseases.

Fleming's work in the field of bacteriology led him to the discovery of lysozyme in 1922, a naturally occurring enzyme in body fluids like tears and saliva that had mild antibacterial properties. While this was a significant finding, it was only a precursor to his most monumental discovery. In 1928, while working at St. Mary's Hospital in London, Fleming's career took an unexpected turn that would change the course of medical history. Upon returning from a holiday, he noticed that a petri dish containing Staphylococcus bacteria had been inadvertently left uncovered. To his surprise, the bacteria surrounding a mold that had contaminated the dish were being destroyed, while colonies farther away were unaffected. Fleming identified the mold as belonging to the *Penicillium* genus, and he correctly surmised that the mold was releasing a substance that was killing the bacteria. This substance was penicillin, the world's first true antibiotic.

Fleming's discovery was revolutionary. Before penicillin, there were no effective treatments for infections such as pneumonia, gonorrhea, or rheumatic fever. Minor injuries and surgeries often led to deadly infections, and diseases that are now easily treatable were frequently fatal. However, despite the profound implications of his discovery, Fleming struggled to purify penicillin and produce it in large quantities. The mold produced only tiny amounts of the substance, and the methods available at the time were insufficient to isolate penicillin effectively for widespread use. Fleming published his findings in 1929, but the medical community largely overlooked them, partly due to the technical difficulties involved in producing the drug and the lack of immediate commercial interest.

It wasn't until the early 1940s that penicillin's potential was fully realized, thanks to the efforts of scientists such as Howard Florey, Ernst Boris Chain, and Norman Heatley, who successfully mass-produced penicillin and demonstrated its effectiveness in treating bacterial infections. Their work, which was crucial during World War II, saved countless lives and earned them, along with Fleming, the Nobel Prize in Physiology or Medicine in 1945. Fleming's role in the discovery of penicillin has often been romanticized, with the story of the moldy petri dish becoming a cornerstone of scientific folklore. Yet, this narrative oversimplifies the years of painstaking work, the challenges faced, and the collective efforts of the scientific community to bring penicillin to the world.

Fleming's humility was well known; he often downplayed his role in the discovery, acknowledging the contributions of others who worked to make penicillin a practical medicine. He was acutely aware of the potential dangers of antibiotic resistance, warning that the misuse of penicillin could lead to resistant strains of bacteria—a warning that resonates strongly in the medical community today. Beyond penicillin, Fleming's contributions to bacteriology and immunology were vast. He was an early advocate of aseptic techniques in medical practice and contributed significantly to our understanding of the body's immune response. His work laid the foundation for modern antibiotic research and opened new avenues for the treatment of infectious diseases.

Fleming's legacy extends beyond his scientific achievements. He is remembered as a diligent, curious, and humble scientist who was dedicated to improving human health. His discovery of penicillin not only revolutionized medicine but also ushered in the age of antibiotics, fundamentally altering the relationship between humans and disease. Penicillin's impact on public health cannot be overstated; it has saved millions of lives and continues to be a cornerstone of medical treatment worldwide. Fleming's life and work serve as a reminder of the power of observation, the importance of scientific inquiry, and the profound impact that one discovery can have on the world.

Fleming passed away on March 11, 1955, but his contributions to science live on. His discovery of penicillin remains one of the greatest medical achievements of the 20th century, and his warnings about antibiotic resistance continue to guide contemporary medical practice. Today, Fleming's name is enshrined in history, not just as the discoverer of penicillin, but as a symbol of scientific perseverance, curiosity, and the relentless pursuit of knowledge. His story inspires scientists and researchers worldwide, illustrating that sometimes the most extraordinary discoveries can come from the most unexpected observations.

Chapter 36: Gerty Cori & Carl Cori

Gerty Cori and Carl Cori were a remarkable scientific duo whose pioneering work in biochemistry earned them the Nobel Prize in Physiology or Medicine in 1947. Their collaborative research not only advanced our understanding of carbohydrate metabolism but also broke significant barriers in the scientific community, particularly for women in science. Gerty Theresa Radnitz was born on August 15, 1896, in Prague, then part of the Austro-Hungarian Empire. She was a brilliant student with a strong interest in science from a young age, but the path to a scientific career was far from straightforward for women during her time. Nonetheless, she pursued her passion and enrolled at the German University in Prague, where she studied medicine. It was here that she met Carl Ferdinand Cori, a fellow medical student with whom she would form both a lifelong partnership in marriage and an extraordinary scientific collaboration.

Carl was born on December 5, 1896, in Prague, and like Gerty, he developed an early interest in science. The two were drawn together by their shared intellectual curiosity and mutual respect for each other's abilities. They married in 1920, shortly after completing their medical degrees, and began their collaborative work, focusing initially on issues related to the thyroid gland. However, their most significant contributions would come in the field of biochemistry, specifically in understanding how the body metabolizes carbohydrates.

After moving to the United States in 1922, the Coris worked at the State Institute for the Study of Malignant Diseases in Buffalo, New York. Despite the institute's limited resources, they embarked on research that would ultimately transform our understanding of metabolic processes. Their early work involved studying how the body converts glucose, a simple sugar, into glycogen, a stored form of energy, and vice versa. This process is crucial for maintaining blood sugar levels and providing energy to muscles during physical activity. In the early 1930s, Gerty and Carl Cori proposed the "Cori cycle," a groundbreaking concept that explained how lactic acid produced by muscles during exercise is converted back into glucose in the liver and then reused by muscles. This cycle is a fundamental aspect of carbohydrate metabolism and remains a cornerstone of biochemistry.

The Coris' work was characterized by meticulous experimentation and an innovative approach to scientific problems. They were able to isolate and identify several key enzymes involved in the conversion of glycogen to glucose, including phosphorylase, an enzyme that plays a critical role in breaking down glycogen into glucose-1-phosphate. This discovery was monumental because it provided the first clear insight into the biochemical steps involved in glycogen metabolism. Their work laid the foundation for understanding various metabolic diseases, including diabetes, where the body's ability to manage glucose is impaired.

Despite their joint contributions, Gerty often faced significant challenges due to her gender. While Carl was appointed to a full professorship at Washington University School of Medicine in St. Louis in 1931, Gerty was initially offered only a position as a research associate, with a salary far lower than that of her male counterparts. This disparity was not uncommon at the time, as women in science were frequently marginalized and their work undervalued. However, Gerty's perseverance, combined with her exceptional scientific abilities, eventually led to her promotion to a full professorship in 1947, the same year she and Carl were awarded the Nobel Prize. The recognition of the Coris' work by the Nobel Committee was a significant milestone, not just for their scientific achievements but also for gender equality in science. Gerty Cori became the third woman to win a Nobel Prize in science, following

Marie Curie and Irène Joliot-Curie. Her award was a powerful statement against the prevailing gender biases of the time and served as an inspiration for future generations of women scientists.

The Coris' scientific legacy extends far beyond their Nobel Prize-winning work. They trained and mentored numerous students and young scientists, many of whom went on to have distinguished careers in biochemistry and medicine. Their approach to collaborative research, where intellectual partnership was valued over individual achievement, set a standard for scientific inquiry that emphasized the importance of teamwork and shared credit. The Coris continued their research after receiving the Nobel Prize, delving deeper into the intricacies of enzyme function and metabolic pathways. Their later work contributed to the broader understanding of how genetic and biochemical factors influence human health, laying the groundwork for the emerging field of molecular biology. Even after Carl's death in 1984, Gerty's influence on science continued to be felt, as her contributions to the understanding of glycogen metabolism and enzyme function remained integral to biochemistry and medicine.

Gerty Cori's death in 1957 from myelosclerosis, a rare form of bone marrow cancer, was a significant loss to the scientific community. However, her legacy endures, not only in the groundbreaking discoveries she made with Carl but also in the barriers she broke down for women in science. Today, the Cori cycle and the enzymes they discovered are taught in biochemistry courses worldwide, a testament to the enduring impact of their work. The Cori's story is one of intellectual partnership, scientific brilliance, and the relentless pursuit of knowledge in the face of adversity. Their lives and work demonstrate the power of collaboration in science and the profound impact that such partnerships can have on our understanding of the natural world. Gerty and Carl Cori remain icons in the history of science, celebrated not just for their Nobel

Prize but for the lasting contributions they made to biochemistry and the inspiration they provided to generations of scientists who followed in their footsteps. Their story is a powerful reminder that the pursuit of knowledge is not bound by gender, and their legacy continues to inspire those who seek to push the boundaries of human understanding.

Chapter 37: Thouless, Haldane, & Kosterlitz

David Thouless, Duncan Haldane, and John Kosterlitz, three brilliant physicists whose groundbreaking work in condensed matter physics earned them the Nobel Prize in Physics in 2016, revolutionized our understanding of phase transitions and the behavior of matter in unusual states. Their research, which initially seemed abstract and far removed from practical applications, has since become foundational to the development of new technologies and the exploration of novel quantum phenomena. These three scientists' contributions are deeply intertwined, and their collective work represents a significant leap forward in the field of theoretical physics.

The story begins in the early 1970s when David Thouless and John Kosterlitz, working at the University of Birmingham in the United Kingdom, embarked on a study of two-dimensional systems, which behave differently from their three-dimensional counterparts. At the time, the prevailing belief in physics was that phase transitions—changes in the state of matter, such as from a liquid to a solid—could not occur in two-dimensional systems due to the disruptive effects of thermal fluctuations. These fluctuations, it was thought, would prevent the orderly patterns required for such transitions from forming. However, Thouless and Kosterlitz challenged this assumption by demonstrating that a new type of phase transition could indeed occur in two-dimensional systems, governed by what are known as topological defects.

Thouless and Kosterlitz introduced the concept of topological phase transitions, which involve the creation and annihilation of pairs of topological defects, such as vortices, rather than the usual breaking of symmetries that occurs in three-dimensional systems.

They showed that, at low temperatures, these defects would pair up, leading to a state with a certain degree of order, but as the temperature increased, the pairs would unbind, causing the system to undergo a phase transition. This transition, now known as the Kosterlitz-Thouless transition, was a profound discovery because it revealed that even in two-dimensional systems, which were previously thought to be too disordered, there could exist a new kind of order governed by topological properties rather than conventional symmetry breaking.

The implications of this discovery were far-reaching, as it provided a new way of thinking about phase transitions and the behavior of matter in lower dimensions. The work of Thouless and Kosterlitz not only explained phenomena that had been observed in thin films of superfluids and superconductors but also opened up new avenues for research in areas such as quantum Hall effects, topological insulators, and other exotic states of matter. Their findings demonstrated that topology, a branch of mathematics concerned with the properties of space that are preserved under continuous deformations, could play a crucial role in understanding physical systems. Topology became a powerful tool in physics, providing insights into how different phases of matter could be classified and how phase transitions could occur in systems where traditional theories of phase transitions did not apply.

While Thouless and Kosterlitz were exploring two-dimensional systems, Duncan Haldane was working on a related but distinct problem in the study of one-dimensional systems. In the early 1980s, Haldane made a breakthrough in understanding the behavior of spin chains, which are systems of particles with quantum spins arranged in a linear array. Conventional wisdom held that the properties of such systems should be similar to those of higher-dimensional systems, but Haldane's work revealed something entirely unexpected. Haldane proposed that in one-dimensional spin chains with integer values of spin, the system would not exhibit the expected long-range magnetic order at low temperatures, even in the absence of thermal fluctuations. Instead, these systems would enter a new phase characterized by a "gap" in the energy spectrum—a range of energies that the system could not access. This gap would prevent the formation of magnetic order, leading to a phase that was fundamentally different from the ordered or disordered phases seen in other dimensions.

Haldane's discovery of what is now known as the "Haldane gap" was a major departure from conventional theories and provided the first example of how topology could influence the properties of one-dimensional quantum systems. This work led to the identification of new phases of matter, known as Haldane phases, which are distinguished by their topological properties rather than by any local order parameter. The significance of Haldane's work lies in its demonstration that even in one-dimensional systems, where traditional phase transitions are absent, there can still exist rich and complex behavior governed by topological principles. This insight has had profound implications for the study of quantum systems and has paved the way for the exploration of topological phases in a wide variety of physical systems.

The collective contributions of Thouless, Haldane, and Kosterlitz have had a lasting impact on condensed matter physics, transforming our understanding of how matter behaves in low-dimensional systems and how topological concepts can be used to describe physical phenomena. Their work has inspired a generation of physicists to explore new and exotic states of matter, leading to the discovery of topological insulators, quantum spin liquids, and other phases that are now at the forefront of research in condensed matter physics. These discoveries have not only deepened our understanding of fundamental physics but have also opened up new possibilities for technological innovation. Topological insulators, for example, have the potential to revolutionize electronics by enabling the development of devices that are more robust against defects and imperfections, while quantum spin liquids could lead to new approaches to quantum computing and information storage.

The Nobel Prize awarded to Thouless, Haldane, and Kosterlitz in 2016 was a recognition of the profound and far-reaching impact of their work. Their discoveries have fundamentally changed the way we think about phase transitions and the behavior of matter in low-dimensional systems, providing new tools and concepts that continue to drive research in condensed matter physics. The work of these three scientists represents a triumph of theoretical physics, demonstrating the power of abstract mathematical concepts to unlock new understanding of the natural world. Their contributions have not only advanced our knowledge of physics but have also had a lasting influence on a wide range of scientific disciplines, from materials science to quantum computing.

Thouless, Haldane, and Kosterlitz's work is a testament to the importance of curiosity-driven research and the value of exploring unconventional ideas. Their discoveries were not the result of a search for immediate practical applications but rather a deep and sustained inquiry into the fundamental principles governing the behavior of matter. This approach has led to insights that have had profound and unexpected consequences, illustrating the often unpredictable nature of scientific discovery. Today, the legacy of Thouless, Haldane, and Kosterlitz lives on in the ongoing research into topological phases of matter and the exploration of new quantum phenomena. Their work continues to inspire physicists around the world, driving the search for new states of matter and new ways of understanding the complex and beautiful behavior of the physical world. Their contributions have earned them a place among the most influential physicists of the 20th and 21st centuries, and their work will undoubtedly continue to shape the future of physics for many years to come.

Chapter 38: Brenner, Sulston, & Horvitz

Sydney Brenner, John Sulston, and H. Robert Horvitz, three extraordinary scientists whose pioneering research into the genetic regulation of organ development and programmed cell death in *Caenorhabditis elegans* (C. elegans) earned them the Nobel Prize in Physiology or Medicine in 2002, revolutionized the field of molecular biology and deepened our understanding of fundamental biological processes. Their work, which combined genetics, developmental biology, and molecular biology, not only provided key insights into how genes control development and cell death but also laid the groundwork for the broader field of developmental biology and influenced cancer research, neurobiology, and genetics.

The journey that led to this monumental achievement began with Sydney Brenner, a South African biologist born on January 13, 1927, in Germiston, South Africa. Brenner's early interest in science and his relentless curiosity about the mechanisms of life drove him to pursue a career in molecular biology. He studied at the University of Witwatersrand in Johannesburg before moving to the University of Oxford, where he completed his DPhil under the supervision of Cyril Hinshelwood. Brenner's postdoctoral work at Cambridge University placed him at the forefront of the emerging field of molecular biology, where he worked alongside luminaries such as Francis Crick and James Watson. Brenner was a critical figure in the early development of molecular genetics, making significant contributions to our understanding of the genetic code and the mechanism of protein synthesis. However, Brenner's most enduring contribution to science would come from his decision to use *C. elegans*, a tiny, transparent nematode, as a model organism to study the genetic basis of development.

Brenner recognized that the simplicity of *C. elegans*—with its roughly 1,000 cells, short life cycle, and transparent body—made it an ideal organism for studying the genetic control of development and behavior. In a landmark 1974 paper, Brenner described the use of *C. elegans* in genetic research, establishing the nematode as a model organism that would revolutionize the study of biology. He showed that by inducing mutations in the worms and observing the resulting phenotypes, one could identify genes involved in specific biological processes. This approach enabled researchers to dissect the genetic pathways that control development, cell division, and cell death. Brenner's work with *C. elegans* laid the foundation for a new era in genetics and developmental biology, as it allowed scientists to study complex biological processes in a simple and tractable organism.

John Sulston, born on March 27, 1942, in Cambridge, England, joined Brenner's lab at the Medical Research Council (MRC) Laboratory of Molecular Biology in Cambridge in the early 1970s. Sulston, who had completed his PhD at the University of Cambridge, was fascinated by Brenner's work with *C. elegans* and quickly became one of the leading researchers in the field. Sulston's most significant contribution came from his meticulous work in mapping the complete cell lineage of *C. elegans*. Over several years, Sulston used a microscope to observe the development of individual *C. elegans* embryos, recording every cell division and movement from the fertilized egg to the adult worm. This painstaking work resulted in the first complete cell lineage of an animal, a map that detailed every cell division and the fate of every cell in the organism. This cell lineage map was a groundbreaking achievement in developmental biology, providing a comprehensive view of how a multicellular organism develops from a single cell.

Sulston's work revealed that certain cells in *C. elegans* underwent programmed cell death, or apoptosis, during development—a process that is crucial for normal development and tissue homeostasis. He showed that specific cells were destined to die as part of the organism's normal development, and that this process was genetically programmed. This discovery of genetically programmed cell death in *C. elegans* had profound implications for understanding how cell death is regulated in all animals, including humans. It also provided a framework for studying how the dysregulation of apoptosis could lead to diseases such as cancer, where cells evade death and continue to proliferate uncontrollably.

H. Robert Horvitz, an American biologist born on May 8, 1947, in Chicago, Illinois, joined the *C. elegans* research community in the 1970s, initially working in the laboratory of Victor Ambros and later establishing his own lab at the Massachusetts Institute of Technology (MIT). Horvitz's research focused on identifying and characterizing the genes involved in programmed cell death in *C. elegans*. Building on the work of Brenner and Sulston, Horvitz used genetic approaches to identify specific genes that controlled whether a cell would live or die during the development of the nematode. Horvitz's landmark discovery was the identification of the *ced-3*, *ced-4*, and *ced-9* genes, which play a central role in regulating apoptosis in *C. elegans*. He showed that *ced-3* and *ced-4* promote cell death, while *ced-9* protects cells from dying by inhibiting the activity of *ced-3* and *ced-4*. Horvitz's work provided the first clear genetic evidence that programmed cell death is a regulated process controlled by specific genes, and it established *C. elegans* as a powerful model for studying apoptosis.

The genes identified by Horvitz in *C. elegans* were later found to have homologs in humans, including the well-known Bcl-2 gene, which plays a key role in preventing apoptosis and is implicated in cancer. This discovery demonstrated the evolutionary conservation of the mechanisms controlling cell death and highlighted the relevance of *C. elegans* research to human biology and disease.

Horvitz's work also laid the foundation for the development of new cancer therapies aimed at modulating apoptosis to kill cancer cells.

The collective contributions of Brenner, Sulston, and Horvitz transformed our understanding of how genes control development and programmed cell death. Their work with *C. elegans* provided a model for studying complex biological processes in a simple organism, and their discoveries have had a lasting impact on a wide range of fields, including developmental biology, genetics, cancer research, and neurobiology. The Nobel Prize awarded to Brenner, Sulston, and Horvitz in 2002 was a recognition of the profound influence their work had on modern biology. Their research not only provided fundamental insights into the genetic control of development and cell death but also established *C. elegans* as a model organism that continues to be used in laboratories around the world.

The legacy of Brenner, Sulston, and Horvitz extends far beyond their Nobel Prize-winning work. Their research has inspired generations of scientists to use *C. elegans* as a model organism for studying a wide range of biological processes, from aging to neurodegenerative diseases. The genetic tools and techniques they developed have become standard in the field, enabling researchers to explore the molecular mechanisms underlying development, behavior, and disease in unprecedented detail. In addition to their scientific contributions, Brenner, Sulston, and Horvitz were also influential mentors who trained and inspired numerous students and postdoctoral fellows, many of whom have gone on to make significant contributions to science in their own right. Their collaborative and interdisciplinary approach to research set a standard for how complex biological problems can be addressed through the integration of genetics, molecular biology, and developmental biology.

The impact of their work is also evident in the broader field of biomedical research. The discovery of the genetic basis of programmed cell death has led to new approaches for treating diseases such as cancer, where the manipulation of apoptotic pathways is a key therapeutic strategy. The insights gained from studying *C. elegans* have also informed our understanding of neurodegenerative diseases, aging, and immunity, demonstrating the relevance of basic research in model organisms to human health. Today, the research initiated by Brenner, Sulston, and Horvitz continues to resonate in the scientific community, driving new discoveries and shaping our understanding of the fundamental processes that govern life. Their work exemplifies the power of model organisms in uncovering the genetic and molecular mechanisms that underlie development and disease, and it serves as a testament to the importance of curiosity-driven research in advancing human knowledge.

The story of Brenner, Sulston, and Horvitz is one of intellectual curiosity, perseverance, and the relentless pursuit of understanding the mysteries of life. Their work has not only transformed our understanding of biology but has also provided a powerful example of how scientific collaboration and the use of simple model organisms can lead to discoveries with far-reaching implications for human health and disease. Their contributions to science are a testament to the impact that fundamental research can have on our understanding of life and our ability to improve human health. Their legacy continues to inspire scientists around the world, and their discoveries will undoubtedly influence the direction of biological research for many years to come.

Chapter 39: Grubbs, Schrock, & Chauvin

Robert Grubbs, Richard Schrock, and Yves Chauvin, three chemists whose pioneering work in the field of organic chemistry revolutionized the understanding and application of metathesis, were awarded the Nobel Prize in Chemistry in 2005. Their contributions not only provided a deeper insight into the mechanisms of chemical reactions but also led to the development of new, more efficient methods for creating complex molecules. These advancements have had a profound impact on industries ranging from pharmaceuticals to materials science, transforming the way chemists approach the synthesis of organic compounds.

The story begins with Yves Chauvin, a French chemist born on October 10, 1930, in Menen, Belgium, who was particularly interested in the mechanisms of chemical reactions. Chauvin, who spent much of his career at the French Petroleum Institute (Institut Français du Pétrole), made his landmark discovery in the early 1970s. At the time, metathesis reactions were known to occur, but the details of how these reactions proceeded were poorly understood. Metathesis, derived from the Greek word meaning "to change places," refers to a chemical process where bonds are broken and reformed in such a way that the substituents of the reacting molecules exchange places. The practical applications of metathesis were already apparent in the chemical industry, particularly in the production of polymers, but the reaction's mechanism remained elusive.

Chauvin proposed a detailed mechanism for the metathesis reaction, which was both elegant and groundbreaking. He suggested that the reaction proceeds through a mechanism involving the formation of a metal carbene complex, an intermediate in which a metal atom is bonded to a carbon atom with a double bond. This intermediate then interacts with an alkene (a molecule containing a carbon-carbon double bond) to form a metallacyclobutane intermediate. The metallacyclobutane then breaks down, allowing the exchange of the alkylidene groups between the reacting molecules, leading to the formation of new alkenes. Chauvin's mechanism elegantly explained the observed outcomes of metathesis reactions and provided a clear theoretical framework for understanding how these reactions occurred.

Chauvin's work laid the groundwork for the development of more efficient and selective catalysts for metathesis reactions. However, while his theoretical contribution was crucial, the practical realization of metathesis as a powerful synthetic tool required the development of robust and effective catalysts. This is where the contributions of Richard Schrock and Robert Grubbs come into play.

Richard Schrock, an American chemist born on January 4, 1945, in Berne, Indiana, made his most significant contributions while working at the Massachusetts Institute of Technology (MIT). In the late 1970s, Schrock developed the first well-defined, highly active metal carbene complexes that could effectively catalyze metathesis reactions. Schrock's catalysts were based on early transition metals, such as tungsten and molybdenum, which he found to be particularly effective for promoting metathesis. These catalysts were highly active and allowed for the precise control of metathesis reactions, enabling chemists to carry out a wide range of transformations that were previously difficult or impossible.

Schrock's development of well-defined metal carbene complexes was a major breakthrough, as it provided a reliable and predictable way to carry out metathesis reactions. His work also demonstrated that these reactions could be conducted under mild conditions, making them more practical for use in organic synthesis. Schrock's catalysts were the first to demonstrate that metathesis could be a general and versatile tool for organic synthesis, paving the way for its widespread adoption in both academic and industrial laboratories.

While Schrock's catalysts were highly effective, they were also sensitive to air and moisture, which limited their practical applications. This challenge was addressed by Robert Grubbs, an American chemist born on February 27, 1942, in Calvert City, Kentucky. Grubbs, who spent most of his career at the California Institute of Technology (Caltech), focused on developing metathesis catalysts that were not only highly active but also more stable and easier to use. In the early 1990s, Grubbs developed a series of ruthenium-based catalysts that proved to be both robust and highly effective for metathesis. These "Grubbs catalysts" were air-stable, meaning they could be handled and stored under normal laboratory conditions without degradation, making them much more practical for everyday use.

Grubbs' catalysts revolutionized the field of metathesis, as they combined the high activity of Schrock's catalysts with the practical advantages of stability and ease of use. These catalysts were not only more accessible to chemists but also allowed for a broader range of reactions to be performed, including reactions with complex and sensitive molecules. The versatility and reliability of Grubbs' catalysts made them a standard tool in synthetic chemistry, leading to their widespread adoption in both academic research and industrial applications.

The impact of the work of Grubbs, Schrock, and Chauvin on the field of organic chemistry cannot be overstated. Metathesis reactions have become one of the most important tools for the construction of carbon-carbon bonds, a fundamental process in the synthesis of organic molecules. The ability to create these bonds in a controlled and predictable manner has enabled the synthesis of complex molecules with a high degree of precision, which is essential for the development of new drugs, materials, and agrochemicals.

In the pharmaceutical industry, metathesis has been used to streamline the synthesis of active pharmaceutical ingredients (APIs), making the production of drugs more efficient and cost-effective. The ability to create complex molecular architectures using metathesis has also facilitated the discovery of new drugs with enhanced potency and selectivity. In the field of materials science, metathesis has been used to create new polymers with unique properties, such as improved strength, flexibility, and thermal stability. These materials have found applications in a wide range of industries, from automotive manufacturing to electronics.

Beyond its practical applications, the work of Grubbs, Schrock, and Chauvin has also had a profound impact on the way chemists think about chemical reactions. Their contributions have deepened our understanding of the mechanisms underlying metathesis and have provided a framework for the development of new catalytic processes. The concept of using metal carbene complexes as intermediates in catalytic reactions has since been extended to a wide range of other chemical transformations, leading to the discovery of new reactions and catalysts that continue to expand the toolbox of synthetic chemistry.

The Nobel Prize in Chemistry awarded to Grubbs, Schrock, and Chauvin in 2005 was a recognition of their transformative contributions to the field of organic chemistry. Their work has not only advanced the science of catalysis but has also had a lasting impact on the broader field of chemistry, influencing research in areas ranging from chemical biology to materials science. The development of metathesis as a powerful and versatile tool for organic synthesis has opened up new possibilities for the creation of complex molecules, enabling chemists to explore new frontiers in drug discovery, materials science, and beyond.

The legacy of Grubbs, Schrock, and Chauvin continues to inspire chemists around the world, driving innovation and discovery in the field of catalysis. Their work exemplifies the power of fundamental research to transform science and industry, demonstrating how a deep understanding of chemical mechanisms can lead to the development of new technologies with far-reaching implications. The impact of their discoveries will undoubtedly continue to shape the future of chemistry for many years to come, as chemists build on their pioneering work to develop new catalysts, reactions, and applications that push the boundaries of what is possible in organic synthesis.

In conclusion, the work of Robert Grubbs, Richard Schrock, and Yves Chauvin represents a milestone in the history of chemistry, marking the emergence of metathesis as a fundamental tool for the synthesis of organic molecules. Their contributions have had a profound impact on both the theory and practice of chemistry, enabling the development of new drugs, materials, and chemical processes that have improved the quality of life for people around the world. The Nobel Prize awarded to these three chemists is a testament to the significance of their work and the enduring legacy of their contributions to science. Their achievements serve as an inspiration to future generations of chemists, who will continue to build on their discoveries and push the boundaries of what is possible in the field of organic chemistry.

Chapter 40: Richard J. Roberts & Phillip A. Sharp

Richard J. Roberts and Phillip A. Sharp, two distinguished molecular biologists, were jointly awarded the Nobel Prize in Physiology or Medicine in 1993 for their groundbreaking discovery of split genes and the mechanism of RNA splicing. Their work fundamentally altered our understanding of the structure of genes and the process by which genetic information is expressed, marking a significant shift in the field of molecular biology. The discovery of split genes and RNA splicing not only deepened our knowledge of gene expression in eukaryotic cells but also had profound implications for genetic research, biotechnology, and medicine.

The journey to this revolutionary discovery began in the early 1970s when the molecular biology community was beginning to unravel the complexities of gene structure and function. At that time, it was widely believed that genes in higher organisms, like those of bacteria, were continuous stretches of DNA that encoded proteins in a straightforward manner. According to this model, a gene would be transcribed into a continuous strand of messenger RNA (mRNA), which would then be translated into a protein by the cellular machinery. This "one gene, one protein" concept had been the cornerstone of molecular biology, and the simplicity of bacterial gene structure reinforced this view.

However, this understanding was about to be challenged by the work of Roberts and Sharp, who independently discovered that the structure of genes in eukaryotic organisms (organisms with complex cells, including humans) was far more intricate than previously thought. Their discovery revealed that the genes of eukaryotes were not continuous but rather were split into segments called exons, which are separated by non-coding regions known as introns. This finding was revolutionary because it showed that the initial RNA transcript produced from a gene—called pre-mRNA—contained both exons and introns. The introns needed to be removed, and the exons spliced together to produce a functional mRNA molecule that could be translated into a protein.

Richard J. Roberts, born on September 6, 1943, in Derby, England, played a pivotal role in this discovery. After earning his PhD in organic chemistry at the University of Sheffield, Roberts moved to the United States, where he worked at Harvard University before joining Cold Spring Harbor Laboratory in New York. It was at Cold Spring Harbor that Roberts, working with his team, made the crucial discovery of split genes in adenovirus, a virus that infects humans and causes respiratory illness. While studying the genome of adenovirus, Roberts and his colleagues noticed something unusual. When they compared the viral DNA to the mRNA produced during infection, they found that the mRNA was not a direct copy of the DNA sequence. Instead, it appeared that the mRNA was shorter than expected, missing large segments of the DNA sequence that were present in the genome.

Roberts and his team hypothesized that the mRNA was being processed in a way that removed certain segments of the DNA before it was translated into protein. This process, which they termed "splicing," involved the excision of introns and the joining of exons to form a continuous mRNA strand. This discovery of split genes and RNA splicing in adenovirus provided the first direct evidence that eukaryotic genes could be discontinuous, with coding sequences interrupted by non-coding regions. This finding challenged the prevailing dogma and opened up a new area of research into the mechanisms of gene expression.

Around the same time, Phillip A. Sharp, an American biochemist born on June 6, 1944, in Falmouth, Kentucky, was conducting similar research at the Massachusetts Institute of

Technology (MIT). Sharp, who had a background in chemistry and biochemistry, was interested in understanding how the genetic material of viruses was expressed in infected cells. Sharp and his team were studying the Simian Virus 40 (SV40), a virus that infects primates, including humans. Like Roberts, Sharp and his colleagues found that the mRNA produced by the virus was not a direct copy of the DNA sequence. Instead, they discovered that the mRNA was formed by splicing together sequences from different parts of the viral genome, a process that involved the removal of non-coding introns.

Sharp's work confirmed the presence of split genes and RNA splicing in eukaryotic cells and demonstrated that this phenomenon was not limited to viruses but was a general feature of gene expression in higher organisms. The discovery that genes could be split into exons and introns, and that RNA splicing was required to produce functional mRNA, revolutionized the understanding of gene structure and function. It also raised new questions about how cells recognized and processed introns and exons, leading to a surge of research into the mechanisms of RNA splicing.

The discovery of RNA splicing had far-reaching implications for molecular biology and genetics. It provided an explanation for the observation that the genomes of higher organisms were much larger and more complex than those of bacteria, yet did not necessarily produce a proportionately greater number of proteins. The presence of introns in eukaryotic genes meant that the genetic information was more modular and flexible, allowing for the production of multiple protein variants from a single gene through a process known as alternative splicing. In alternative splicing, different combinations of exons can be joined together, resulting in the production of different mRNA molecules and, consequently, different proteins. This process greatly increases the diversity of proteins that can be produced from a single gene, contributing to the complexity of eukaryotic organisms.

The implications of RNA splicing extend beyond basic research into practical applications in biotechnology and medicine. Understanding the mechanisms of splicing has led to the development of new techniques for gene therapy, where splicing errors can be corrected to treat genetic diseases. It has also provided insights into the regulation of gene expression and the role of splicing in disease processes such as cancer, where aberrant splicing can lead to the production of dysfunctional proteins that drive tumor growth.

Furthermore, the discovery of split genes and RNA splicing has had a profound impact on the study of human genetics. The Human Genome Project, which aimed to sequence the entire human genome, was greatly influenced by the understanding that genes were not continuous stretches of DNA but could be interrupted by introns. This realization required new strategies for sequencing and interpreting the genome, as well as new computational tools for identifying exons and predicting splicing patterns.

Roberts and Sharp's discovery also highlighted the evolutionary significance of RNA splicing. It suggested that introns and exons might play a role in the evolution of new genes and proteins by allowing for the rearrangement and recombination of genetic material. This modularity of gene structure could facilitate the evolution of new functions and the adaptation of organisms to changing environments. The presence of introns in eukaryotic genes may also have provided a selective advantage by enabling the regulation of gene expression at multiple levels, including during RNA processing and splicing.

The Nobel Prize awarded to Richard J. Roberts and Phillip A. Sharp in 1993 was a recognition of the transformative impact of their work on the field of molecular biology. Their discovery of split genes and RNA splicing fundamentally changed the understanding of gene expression and opened up new avenues of research into the regulation of genetic information. The implications of their work continue to resonate in the scientific community, influencing research in genetics, molecular biology, and biotechnology.

The legacy of Roberts and Sharp's discovery extends beyond their Nobel Prize-winning work. It has inspired generations of scientists to explore the complexities of gene expression and the role of RNA processing in health and disease. Their work has also laid the foundation for the development of new technologies and therapeutic strategies that harness the power of RNA splicing to treat genetic disorders and improve human health.

In conclusion, the discovery of split genes and RNA splicing by Richard J. Roberts and Phillip A. Sharp represents a major milestone in the history of molecular biology. Their work has had a profound impact on the understanding of gene structure and function, transforming the way scientists think about genetic information and its expression in eukaryotic cells. The implications of their discovery continue to shape the direction of research in molecular biology, genetics, and biotechnology, and their contributions to science will be remembered as one of the most significant advances in the field of gene expression.

Chapter 41: Paul Dirac

Paul Dirac, a British theoretical physicist, is one of the most influential figures in the history of science, known for his monumental contributions to quantum mechanics and quantum electrodynamics. Dirac's work is characterized by its mathematical rigor and profound insights, which laid the foundation for much of modern physics. Born on August 8, 1902, in Bristol, England, Dirac was the son of Charles Adrien Ladislas Dirac, a Swiss-born teacher, and Florence Hannah Holten, an Englishwoman. From an early age, Dirac displayed an extraordinary aptitude for mathematics, a talent that would later become the hallmark of his scientific career.

Dirac's academic journey began at the University of Bristol, where he initially studied electrical engineering, earning a degree in 1921. His interest in mathematics, however, soon led him to pursue a second degree in the subject, which he completed in 1923. It was during this time that Dirac developed a deep interest in theoretical physics, particularly in the emerging field of quantum mechanics. After graduating from Bristol, Dirac moved to St John's College, Cambridge, where he began his doctoral studies under the supervision of Ralph Fowler, a prominent physicist who was instrumental in guiding Dirac's early research.

The 1920s were a period of intense activity and rapid development in quantum theory, a field that was undergoing a revolutionary transformation. In 1925, the German physicist Werner Heisenberg formulated matrix mechanics, one of the earliest and most successful formulations of quantum mechanics. Heisenberg's work, along with the contributions of physicists like Erwin Schrödinger and Max Born, set the stage for a new understanding of the subatomic world. However, the mathematical framework of quantum mechanics was still in its infancy, and many physicists were grappling with the implications of this new theory.

It was in this context that Dirac made his first major contribution to quantum mechanics. In 1926, while still a doctoral student, he independently developed a formulation of quantum mechanics that was based on the theory of classical mechanics. Dirac's approach, known as the transformation theory, was a generalization of Heisenberg's matrix mechanics and Schrödinger's wave mechanics. Transformation theory provided a unified framework for understanding quantum mechanics, showing that the different formulations of the theory were equivalent. This work, which was published in a series of papers, established Dirac as one of the leading theoretical physicists of his time.

Dirac's most famous and groundbreaking work came in 1928 when he formulated the Dirac equation, a relativistic wave equation for the electron. The Dirac equation is one of the cornerstones of quantum mechanics and quantum electrodynamics, and it represents a profound synthesis of quantum theory and the theory of special relativity. Before Dirac's work, quantum mechanics was successful in describing the behavior of particles at low speeds, but it struggled to incorporate the principles of relativity, which govern the behavior of particles moving at speeds close to that of light.

Dirac's equation elegantly solved this problem by providing a relativistic description of the electron. The equation not only predicted the existence of the electron's intrinsic angular momentum, or spin, but also led to the prediction of the existence of antimatter, a discovery that would have far-reaching implications for both theoretical and experimental physics. The Dirac equation showed that for every particle, there exists a corresponding antiparticle with the same mass but opposite charge. This prediction was later confirmed experimentally with the discovery of the positron, the antiparticle of the electron, by Carl Anderson in 1932.

The discovery of antimatter was a monumental achievement that fundamentally changed our understanding of the universe. It suggested that the universe is not composed solely of the matter we observe but also contains a vast amount of antimatter, a concept that has inspired countless theories and experiments in particle physics and cosmology. Dirac's equation also played a crucial role in the development of quantum electrodynamics (QED), the quantum field theory of the electromagnetic force. QED is one of the most successful theories in physics, providing extremely accurate predictions of phenomena such as the anomalous magnetic moment of the electron and the Lamb shift in the hydrogen atom.

Dirac's contributions to quantum mechanics extended beyond the Dirac equation. He introduced the concept of the Fermi-Dirac statistics, which describes the behavior of particles known as fermions—particles that obey the Pauli exclusion principle, such as electrons, protons, and neutrons. The Fermi-Dirac distribution is a statistical distribution that describes the probability of occupancy of quantum states by fermions at a given temperature. This concept is fundamental to the understanding of the behavior of systems composed of many fermions, such as electrons in a metal or the particles in a degenerate star like a white dwarf.

Dirac's work in quantum mechanics was characterized by its mathematical elegance and simplicity, qualities that he believed were essential to a correct physical theory. He often emphasized the importance of mathematical beauty in the development of physical theories, arguing that the most successful theories are those that are mathematically beautiful. This philosophy guided much of Dirac's work, leading him to make several other significant contributions to theoretical physics, including his work on quantum field theory and the quantization of the electromagnetic field.

In the 1930s, Dirac continued to make important contributions to quantum mechanics and quantum field theory. He developed the concept of second quantization, a formalism that is used to describe quantum fields and the creation and annihilation of particles.

Second quantization is a key component of quantum field theory and is essential for understanding the interactions between particles and fields. Dirac also introduced the idea of the vacuum as a sea of negative energy states, known as the Dirac sea. This concept was an attempt to explain the existence of negative energy solutions to the Dirac equation, and it played a significant role in the development of quantum electrodynamics.

Despite his many contributions to theoretical physics, Dirac was known for his reticence and modesty. He was a man of few words, often preferring to let his work speak for itself. Dirac's personality was reflected in his approach to science, which was characterized by a focus on clarity, precision, and mathematical rigor. He had little patience for speculative or imprecise theories, and he was known for his ability to identify and correct errors in the work of others.

Dirac's achievements were recognized with numerous awards and honors throughout his career. In 1933, he was awarded the Nobel Prize in Physics, which he shared with Erwin Schrödinger, for their contributions to the development of quantum mechanics. The Nobel Committee specifically cited Dirac's discovery of new productive forms of atomic theory, including his relativistic wave equation for the electron. At the time, Dirac was one of the youngest recipients of the Nobel Prize, and his work was already considered a major milestone in the history of physics.

After receiving the Nobel Prize, Dirac continued to make significant contributions to theoretical physics. In the late 1930s and 1940s, he worked on the development of quantum electrodynamics and explored the implications of his earlier work on the Dirac equation. He also made important contributions to the study of magnetic monopoles, hypothetical particles that have a single magnetic pole. Although magnetic monopoles have not been observed experimentally, Dirac's work on the subject has had a lasting impact on theoretical physics, influencing the development of gauge theories and the study of topological defects in field theory.

Dirac's influence on theoretical physics extended beyond his own research. He was a mentor and inspiration to many of the leading physicists of the 20th century, including Richard Feynman, Julian Schwinger, and Freeman Dyson, who made significant contributions to quantum electrodynamics and quantum field theory. Dirac's emphasis on mathematical beauty and rigor also had a profound impact on the development of theoretical physics, shaping the way that future generations of physicists approached the study of the fundamental laws of nature.

In addition to his scientific achievements, Dirac was also known for his contributions to the philosophy of science. He believed that the laws of physics should be expressed in the language of mathematics and that the most successful physical theories are those that are mathematically elegant and simple. Dirac's belief in the importance of mathematical beauty was not merely an aesthetic preference but was based on his conviction that the fundamental laws of nature are inherently simple and that the complexity of the physical world arises from the application of these simple laws.

Dirac's later years were marked by a continued engagement with theoretical physics, although he became increasingly critical of some of the directions that the field was taking. He was particularly skeptical of the renormalization techniques used in quantum field theory, which he viewed as mathematically unsatisfactory. Despite his reservations, Dirac's work on quantum field theory laid the groundwork for many of the developments in the field, including the formulation of the Standard Model of particle physics.

Paul Dirac passed away on October 20, 1984, in Tallahassee, Florida, where he had spent the last years of his life as a professor at Florida State University. His death marked the end of an era in theoretical physics, but his legacy lives on in the many contributions he made to the field. Dirac's work continues to be a source of inspiration for physicists and mathematicians, and his ideas have had a lasting impact on the development of modern physics.

In summary, Paul Dirac's contributions to theoretical physics are among the most significant in the history of science. His work on quantum mechanics, quantum electrodynamics, and the Dirac equation has had a profound impact on our understanding of the fundamental laws of nature. Dirac's emphasis on mathematical beauty and rigor has shaped the way that physicists approach the study of the physical world, and his legacy continues to influence the field of theoretical physics. Dirac's life and work are a testament to the power of human intellect and creativity, and his contributions to science will be remembered for generations to come.

Chapter 42: Harold Varmus & Michael Bishop

Harold Varmus and Michael Bishop are two distinguished American scientists whose groundbreaking research in the field of cancer biology led to the discovery of oncogenes, genes that have the potential to cause cancer when mutated or expressed at high levels. Their work fundamentally transformed the understanding of cancer as a genetic disease and opened new avenues for cancer research, diagnosis, and treatment. In recognition of their contributions, Varmus and Bishop were jointly awarded the Nobel Prize in Physiology or Medicine in 1989. Their discovery not only revolutionized the field of oncology but also had a profound impact on molecular biology, genetics, and medicine as a whole.

The story of Varmus and Bishop's discovery begins in the 1960s and 1970s, a time when cancer was a poorly understood disease with few effective treatments. The prevailing theories of cancer causation were largely based on the idea that cancer was caused by external factors such as chemicals, radiation, or viruses, which somehow triggered uncontrolled cell growth. While these factors were known to be associated with cancer, the underlying mechanisms by which normal cells became cancerous remained elusive. There was little understanding of the role that genes played in the development of cancer, and the field of molecular oncology was still in its infancy.

Harold Varmus, born on December 18, 1939, in Oceanside, New York, and Michael Bishop, born on February 22, 1936, in Pennsylvania, both came from academic backgrounds that would eventually lead them to the study of cancer. Varmus earned his undergraduate degree in English literature from Amherst College before deciding to pursue a career in medicine. He received his MD from Columbia University in 1966 and, after a brief stint in clinical practice, shifted his focus to research. Varmus joined the National Institutes of Health (NIH) as a clinical associate and later worked at the University of California, San Francisco (UCSF), where he would make his most significant contributions to cancer research.

Michael Bishop, on the other hand, pursued a more traditional path in the sciences. After earning his undergraduate degree in chemistry from Gettysburg College, Bishop went on to study medicine at Harvard Medical School, where he developed an interest in virology and molecular biology. Following his medical degree, Bishop conducted research at the NIH and later joined UCSF, where he would eventually collaborate with Varmus on their pioneering research into the genetic basis of cancer.

The collaboration between Varmus and Bishop began in the early 1970s at UCSF, where they were both faculty members in the Department of Microbiology and Immunology. At that time, one of the most active areas of cancer research was the study of cancer-causing viruses, known as oncoviruses, which had been shown to induce tumors in animals. One of the most well-known oncoviruses was the Rous sarcoma virus (RSV), a retrovirus that caused cancer in chickens. RSV had been discovered by Peyton Rous in 1911, and subsequent research had shown that the virus could transform normal cells into cancerous ones. However, the mechanism by which RSV and other oncoviruses caused cancer was not understood.

Varmus and Bishop set out to investigate how RSV induced cancer at the molecular level. Their research focused on the viral genome, which they hypothesized contained a gene responsible for the virus's ability to transform cells. This gene, they believed, might be similar to a gene found in the host cells that the virus infected. To test this hypothesis, they used molecular hybridization techniques to compare the viral genome with the DNA of normal, uninfected cells. What they discovered was astonishing: the RSV genome contained a gene that was nearly identical to a gene found in the DNA of normal chicken cells. This gene, which they called v-src (for viral src), was responsible for the virus's ability to cause cancer. Even more surprising, the normal cellular gene, which they named c-src (for cellular src), was present in all cells, not just those infected by the virus.

The discovery of the c-src gene was a major breakthrough because it suggested that the ability to cause cancer was not unique to viruses but was instead related to a gene that was normally present in the cells of healthy organisms. Varmus and Bishop proposed that the c-src gene was a proto-oncogene—a normal gene that, when mutated or abnormally activated, could become an oncogene and drive the uncontrolled cell division characteristic of cancer. This was a radical departure from the prevailing view that cancer was caused primarily by external agents. Instead, Varmus and Bishop's work suggested that cancer could arise from the mutation or misregulation of genes that were essential for normal cellular function.

The implications of this discovery were profound. If cancer could result from the activation of proto-oncogenes, then it meant that cancer was, at its core, a genetic disease. This realization opened up a new field of research focused on identifying other proto-oncogenes and understanding how their mutation or activation led to cancer. Over the following years, Varmus, Bishop, and their colleagues identified several other proto-oncogenes and demonstrated that they were involved in a variety of cancers. These discoveries laid the groundwork for the development of targeted therapies, which aim to specifically inhibit the activity of oncogenes or the pathways they control.

One of the key insights from Varmus and Bishop's work was the understanding that proto-oncogenes play essential roles in normal cell growth and development. Proto-oncogenes are involved in regulating cell division, differentiation, and survival, processes that are critical for the maintenance of healthy tissues. However, when these genes are mutated, overexpressed, or otherwise dysregulated, they can drive the uncontrolled proliferation of cells, leading to the formation of tumors. This concept helped explain why cancer can develop spontaneously in the absence of viral infection and why certain genetic mutations are associated with an increased risk of cancer.

The discovery of oncogenes also had significant implications for cancer diagnosis and treatment. The identification of specific oncogenes associated with particular types of cancer allowed for the development of molecular diagnostic tools that could detect the presence of these genes in patients. This led to more accurate diagnoses and the ability to tailor treatment to the specific genetic profile of a patient's cancer. Additionally, the understanding that oncogenes could be targeted by drugs led to the development of targeted therapies, which have become a cornerstone of modern cancer treatment. These therapies aim to specifically inhibit the activity of oncogenes or the signaling pathways they control, thereby halting the growth and spread of cancer cells while minimizing damage to normal cells.

Varmus and Bishop's discovery of oncogenes was not only a scientific breakthrough but also a turning point in the fight against cancer. Their work shifted the focus of cancer research from external factors to the genetic and molecular mechanisms that drive the disease. This shift has led to significant advances in cancer biology, including the identification of tumor suppressor genes, the development of precision medicine, and the advent of immunotherapy.

Harold Varmus and Michael Bishop's contributions to science extend beyond their discovery of oncogenes. Throughout their careers, both scientists have been leaders in the scientific community, advocating for the importance of basic research and the need for interdisciplinary collaboration in the pursuit of scientific knowledge. Varmus, in particular, has been a prominent figure in science policy and administration. After winning the Nobel Prize, he served as the Director of the National Institutes of Health (NIH) from 1993 to 1999, where he was instrumental in launching several major initiatives, including the Human Genome Project and the creation of the NIH Roadmap for Medical Research.

Following his tenure at the NIH, Varmus continued to play a key role in the scientific community, serving as the President of Memorial Sloan Kettering Cancer Center in New York City and later as the Director of the National Cancer Institute (NCI). In these roles, Varmus has been a vocal advocate for the importance of cancer research and the need to translate scientific discoveries into clinical applications that can benefit patients.

Michael Bishop, too, has made significant contributions to the field of cancer research and has held leadership positions in the academic and scientific communities. He served as the Chancellor of the University of California, San Francisco (UCSF) from 1998 to 2009, where he played a key role in expanding the university's research programs and fostering collaborations between scientists and clinicians. Under Bishop's leadership, UCSF became one of the leading biomedical research institutions in the world, known for its pioneering work in cancer biology, neuroscience, and regenerative medicine.

The legacy of Harold Varmus and Michael Bishop's discovery of oncogenes is evident in the ongoing research into the genetic and molecular basis of cancer. Their work has inspired countless scientists to explore the complex interplay between genes, signaling pathways, and cellular processes that drive the development of cancer. The identification of oncogenes and the understanding of their role in cancer has led to the development of numerous targeted therapies that have improved the outcomes for many cancer patients.

One of the most notable examples of targeted therapy is the development of tyrosine kinase inhibitors, such as imatinib (Gleevec), which specifically target the BCR-ABL oncogene in chronic myeloid leukemia (CML). The success of imatinib has demonstrated the potential of targeted therapies to transform the treatment of cancer, turning what was once a fatal disease into a manageable condition for many patients. This approach has since been expanded to other types of cancer, with drugs designed to target specific oncogenes or the signaling pathways they control.

In addition to targeted therapies, the discovery of oncogenes has also paved the way for the development of precision medicine, an approach to healthcare that takes into account an individual's genetic makeup, lifestyle, and environment to tailor treatment. Precision medicine has become an integral part of cancer care, with genetic testing used to identify the specific mutations driving a patient's cancer and guide the selection of the most effective treatment. This personalized approach has improved the efficacy of cancer therapies and reduced the side effects associated with conventional treatments.

The impact of Varmus and Bishop's work extends beyond cancer. Their discovery of oncogenes has had far-reaching implications for the broader field of molecular biology and genetics. The concept of proto-oncogenes has provided a framework for understanding how genes regulate cell growth and development, and how their dysregulation can lead to disease. This knowledge has been applied to a wide range of biological processes, from embryonic development to aging, and has informed research into other diseases, such as neurodegenerative disorders and autoimmune conditions.

Moreover, the techniques and methodologies developed by Varmus, Bishop, and their colleagues have become fundamental tools in molecular biology research. The use of molecular hybridization, gene cloning, and transgenic models to study gene function and regulation has become standard practice in laboratories around the world. These tools have enabled scientists to unravel the complex networks of genes and proteins that govern cellular behavior and to develop new strategies for manipulating these networks for therapeutic purposes.

In recognition of their contributions to science and medicine, Harold Varmus and Michael Bishop have received numerous honors and awards in addition to the Nobel Prize. Varmus has been elected to the National Academy of Sciences, the American Academy of Arts and Sciences, and the Institute of Medicine, among other prestigious organizations. Bishop has also been recognized with membership in the National Academy of Sciences and the American Academy of Arts and Sciences, as well as the Lasker Award, one of the most respected prizes in medical research.

The discovery of oncogenes by Harold Varmus and Michael Bishop represents a pivotal moment in the history of cancer research and molecular biology. Their work has provided a deeper understanding of the genetic basis of cancer and has led to the development of targeted therapies that have saved countless lives. Their legacy continues to inspire new generations of scientists to explore the genetic and molecular mechanisms of disease, with the ultimate goal of improving human health. As the field of oncology continues to evolve, the contributions of Varmus and Bishop will remain a cornerstone of our understanding of cancer and its treatment.

Chapter 43: Andre Geim & Konstantin Novoselov

Andre Geim and Konstantin Novoselov are renowned physicists whose pioneering work in the field of condensed matter physics led to the discovery of graphene, a material that has been heralded as a "wonder material" due to its extraordinary properties. Their groundbreaking research on graphene earned them the Nobel Prize in Physics in 2010, making them two of the most celebrated scientists of the 21st century. Their discovery not only revolutionized the field of material science but also opened up new possibilities in electronics, nanotechnology, and a wide range of other scientific and industrial applications. The story of their discovery is one of curiosity, creativity, and a relentless pursuit of knowledge, which ultimately led to the isolation of graphene and the exploration of its remarkable characteristics.

Andre Geim was born on October 21, 1958, in Sochi, Russia, and he developed an interest in physics at a young age. After completing his undergraduate studies at the Moscow Institute of Physics and Technology, Geim pursued a Ph.D. at the Institute of Solid-State Physics in Chernogolovka, where he began to explore the properties of different materials. His early research focused on magnetism and superconductivity, fields that would later play a significant role in his scientific career. Geim's curiosity and willingness to explore unconventional ideas set him apart from his peers, and he quickly gained a reputation as an innovative and creative thinker.

Konstantin Novoselov, born on August 23, 1974, in Nizhny Tagil, Russia, also showed a strong interest in science from an early age. Novoselov pursued his education in physics, obtaining his undergraduate degree from the Moscow Institute of Physics and

Technology, where he first met Geim. Impressed by Geim's approach to research and his willingness to take risks in the pursuit of new knowledge, Novoselov joined Geim's research group as a Ph.D. student. This partnership would prove to be highly fruitful, as the two scientists shared a mutual passion for exploring the unknown and pushing the boundaries of what was possible in material science.

The collaboration between Geim and Novoselov took off when both were at the University of Manchester in the United Kingdom. It was here that they began to investigate the properties of various materials in their search for new phenomena and potential applications. One of the key aspects of their research was their use of a method known as "micromechanical cleavage," which involved using adhesive tape to peel off layers from bulk materials to obtain thinner and thinner samples. This seemingly simple technique would eventually lead to one of the most important discoveries in modern physics.

In 2004, Geim and Novoselov made their landmark discovery when they successfully isolated a single layer of carbon atoms arranged in a two-dimensional honeycomb lattice, a material that came to be known as graphene. Graphene is the thinnest material known to science, consisting of just one layer of carbon atoms, yet it is also incredibly strong, with a tensile strength over 100 times greater than that of steel. Moreover, graphene exhibits remarkable electrical conductivity, surpassing even copper, and is nearly transparent, making it an ideal candidate for a wide range of electronic and optoelectronic applications.

The isolation of graphene was a significant breakthrough because it defied the conventional wisdom of the time. Prior to Geim and Novoselov's work, it was widely believed that two-dimensional materials could not exist in a free-standing form because they would be too unstable and prone to collapsing into three-dimensional structures. However, the success of Geim and Novoselov's micromechanical cleavage technique demonstrated that graphene could indeed be isolated and studied in its pure form, opening up a new realm of possibilities in material science.

The discovery of graphene had profound implications for both fundamental physics and applied science. From a theoretical standpoint, graphene provides a unique platform for studying quantum mechanical effects in two dimensions. The electrons in graphene behave as massless relativistic particles, known as Dirac fermions, which move at an effective speed of light. This has led to the observation of phenomena such as the anomalous quantum Hall effect and Klein tunneling, which have deepened our understanding of quantum mechanics and condensed matter physics.

On the applied side, graphene's exceptional properties have made it a highly sought-after material for a wide range of applications. In the field of electronics, graphene's high electrical conductivity and flexibility have the potential to revolutionize the development of next-generation electronic devices, such as flexible displays, high-speed transistors, and advanced sensors. Graphene's transparency and strength also make it an ideal material for transparent conductive coatings, which are used in touchscreens, solar cells, and other optoelectronic devices.

The potential applications of graphene extend beyond electronics and optoelectronics. In the field of energy storage, graphene has shown promise as a material for improving the performance of batteries and supercapacitors. Its high surface area and conductivity enable faster charging and discharging rates, as well as higher energy densities, which could lead to more efficient and longer-lasting energy storage devices. In the realm of composite materials, graphene's strength and lightweight nature make it an attractive additive for enhancing the mechanical properties of polymers, metals, and ceramics, leading to the development of stronger and lighter materials for use in aerospace, automotive, and other industries.

Despite the immense promise of graphene, the path from discovery to commercialization has not been without challenges. One of the key hurdles has been the development of scalable and cost-effective methods for producing high-quality graphene. The micromechanical cleavage technique used by Geim and Novoselov to isolate graphene is not suitable for large-scale production, and alternative methods, such as chemical vapor deposition (CVD) and liquid-phase exfoliation, have been explored to address this issue. While significant progress has been made in scaling up graphene production, challenges remain in ensuring the consistency and quality of the material, which are critical for its successful integration into commercial products.

Another challenge lies in the integration of graphene into existing manufacturing processes and technologies. While graphene's properties are exceptional, its implementation in devices and systems requires overcoming technical and engineering challenges, such as ensuring compatibility with other materials, controlling its behavior in different environments, and developing new fabrication techniques that can take full advantage of its unique characteristics. Researchers and engineers continue to work on these issues, and significant advances have been made in recent years, bringing graphene closer to widespread commercial use.

Geim and Novoselov's discovery of graphene has not only had a profound impact on material science but has also inspired a new generation of researchers to explore the possibilities of other two-dimensional materials. Following the discovery of graphene, scientists have identified and studied a variety of other 2D materials, such as transition metal dichalcogenides (TMDs), hexagonal boron nitride (h-BN), and black phosphorus, each with its own unique set of properties and potential applications. This burgeoning field of research, known as "2D materials," is rapidly expanding, with new materials and phenomena being discovered at an unprecedented pace.

In addition to their work on graphene, both Andre Geim and Konstantin Novoselov have made significant contributions to other areas of physics and material science. Geim, for example, is known for his work on diamagnetic levitation, which led to the famous "flying frog" experiment, where a live frog was levitated using a powerful magnetic field. This playful experiment, conducted in the late 1990s, not only demonstrated the principle of diamagnetic levitation but also highlighted Geim's willingness to explore unconventional ideas and push the boundaries of scientific research.

Novoselov, for his part, has continued to explore the properties of graphene and other 2D materials, focusing on their potential applications in various fields, including nanoelectronics, photonics, and biomedical engineering. His research has helped to advance the understanding of how 2D materials interact with each other and with other substances, leading to the development of new materials and devices with novel properties and functionalities.

The impact of Geim and Novoselov's work extends beyond the scientific community. Their discovery of graphene has captured the imagination of the public and has been widely recognized as a major scientific achievement. In addition to the Nobel Prize, both scientists have received numerous awards and honors for their contributions to science and technology. Geim was knighted by Queen Elizabeth II in 2012, and Novoselov was knighted in 2013, both in recognition of their services to science.

The story of Andre Geim and Konstantin Novoselov is a testament to the power of curiosity, creativity, and collaboration in scientific discovery. Their work on graphene has not only expanded the frontiers of material science but has also demonstrated the importance of taking risks and exploring new ideas, even when they challenge conventional wisdom. Their discovery has opened up new possibilities for technological innovation and has inspired a generation of scientists to continue exploring the fascinating world of 2D materials.

As research into graphene and other 2D materials continues to advance, the full potential of these materials is still being uncovered. While many challenges remain, the possibilities for new applications and technologies are vast. Whether in electronics, energy, healthcare, or beyond, the discovery of graphene by Geim and Novoselov has laid the foundation for a new era of material science, one that promises to shape the future in ways that we can only begin to imagine. Their legacy will undoubtedly continue to influence the field for decades to come, as scientists and engineers build upon their pioneering work to unlock the full potential of 2D materials and bring their benefits to society.

Chapter 44: Kroto, Curl, & Smalley

Harold Kroto, Robert Curl, and Richard Smalley are celebrated for their discovery of fullerenes, a new form of carbon that opened an entirely new field of chemistry and materials science. Their groundbreaking work, which was honored with the Nobel Prize in Chemistry in 1996, not only expanded our understanding of carbon's versatility but also led to significant advancements in nanotechnology and various applied sciences. The journey to this discovery is a story of curiosity, interdisciplinary collaboration, and the profound impact that a single breakthrough can have on multiple fields of study.

Sir Harold W. Kroto, born in England in 1939, was a chemist whose work was characterized by a fascination with the structures of molecules, particularly carbon-based ones. His career path took him through various institutions, where he developed expertise in spectroscopy, which he would later use to investigate the composition of interstellar space. Kroto's interest in astronomy and the formation of carbon chains in the universe was a crucial factor that led to the discovery of fullerenes.

Robert F. Curl Jr., born in 1933 in Texas, was an American chemist with a deep interest in physical chemistry and molecular spectroscopy. He spent much of his academic career at Rice University, where he focused on the study of chemical reactions and the properties of small molecules. Curl's expertise in spectroscopy made him a natural partner for Kroto in their joint research endeavors.

Richard E. Smalley, born in 1943 in Ohio, was a pioneering American chemist and physicist. His work at Rice University was instrumental in developing new techniques for investigating the properties of materials at the atomic level. Smalley was particularly known for his development of laser vaporization cluster beams, a technique that allowed the study of clusters of atoms and molecules, and which would play a pivotal role in the discovery of fullerenes.

The story of the discovery of fullerenes begins with Harold Kroto's interest in the long carbon chains observed in the spectra of interstellar space. These carbon chains, thought to be formed in the atmospheres of cool, carbon-rich stars, fascinated Kroto, who hypothesized that similar processes might be responsible for the formation of unusual carbon molecules. To investigate this, he sought the collaboration of Robert Curl and Richard Smalley, who had developed a technique using laser vaporization to study clusters of atoms.

In September 1985, Kroto, Curl, and Smalley, along with graduate students James Heath, Sean O'Brien, and Yuan Liu, conducted experiments at Rice University that would lead to a momentous discovery. They used Smalley's laser vaporization apparatus to simulate the conditions that might exist in the atmospheres of carbon-rich stars. By vaporizing graphite and cooling the resulting carbon vapor in a stream of helium gas, they created clusters of carbon atoms that could be analyzed using mass spectrometry.

What they found was astonishing. Among the various carbon clusters produced, one particular cluster stood out for its stability and abundance: a molecule composed of 60 carbon atoms. This molecule, later named buckminsterfullerene, or C60, had a structure unlike any previously known form of carbon. Instead of forming the familiar planar sheets of graphite or the rigid three-dimensional lattice of diamond, C60 consisted of carbon atoms arranged in a hollow, spherical structure resembling a soccer ball, with 12 pentagons and 20 hexagons, similar to the geodesic domes designed by architect Buckminster Fuller, after whom the molecule was named.

The discovery of C60 was more than just the identification of a new molecule; it represented the realization of a completely new form of carbon. Unlike the previously known allotropes of carbon—diamond and graphite—C60 and other fullerenes were molecules with entirely different properties. The spherical structure of C60, for example, gives it unique stability and the ability to resist compression, making it an extraordinarily resilient molecule.

The implications of this discovery were profound. Fullerenes, often referred to as "buckyballs" due to their resemblance to soccer balls, opened up a new field of chemistry that focused on the synthesis, characterization, and functionalization of carbon-based nanostructures. The discovery of fullerenes led to a broader exploration of carbon's ability to form other novel structures, including carbon nanotubes, which are essentially elongated fullerenes and have remarkable mechanical, electrical, and thermal properties. Carbon nanotubes have since found applications in a wide range of fields, from materials science to electronics to medicine.

The discovery of fullerenes also had significant implications for our understanding of chemistry and the potential for the existence of other carbon-based structures. Prior to this discovery, the chemistry of carbon was thought to be largely understood, with the focus being on organic molecules, polymers, and the well-known allotropes of carbon. The identification of fullerenes shattered this notion and demonstrated that carbon was capable of forming an entirely new class of molecules with unique properties. This realization led to an explosion of research into carbon nanostructures and materials, which continues to this day.

The research conducted by Kroto, Curl, and Smalley not only led to the discovery of fullerenes but also advanced our understanding of the processes that govern the formation of complex molecules in space. The conditions under which fullerenes were synthesized in the laboratory—high temperatures and carbon-rich environments—are similar to those found in the atmospheres of certain types of stars. This connection between laboratory chemistry and astrophysics provided insights into the possible origins of complex organic molecules in space and their potential role in the formation of life.

The recognition of fullerenes as a new form of carbon also spurred interest in the potential applications of these molecules. Fullerenes possess a range of interesting properties, including the ability to act as superconductors, their potential use in drug delivery systems due to their ability to encapsulate other molecules, and their effectiveness as antioxidants. Researchers have also explored the use of fullerenes in photovoltaic devices, where their ability to accept electrons makes them useful in the design of more efficient solar cells.

The work of Kroto, Curl, and Smalley was characterized by a spirit of interdisciplinary collaboration and a willingness to explore the unknown. Their discovery was not the result of a planned search for a new form of carbon, but rather a consequence of their curiosity and openness to unexpected results. The use of Smalley's laser vaporization technique, combined with Kroto's interest in interstellar chemistry and Curl's expertise in spectroscopy, created the perfect environment for this serendipitous discovery.

The Nobel Prize awarded to Harold Kroto, Robert Curl, and Richard Smalley in 1996 was a recognition of the significance of their discovery and the impact it had on the field of chemistry. Beyond the scientific community, their work has inspired a new generation of researchers to explore the possibilities of carbon nanostructures and has led to the development of new technologies that harness the unique properties of fullerenes and related materials.

Harold Kroto continued to be an advocate for science education and the public understanding of science throughout his career. He was passionate about inspiring young people to pursue careers in science and was involved in numerous educational initiatives. His legacy extends beyond his scientific contributions to his efforts to promote science as a vital part of society and culture.

Robert Curl, while continuing his academic career, has been known for his contributions to the field of physical chemistry and his mentorship of students and researchers. His work on fullerenes and his broader contributions to molecular spectroscopy have left a lasting impact on the field.

Richard Smalley, who passed away in 2005, was a visionary in the field of nanotechnology. He recognized early on the potential of nanoscience to revolutionize a wide range of industries and was a vocal advocate for increased funding and research in this area. His work on fullerenes and carbon nanotubes laid the foundation for many of the advances in nanotechnology that we see today.

The discovery of fullerenes by Kroto, Curl, and Smalley represents a milestone in the history of science. It is a testament to the power of curiosity-driven research and the importance of interdisciplinary collaboration. Their work has had a profound impact on our understanding of carbon and its potential to form a vast array of structures with unique and useful properties. As research in nanotechnology and materials science continues to evolve, the legacy of Harold Kroto, Robert Curl, and Richard Smalley will continue to influence the direction of scientific inquiry and the development of new technologies that have the potential to change the world. Their discovery of fullerenes stands as a shining example of how a single scientific breakthrough can open up entirely new fields of study and lead to innovations that benefit society as a whole.

Chapter 45: James Peebles

James Peebles, a Canadian-American astrophysicist, has profoundly influenced our understanding of the universe and its origins. His groundbreaking contributions to cosmology have shaped much of what we know today about the cosmos, including the Big Bang theory, the cosmic microwave background radiation, dark matter, and dark energy. Peebles' work is a testament to the power of theoretical physics to uncover the fundamental principles governing the universe, and his insights have earned him the Nobel Prize in Physics in 2019. His career, spanning over five decades, is characterized by a relentless pursuit of knowledge, a deep curiosity about the cosmos, and an unparalleled ability to translate complex mathematical theories into profound physical insights.

James Peebles was born on April 25, 1935, in Winnipeg, Manitoba, Canada. He grew up during a time when the field of cosmology was still in its infancy, and many of the questions that drive modern astrophysics had yet to be formulated. Peebles' early education in Canada laid the foundation for his later achievements in physics. He earned his undergraduate degree in 1958 from the University of Manitoba, where his interest in theoretical physics began to take shape. Peebles then moved to the United States to pursue graduate studies at Princeton University, a decision that would set the stage for his transformative contributions to cosmology.

At Princeton, Peebles studied under the guidance of Robert Dicke, a physicist known for his work on the theory of gravity and the search for evidence of the Big Bang. Dicke was instrumental in fostering Peebles' interest in cosmology and encouraging him to explore the implications of the Big Bang theory, which, at that time, was still a relatively new idea. The early 1960s were a period of intense intellectual activity in cosmology, with many competing theories about the origin and evolution of the universe. Peebles' work during this period would help solidify the Big Bang theory as the leading explanation for the origin of the cosmos.

One of Peebles' most significant contributions to cosmology was his work on the cosmic microwave background (CMB) radiation, which is the faint afterglow of the Big Bang. The existence of the CMB had been predicted by George Gamow, Ralph Alpher, and Robert Herman in the late 1940s, but it had not yet been observed. Peebles, working with Dicke and other colleagues at Princeton, realized that if the Big Bang theory were correct, the universe should be filled with this radiation, and it should be detectable with radio telescopes. This insight led to a search for the CMB, which culminated in its accidental discovery in 1965 by Arno Penzias and Robert Wilson at Bell Labs. Although Penzias and Wilson were awarded the Nobel Prize for their discovery, Peebles' theoretical work provided the framework for understanding the significance of the CMB as evidence for the Big Bang.

The discovery of the CMB was a watershed moment in cosmology, and Peebles' subsequent work on the topic helped to establish it as one of the most important pieces of evidence supporting the Big Bang theory. Peebles developed detailed models of the early universe that explained how the CMB was generated and how its properties could be used to infer information about the universe's age, composition, and structure. His work on the CMB also led to the development of the theory of cosmic inflation, which posits that the universe underwent a rapid expansion in the first fraction of a second after the Big Bang. This theory helps to explain why the universe appears to be so homogeneous and isotropic on large scales.

In addition to his work on the CMB, Peebles made significant contributions to our understanding of dark matter, an invisible substance that makes up most of the mass in the universe. In the

1970s, astronomers began to realize that the visible matter in galaxies could not account for their observed rotation curves. The stars in galaxies were moving too quickly to be held together by the gravity of the visible matter alone, implying the presence of an unseen mass. Peebles was one of the first theorists to explore the implications of this discovery, and he developed models that incorporated dark matter into the standard cosmological framework. His work showed that dark matter played a crucial role in the formation of galaxies and large-scale structures in the universe. Without dark matter, the gravitational forces needed to pull matter together and form galaxies would not be sufficient.

Peebles also contributed to the understanding of dark energy, a mysterious force that is driving the accelerated expansion of the universe. In the late 1990s, observations of distant supernovae revealed that the expansion of the universe was not slowing down, as had been expected, but was instead accelerating. This unexpected discovery suggested the existence of a new form of energy, dubbed dark energy, which exerts a repulsive force on the cosmos. Peebles was among the first to recognize the significance of this discovery and to integrate it into the broader cosmological framework. He developed theoretical models that explained how dark energy could be responsible for the accelerated expansion and explored its implications for the fate of the universe.

Throughout his career, Peebles has been a key figure in the development of the standard model of cosmology, often referred to as the Lambda Cold Dark Matter (ΛCDM) model. This model incorporates the Big Bang theory, dark matter, dark energy, and the inflationary universe model to provide a comprehensive explanation of the observed properties of the universe. The ΛCDM model has been remarkably successful in explaining a wide range of cosmological observations, from the large-scale structure of the universe to the distribution of galaxies and the fluctuations in the

CMB. Peebles' contributions to this model have been instrumental in shaping our current understanding of the universe's evolution.

In addition to his scientific achievements, Peebles has been an influential educator and mentor. He has trained numerous students and postdoctoral researchers who have gone on to make significant contributions to cosmology and astrophysics. Peebles' approach to teaching is characterized by a deep commitment to fostering critical thinking and encouraging his students to explore new ideas. He has authored several seminal textbooks on cosmology, including "Physical Cosmology" (1971) and "Principles of Physical Cosmology" (1993), which have been widely used by students and researchers alike.

Peebles' work has been recognized with numerous awards and honors, including the Nobel Prize in Physics in 2019, which he shared with Michel Mayor and Didier Queloz. The Nobel Committee cited Peebles for his "theoretical discoveries in physical cosmology," acknowledging his contributions to our understanding of the universe's origins and evolution. The award was a fitting recognition of Peebles' lifelong dedication to uncovering the mysteries of the cosmos and his role in transforming cosmology into a precise and predictive science.

Despite his many achievements, Peebles is known for his humility and his emphasis on the collaborative nature of scientific research. He has often remarked that his work builds on the contributions of others and that progress in science is the result of the collective efforts of many researchers. This modesty, combined with his intellectual rigor and curiosity, has made him a respected and admired figure in the scientific community.

Peebles' influence extends beyond the realm of cosmology. His work has had a profound impact on related fields such as astrophysics, particle physics, and general relativity. The concepts he developed, such as dark matter and dark energy, have become central to our understanding of the universe and have inspired new lines of inquiry in both theoretical and experimental physics. Peebles' contributions to the study of the CMB have also paved the way for a new generation of observational experiments, such as the Planck satellite, which have provided detailed measurements of the CMB and further refined our understanding of the early universe.

James Peebles' legacy is one of profound scientific achievement and intellectual curiosity. His work has transformed cosmology from a speculative field into a rigorous science grounded in observation and theory. Peebles' insights into the nature of the universe have expanded our understanding of the cosmos and have opened up new avenues of exploration that will continue to shape the future of astrophysics and cosmology. His contributions to our knowledge of the universe's origins, the nature of dark matter and dark energy, and the structure of the cosmos will remain a cornerstone of modern physics for generations to come. As we continue to explore the mysteries of the universe, the work of James Peebles will undoubtedly serve as a guiding light, inspiring future generations of scientists to push the boundaries of human knowledge and to seek answers to the deepest questions about the nature of the cosmos.

Chapter 46: Steven Weinberg

Steven Weinberg was one of the most influential theoretical physicists of the 20th and early 21st centuries. His contributions to the unification of fundamental forces, particularly through his work on the electroweak theory, significantly shaped modern physics and earned him the Nobel Prize in Physics in 1979. Weinberg's intellectual pursuits extended beyond theoretical physics; he was also a prolific author, an advocate for science, and a critical voice in discussions about science's role in society. His work exemplifies the deep connections between abstract theoretical ideas and the empirical realities of the physical universe.

Steven Weinberg was born on May 3, 1933, in New York City to Jewish immigrant parents. He grew up in the Bronx, where he attended the Bronx High School of Science, an institution known for nurturing many future scientists. It was here that his interest in science, particularly physics, began to take shape. His early fascination with the workings of the universe led him to pursue a career in theoretical physics, a path that would take him to the heights of scientific achievement.

Weinberg attended Cornell University, where he earned his undergraduate degree in 1954. He then moved to the Institute for Theoretical Physics at the University of Copenhagen, where he studied under Niels Bohr, one of the founding figures of quantum mechanics. This experience was formative, exposing him to the frontiers of quantum theory and the deep conceptual questions that would later define his work. After a brief period at the Institute for Advanced Study in Princeton, Weinberg completed his Ph.D. at Princeton University in 1957, under the supervision of Sam Treiman.

Weinberg's early career was marked by a series of influential positions at institutions such as Columbia University, the University of California, Berkeley, and the Massachusetts Institute of Technology (MIT). During these years, he developed a reputation as a brilliant theoretical physicist with a keen ability to tackle some of the most challenging problems in the field. His research interests were broad, spanning particle physics, cosmology, and quantum field theory.

One of Weinberg's most significant contributions to physics came in 1967 when he published a groundbreaking paper titled "A Model of Leptons." In this paper, Weinberg proposed a theoretical framework that unified the electromagnetic force and the weak nuclear force into a single force known as the electroweak force. This unification was a crucial step in the development of the Standard Model of particle physics, which describes the fundamental particles and forces that govern the behavior of matter in the universe.

Weinberg's electroweak theory built upon earlier work by Sheldon Glashow, who had developed a model that combined the electromagnetic and weak forces, and Abdus Salam, who independently arrived at similar conclusions. Weinberg's key insight was to introduce the concept of spontaneous symmetry breaking, a mechanism that explains how the unified electroweak force can give rise to the distinct electromagnetic and weak forces observed in nature. This mechanism involves the Higgs field, a scalar field that permeates all of space. When the Higgs field acquires a nonzero value in its lowest energy state, it breaks the symmetry of the electroweak force, giving mass to the W and Z bosons (the carriers of the weak force) while leaving the photon (the carrier of the electromagnetic force) massless.

The electroweak theory was a monumental achievement, providing a unified description of two of the four fundamental forces of nature and making precise predictions that could be tested experimentally. One of the most striking predictions of the theory was the existence of the Higgs boson, a particle associated with the

Higgs field. Although the Higgs boson would not be discovered until 2012, the success of the electroweak theory in explaining the properties of elementary particles and the interactions between them was evident long before that.

Weinberg's work on the electroweak theory, along with the contributions of Glashow and Salam, was recognized with the Nobel Prize in Physics in 1979. The Nobel Committee praised their efforts for "their contributions to the theory of the unified weak and electromagnetic interaction between elementary particles, including, inter alia, the prediction of the weak neutral current." The discovery of the weak neutral current in experiments conducted at CERN in 1973 provided critical experimental confirmation of the electroweak theory and solidified its status as a cornerstone of modern physics.

Beyond his work on the electroweak theory, Weinberg made significant contributions to many other areas of theoretical physics. He was a key figure in the development of quantum field theory, the framework that underlies the Standard Model. His textbook "The Quantum Theory of Fields," published in three volumes between 1995 and 2000, is considered a seminal work in the field and is widely used by physicists and students alike. In these books, Weinberg provided a comprehensive and rigorous treatment of quantum field theory, covering topics such as renormalization, gauge theories, and spontaneous symmetry breaking.

Weinberg also made important contributions to cosmology, the study of the origin, evolution, and large-scale structure of the universe. He was one of the pioneers in applying quantum field theory to cosmological problems, helping to bridge the gap between particle physics and cosmology. His 1972 book "Gravitation and Cosmology: Principles and Applications of the General Theory of Relativity" became a standard reference in the field and was instrumental in shaping the study of cosmology during a period when it was rapidly evolving into a precision science.

One of Weinberg's most notable contributions to cosmology was his work on the cosmological constant problem, which addresses the question of why the observed value of the cosmological constant, a term in Einstein's equations of general relativity that represents the energy density of empty space, is so much smaller than theoretical predictions. Weinberg's research on this topic, particularly his introduction of the anthropic principle as a possible explanation for the smallness of the cosmological constant, has had a lasting impact on the field.

Weinberg was also deeply interested in the quest for a grand unified theory (GUT) that would unify the strong nuclear force, the weak nuclear force, and the electromagnetic force into a single theoretical framework. While such a theory has yet to be fully realized, Weinberg's work laid important groundwork for future research in this area. His ideas about grand unification and his exploration of the relationship between particle physics and cosmology have inspired generations of physicists to pursue the goal of a deeper understanding of the fundamental forces of nature.

In addition to his scientific work, Weinberg was a prolific writer and communicator of science. He was passionate about making the complex ideas of theoretical physics accessible to a broader audience, and he authored several popular science books, including "The First Three Minutes: A Modern View of the Origin of the Universe" (1977), "Dreams of a Final Theory" (1992), and "To Explain the World: The Discovery of Modern Science" (2015). In these books, Weinberg explored the origins of the universe, the quest for a unified theory of physics, and the history of scientific thought, offering readers a glimpse into the profound questions that have driven scientific inquiry for centuries.

Weinberg was also an outspoken advocate for the role of science in society. He was a vocal critic of pseudoscience, religious dogma, and the misuse of science for political or ideological purposes. He believed strongly in the importance of scientific reasoning and evidence-based thinking as foundations for understanding the world and making informed decisions. In his essays and public lectures, Weinberg often addressed the challenges facing science in the modern world, including the need for adequate funding for scientific research, the dangers of anti-scientific attitudes, and the ethical implications of scientific advances.

Weinberg's contributions to science and his advocacy for the importance of scientific thinking were recognized with numerous awards and honors throughout his career. In addition to the Nobel Prize, he received the National Medal of Science, the Franklin Medal, the Heineman Prize for Mathematical Physics, and the J. Robert Oppenheimer Memorial Prize, among others. He was elected to the National Academy of Sciences, the American Academy of Arts and Sciences, and the Royal Society of London, reflecting his status as one of the most respected and influential scientists of his time.

Steven Weinberg's legacy is one of profound intellectual achievement and a deep commitment to the pursuit of knowledge. His work has fundamentally altered our understanding of the universe and has laid the foundation for much of modern theoretical physics. Weinberg's contributions to the unification of forces, quantum field theory, and cosmology have had a lasting impact on the field, shaping the way physicists think about the fundamental laws of nature. His writings, both technical and popular, have inspired countless individuals to explore the mysteries of the cosmos and to appreciate the beauty and power of scientific reasoning.

Weinberg's influence extended beyond the scientific community; he was a public intellectual who used his platform to advocate for science and to engage with the broader cultural and philosophical implications of scientific discoveries. His clear and articulate explanations of complex scientific ideas made him a powerful voice in the conversation about the role of science in society, and his work continues to resonate with those who seek to understand the deepest questions about the nature of reality.

As we look to the future, Steven Weinberg's contributions to physics and his legacy as a thinker, educator, and advocate for science will continue to inspire new generations of scientists and scholars. His life and work serve as a reminder of the power of human curiosity and the importance of the scientific endeavor in our quest to comprehend the universe and our place within it.

Chapter 47: James P. Allison & Tasuku Honjo

James P. Allison and Tasuku Honjo are two remarkable scientists whose pioneering work in the field of immunotherapy revolutionized cancer treatment, offering new hope to millions of patients around the world. Their groundbreaking discoveries on how to harness the body's own immune system to fight cancer have opened up entirely new avenues in oncology, transforming the landscape of cancer treatment and earning them the Nobel Prize in Physiology or Medicine in 2018. The journey of their scientific endeavors is a testament to the power of basic research, perseverance, and the pursuit of knowledge for the betterment of human health.

James P. Allison, born on August 7, 1948, in Alice, Texas, grew up in a small town where he developed a keen interest in science at a young age. His fascination with biology, combined with a personal experience of loss due to cancer—his mother passed away from lymphoma when he was a boy—fueled his desire to understand the mechanisms of disease and to find ways to combat it. After earning his bachelor's degree in microbiology from the University of Texas at Austin in 1969, Allison pursued a Ph.D. in biological science at the University of Texas, MD Anderson Cancer Center, where he began to delve into the intricacies of the immune system.

Allison's research focused on T cells, a type of white blood cell that plays a critical role in the immune system by identifying and attacking infected or malignant cells. During the 1980s and early 1990s, much of the scientific community believed that T cells were tightly regulated and could not be easily manipulated to attack cancer cells. However, Allison was intrigued by the possibility that T cells could be activated in a way that would allow them to recognize and destroy cancer cells more effectively. His curiosity led him to explore the role of a protein called CTLA-4, which was thought to be a crucial regulator of T cell activity.

In a series of experiments, Allison discovered that CTLA-4 acts as a brake on T cells, preventing them from attacking cancer cells aggressively. He hypothesized that by blocking CTLA-4, it might be possible to unleash the full potential of T cells to fight cancer. This idea was groundbreaking because it suggested a new approach to cancer treatment—one that focused not on directly targeting the cancer cells themselves, but rather on modulating the patient's immune system to enhance its ability to combat the disease.

Allison's bold hypothesis led to the development of a new class of cancer therapies known as immune checkpoint inhibitors. In 1996, he and his colleagues published a seminal paper in which they demonstrated that blocking CTLA-4 with an antibody could significantly shrink tumors in mice. This discovery marked the beginning of a new era in cancer treatment, as it provided the first clear evidence that immune checkpoint blockade could be an effective strategy for combating cancer.

However, the road from this initial discovery to clinical application was not straightforward. Allison faced significant skepticism from the scientific and medical communities, as many believed that targeting the immune system in this way could lead to severe autoimmune side effects or might not be effective in human patients. Undeterred by these challenges, Allison continued to refine his approach, working closely with pharmaceutical companies to develop a CTLA-4 inhibitor that could be tested in clinical trials.

The breakthrough came in 2011 when the U.S. Food and Drug Administration (FDA) approved the first immune checkpoint inhibitor, ipilimumab (marketed as Yervoy), for the treatment of advanced melanoma. Clinical trials showed that ipilimumab could induce long-lasting remissions in a subset of patients with metastatic melanoma, a disease that was previously considered almost uniformly fatal. This approval was a landmark moment in oncology, as it demonstrated that immunotherapy could provide durable responses and even cures for some patients with advanced cancer.

While James Allison was pioneering the field of immune checkpoint blockade, Tasuku Honjo, a Japanese immunologist born on January 27, 1942, in Kyoto, Japan, was making equally transformative discoveries on the other side of the world. Honjo's work focused on another protein involved in the regulation of T cells, known as programmed cell death protein 1 (PD-1). Like CTLA-4, PD-1 acts as a brake on the immune system, but it operates through a different mechanism and plays a distinct role in the regulation of immune responses.

After earning his M.D. in 1966 and Ph.D. in 1975 from Kyoto University, Honjo embarked on a research career that would take him to several prestigious institutions, including the National Institutes of Health (NIH) in the United States, where he worked on the genetic mechanisms underlying the immune response. In the early 1990s, Honjo discovered PD-1 while studying the mechanisms of programmed cell death in immune cells. Initially, the function of PD-1 was not well understood, but Honjo's subsequent research revealed that it played a critical role in preventing the immune system from attacking the body's own tissues, thereby maintaining self-tolerance.

Honjo's discovery of PD-1 was a key breakthrough in the understanding of immune regulation, but its potential application in cancer therapy was not immediately recognized. It was only later that Honjo and his team realized that blocking PD-1 could be a powerful strategy for unleashing the immune system to attack cancer cells. In 2002, Honjo published a landmark paper demonstrating that mice lacking PD-1 were more resistant to tumor formation, suggesting that PD-1 blockade could enhance anti-tumor immunity.

The development of PD-1 inhibitors as cancer therapies soon followed, with the first clinical trials showing remarkable results in patients with advanced cancers, including melanoma, non-small cell lung cancer, and kidney cancer. In 2014, the FDA approved the first PD-1 inhibitor, pembrolizumab (marketed as Keytruda), followed by the approval of another PD-1 inhibitor, nivolumab (marketed as Opdivo), shortly thereafter. These drugs have since become standard treatments for several types of cancer, offering new hope to patients who previously had few options.

The combination of CTLA-4 and PD-1 blockade, known as combination immunotherapy, has proven to be even more effective than either approach alone. Clinical trials have shown that combining these two therapies can lead to synergistic effects, resulting in higher response rates and longer-lasting remissions in patients with certain types of cancer. This combination therapy has been particularly successful in treating melanoma, where it has significantly improved survival rates and provided durable responses in a substantial proportion of patients.

The work of James Allison and Tasuku Honjo has fundamentally changed the way we think about cancer treatment. Their discoveries have established immunotherapy as a cornerstone of modern oncology, alongside surgery, radiation, and chemotherapy. Immunotherapy's ability to harness the power of the immune system to fight cancer has led to a paradigm shift in cancer treatment, offering new hope for patients with cancers that were previously considered untreatable.

Moreover, the impact of their work extends far beyond cancer. The principles underlying immune checkpoint blockade have opened up new avenues for treating other diseases characterized by immune dysfunction, such as autoimmune disorders and infectious diseases. Ongoing research is exploring the potential of immune checkpoint inhibitors in these areas, with the hope of developing new therapies that can modulate the immune system in beneficial ways.

Allison and Honjo's achievements have been recognized with numerous awards and honors in addition to the Nobel Prize. James Allison has received the Lasker-DeBakey Clinical Medical Research Award, the Breakthrough Prize in Life Sciences, and the Canada Gairdner International Award, among others. Tasuku Honjo has been honored with the Order of Culture from the Emperor of Japan, the Kyoto Prize, and the Keio Medical Science Prize. Both scientists have also been elected to prestigious scientific academies, including the National Academy of Sciences in the United States and the Japan Academy.

Their contributions to science and medicine have not only saved countless lives but have also inspired a new generation of researchers to explore the potential of the immune system in treating disease. Their work exemplifies the power of basic research—investigating fundamental biological processes—to yield unexpected and transformative medical breakthroughs. The legacy of James Allison and Tasuku Honjo will continue to influence the field of immunology and oncology for decades to come, as scientists build on their discoveries to develop even more effective and targeted therapies.

In addition to their scientific achievements, both Allison and Honjo have been active in advocating for the importance of scientific research and the need for continued investment in basic science. They have emphasized the unpredictable nature of scientific discovery, where breakthroughs often arise from curiosity-driven research rather than targeted efforts to solve specific problems. Their own careers are a testament to the value of pursuing knowledge for its own sake, with the understanding that such pursuits can lead to profound and unforeseen advances in human health.

James Allison and Tasuku Honjo's work also underscores the importance of international collaboration in science. While they made their discoveries independently, the global impact of their work and the subsequent development of immunotherapies have relied on the contributions of researchers, clinicians, and pharmaceutical companies from around the world. Their stories highlight the interconnectedness of the scientific enterprise and the ways in which discoveries in one part of the world can resonate globally, leading to innovations that benefit all of humanity.

As we look to the future, the field of cancer immunotherapy continues to evolve, with ongoing research aimed at improving the effectiveness and safety of these treatments. Scientists are exploring new combinations of immunotherapies, identifying biomarkers to predict patient response, and developing strategies to overcome resistance to treatment. The work of Allison and Honjo has laid the foundation for these efforts, and their discoveries will continue to guide the development of new therapies that harness the power of the immune system to fight disease.

The story of James P. Allison and Tasuku Honjo is one of perseverance, innovation, and the relentless pursuit of knowledge in the face of skepticism and uncertainty. Their groundbreaking work has not only transformed the treatment of cancer but has also expanded our understanding of the immune system and its potential to combat disease. Their legacy will endure as a beacon of hope for patients and a source of inspiration for scientists around the world, reminding us of the profound impact that scientific discovery can have on human health and well-being.

Chapter 48: George F. Smoot & John C. Mather

George F. Smoot and John C. Mather are two distinguished physicists whose groundbreaking work in cosmology, particularly their contributions to the understanding of the Cosmic Microwave Background (CMB) radiation, has profoundly influenced our comprehension of the universe. Their research has provided critical evidence for the Big Bang theory and deepened our understanding of the early universe, earning them the Nobel Prize in Physics in 2006. The story of their scientific journey is one of remarkable collaboration, innovative experimentation, and a relentless pursuit of answers to some of the most fundamental questions about the cosmos.

George Fitzgerald Smoot III was born on February 20, 1945, in Yukon, Florida, and grew up in a family that valued education and scientific inquiry. He developed a keen interest in science from a young age, particularly in physics and astronomy. After earning his undergraduate degree in mathematics and physics from the Massachusetts Institute of Technology (MIT) in 1966, Smoot pursued graduate studies at MIT, where he completed his Ph.D. in particle physics in 1970. His early research focused on high-energy physics, but he soon became fascinated by cosmology, a field that was rapidly advancing thanks to new observational techniques and theoretical developments.

John Cromwell Mather was born on August 7, 1946, in Roanoke, Virginia. Like Smoot, Mather was deeply interested in science from a young age, particularly in physics and astronomy. He earned his bachelor's degree in physics from Swarthmore College in 1968 and went on to complete his Ph.D. in physics at the University of California, Berkeley, in 1974. Mather's doctoral research focused on the development of instruments for measuring the properties of the cosmic microwave background radiation, which was becoming an increasingly important area of study in cosmology.

The Cosmic Microwave Background (CMB) radiation is the afterglow of the Big Bang, the faint microwave radiation that fills the universe and serves as a snapshot of the universe when it was just 380,000 years old. Discovered in 1965 by Arno Penzias and Robert Wilson, the CMB provided strong evidence for the Big Bang theory, which posits that the universe began as an extremely hot and dense point and has been expanding ever since. The study of the CMB is crucial for understanding the early universe, as it contains information about the conditions that existed just after the Big Bang.

Despite its significance, the CMB remained largely unexplored in the years following its discovery due to the lack of precise instruments capable of measuring its properties. This began to change in the 1970s and 1980s, as advances in technology made it possible to study the CMB with greater accuracy. It was during this period that Smoot and Mather began their work on what would become one of the most important experiments in cosmology: the Cosmic Background Explorer (COBE) satellite.

The COBE satellite was a NASA mission designed to measure the CMB with unprecedented precision. The project was proposed in the late 1970s, and both Smoot and Mather played pivotal roles in its development and execution. John Mather served as the project's Principal Investigator, leading the team responsible for designing and building the satellite's instruments. George Smoot was the leader of the Differential Microwave Radiometer (DMR) team, which was tasked with measuring the tiny fluctuations in the temperature of the CMB across the sky.

One of the key objectives of the COBE mission was to test the predictions of the Big Bang theory and to search for evidence of the early stages of cosmic structure formation. According to the Big

Bang theory, the early universe was a hot, dense plasma where matter and radiation were tightly coupled. As the universe expanded and cooled, it eventually reached a point where protons and electrons combined to form neutral atoms, allowing radiation to travel freely through space. This radiation, now observed as the CMB, was expected to be remarkably uniform, but with tiny fluctuations that would provide clues about the formation of galaxies and other large-scale structures in the universe.

The COBE satellite was launched on November 18, 1989, and began collecting data shortly thereafter. Over the next few years, the mission returned a wealth of information about the CMB, leading to several groundbreaking discoveries. One of the most significant results came from the DMR instrument, which measured temperature variations in the CMB at a level of precision never before achieved. These measurements revealed the existence of tiny fluctuations, or anisotropies, in the temperature of the CMB—differences of just one part in 100,000.

These temperature fluctuations were exactly what the Big Bang theory predicted: they were the seeds of the galaxies and clusters of galaxies that we see today. The tiny variations in the density of matter in the early universe led to gravitational instabilities, which caused matter to clump together and form the large-scale structures we observe in the universe. The detection of these fluctuations was a major triumph for the Big Bang theory and provided a critical piece of evidence for our understanding of cosmic evolution.

In addition to the discovery of CMB anisotropies, the COBE mission also made another groundbreaking discovery: it confirmed that the spectrum of the CMB is that of a nearly perfect blackbody, with a temperature of approximately 2.725 K. This finding was significant because it provided further support for the Big Bang theory and ruled out alternative models of the universe, such as the steady-state theory, which proposed that the universe has no beginning or end and has always existed in a more or less steady state.

The results from COBE were published in a series of papers in the early 1990s and had a profound impact on the field of cosmology. The discovery of CMB anisotropies opened up new avenues of research, leading to the development of more sophisticated models of cosmic structure formation and the refinement of cosmological parameters such as the age, composition, and geometry of the universe. The COBE results also paved the way for future missions, such as the Wilkinson Microwave Anisotropy Probe (WMAP) and the Planck satellite, which have provided even more detailed maps of the CMB and further enhanced our understanding of the universe.

For their contributions to the COBE mission and the study of the CMB, George Smoot and John Mather were awarded the Nobel Prize in Physics in 2006. The Nobel Committee recognized their work as a major milestone in cosmology, describing it as "an outstanding example of how advanced technology can be used to address fundamental questions about the nature of the universe." The award highlighted the importance of precision measurements in cosmology and underscored the role of observational data in testing and refining theoretical models.

The impact of Smoot and Mather's work extends far beyond the realm of cosmology. Their discoveries have influenced a wide range of scientific fields, including particle physics, astrophysics, and even philosophy, as they have provided new insights into the origins and nature of the universe. The detection of CMB anisotropies has also had practical implications, as it has informed our understanding of dark matter, dark energy, and the overall structure of the cosmos.

In addition to their scientific achievements, both Smoot and Mather have been active in public outreach and education, sharing their discoveries with the broader public and inspiring a new generation of scientists. George Smoot, for example, has given numerous lectures and talks around the world, explaining the significance of the CMB and the importance of cosmology in understanding our place in the universe. He has also appeared in popular media, including the television show "The Big Bang Theory," where he made a guest appearance as himself, helping to bring the excitement of cosmological research to a wider audience.

John Mather has similarly been involved in outreach efforts, emphasizing the importance of basic research and the need for continued investment in scientific exploration. He has worked on several high-profile NASA missions, including the James Webb Space Telescope, where he serves as Senior Project Scientist. The Webb telescope, set to launch in the near future, is expected to build on the legacy of COBE by providing even more detailed observations of the early universe, including the formation of the first galaxies and stars.

The legacy of George Smoot and John Mather's work continues to influence the field of cosmology and beyond. Their discoveries have provided a foundation for ongoing research into the origins and evolution of the universe, and their contributions to the COBE mission have set a standard for precision measurements in observational cosmology. The data collected by COBE, and the subsequent missions it inspired, have transformed our understanding of the universe, offering new insights into its age, composition, and ultimate fate.

As we look to the future, the questions raised by Smoot and Mather's work continue to inspire new lines of inquiry. Scientists are now exploring the nature of dark matter and dark energy, the forces that drive cosmic acceleration, and the potential existence of parallel universes or multiverses. These investigations are guided by the principles of precision measurement and observational evidence that Smoot and Mather championed, demonstrating the lasting impact of their contributions to science.

In summary, George F. Smoot and John C. Mather's work on the Cosmic Microwave Background radiation represents a monumental achievement in cosmology. Their discoveries have not only confirmed key predictions of the Big Bang theory but have also opened up new avenues of research that continue to shape our understanding of the universe. Their legacy is one of scientific rigor, collaboration, and the relentless pursuit of knowledge, inspiring future generations of scientists to explore the mysteries of the cosmos and beyond. Their contributions will be remembered as a cornerstone of modern cosmology, providing a foundation for the ongoing quest to understand the origins and evolution of the universe.

Chapter 49: Niels Bohr

Niels Bohr, one of the most influential figures in the history of science, made profound contributions to our understanding of atomic structure and quantum mechanics. Born on October 7, 1885, in Copenhagen, Denmark, Bohr was raised in a family that valued education and intellectual inquiry. His father, Christian Bohr, was a professor of physiology, and his mother, Ellen Adler Bohr, came from a wealthy and prominent Jewish family. This intellectually stimulating environment fostered Bohr's early interest in science and set the stage for his future achievements.

Bohr's academic journey began at the University of Copenhagen, where he initially studied philosophy and mathematics before shifting his focus to physics. His doctoral thesis, completed in 1911, was on the electron theory of metals, where he sought to understand the properties of metals through the behavior of electrons. Although this work did not lead to any major breakthroughs at the time, it demonstrated Bohr's ability to tackle complex problems and laid the groundwork for his future research.

In 1912, Bohr traveled to England to work with J.J. Thomson at the Cavendish Laboratory in Cambridge. Thomson, who had discovered the electron, was one of the leading physicists of the time, and Bohr was eager to learn from him. However, their collaboration did not prove to be as fruitful as Bohr had hoped, largely because Thomson's approach was more experimental, while Bohr was primarily a theorist. Despite this, Bohr's time in Cambridge was not wasted, as it allowed him to immerse himself in the latest developments in atomic theory.

Later in 1912, Bohr moved to Manchester to work with Ernest Rutherford, another giant in the field of physics. Rutherford had recently proposed a new model of the atom, based on his famous gold foil experiment, which suggested that atoms consist of a small, dense nucleus surrounded by electrons. This was a radical departure from the earlier plum pudding model proposed by Thomson, and it laid the foundation for Bohr's most significant work.

Bohr quickly realized that Rutherford's model, while groundbreaking, was incomplete. It could not explain why electrons did not simply spiral into the nucleus, as classical physics would predict, nor could it account for the discrete spectral lines observed in atomic spectra. These lines, which were unique to each element, suggested that electrons could only occupy certain energy levels, a concept that was difficult to reconcile with classical physics.

In 1913, Bohr published a series of three papers that introduced his revolutionary model of the atom, which combined Rutherford's nuclear model with the emerging ideas of quantum theory. Bohr proposed that electrons orbit the nucleus in specific, quantized orbits, or energy levels, and that they could only gain or lose energy by jumping from one orbit to another. This explained the stability of atoms and the discrete spectral lines observed in atomic spectra. When an electron moved from a higher energy level to a lower one, it emitted a photon of light with a specific wavelength, corresponding to the difference in energy between the two levels. This was a major breakthrough that provided a theoretical foundation for understanding atomic structure and radiation.

Bohr's model, known as the Bohr model of the atom, was initially applied to the hydrogen atom, the simplest of all atoms, with just one proton and one electron. The success of the Bohr model in explaining the spectral lines of hydrogen was a triumph of quantum theory and marked the beginning of a new era in atomic physics. Although the Bohr model was later refined and replaced by more advanced theories, such as quantum mechanics, it remains a crucial step in the development of modern physics.

The Bohr model had far-reaching implications for both science and philosophy. It challenged the classical view of nature as deterministic and continuous, introducing the idea that certain properties, such as energy, could only take on discrete values. This was a radical departure from the Newtonian paradigm that had dominated physics for centuries, and it opened the door to the probabilistic and non-deterministic nature of quantum mechanics. Bohr's work laid the foundation for the development of quantum mechanics, a theory that would revolutionize our understanding of the microscopic world.

In the years following the publication of his atomic model, Bohr continued to refine and extend his ideas. He recognized that his model, while successful for hydrogen, could not fully explain the spectra of more complex atoms. This led him to collaborate with other physicists, such as Arnold Sommerfeld and Wolfgang Pauli, who introduced modifications to the Bohr model, including elliptical orbits and the concept of electron spin. These refinements were essential in the development of quantum mechanics, a more comprehensive theory that could explain the behavior of electrons in all atoms.

Bohr's contributions to physics extended beyond his work on atomic structure. He was also deeply involved in the development of quantum mechanics, the theory that describes the behavior of particles on the atomic and subatomic scale. One of Bohr's most significant contributions to quantum mechanics was the principle of complementarity, which he introduced in the 1920s. This principle states that certain pairs of physical properties, such as position and momentum, or energy and time, cannot be precisely measured simultaneously. Instead, these properties are complementary, meaning that the more precisely one is measured, the less precisely the other can be known.

The principle of complementarity was a cornerstone of the Copenhagen interpretation of quantum mechanics, which Bohr developed in collaboration with Werner Heisenberg, another leading physicist of the time. The Copenhagen interpretation, which remains one of the most widely accepted interpretations of quantum mechanics, posits that the behavior of quantum systems is fundamentally probabilistic and that the act of measurement plays a crucial role in determining the outcome of quantum events. This interpretation challenged the classical notion of an objective reality independent of observation and introduced the concept of wave-particle duality, which states that particles such as electrons can exhibit both wave-like and particle-like behavior depending on the experimental setup.

Bohr's principle of complementarity and the Copenhagen interpretation were not without controversy. They sparked intense debates among physicists, most notably with Albert Einstein, who famously quipped, "God does not play dice with the universe." Einstein was uncomfortable with the idea of inherent randomness in nature and the notion that reality depended on observation. These debates between Bohr and Einstein, often referred to as the Bohr-Einstein debates, became one of the most famous and philosophically profound discussions in the history of science.

Despite their disagreements, Bohr and Einstein had great respect for each other, and their debates helped to clarify and refine the concepts of quantum mechanics. Bohr's insistence on the importance of complementarity and the role of observation in quantum mechanics played a crucial role in shaping the direction of physics in the 20th century. The ideas he championed continue to influence our understanding of the quantum world and have found applications in fields as diverse as quantum computing, cryptography, and information theory.

In addition to his contributions to theoretical physics, Bohr was also a key figure in the establishment of several important scientific institutions. In 1920, he founded the Institute for Theoretical Physics in Copenhagen, which became one of the leading centers for research in quantum mechanics and attracted many of the brightest minds in physics, including Heisenberg, Pauli, and Erwin Schrödinger. The institute played a pivotal role in the development of quantum theory and was a hub of intellectual activity during the 1920s and 1930s.

Bohr's influence extended beyond his own research and the institutions he helped establish. He was a mentor and collaborator to many of the leading physicists of his time, and his ideas had a profound impact on the development of quantum mechanics and related fields. His ability to think deeply about the philosophical implications of scientific theories, combined with his rigorous approach to problem-solving, made him a respected and influential figure in the scientific community.

Bohr's contributions to science were recognized with numerous awards and honors. In 1922, he was awarded the Nobel Prize in Physics for his work on the structure of atoms and the radiation they emit. The Nobel Committee cited his model of the atom and his contributions to our understanding of quantum theory as reasons for the award. The Nobel Prize solidified Bohr's reputation as one of the foremost physicists of his time and brought his work to the attention of a broader audience.

During World War II, Bohr's life and work took on a new dimension as he became involved in the political and ethical implications of scientific research. As the Nazi regime occupied Denmark, Bohr, who had Jewish ancestry through his mother, was in grave danger. In 1943, he and his family fled to Sweden with the help of the Danish resistance. From there, Bohr traveled to the United States, where he became involved in the Manhattan Project, the Allied effort to develop the atomic bomb.

Bohr's involvement in the Manhattan Project was driven by his deep concern about the potential misuse of nuclear energy. Although he recognized the necessity of developing the bomb to counter the threat posed by Nazi Germany, he was acutely aware of the moral and ethical dilemmas associated with nuclear weapons. After the war, Bohr became an advocate for the peaceful use of nuclear energy and for international cooperation in the control of nuclear weapons. He believed that scientific knowledge should be used to promote peace and that the dangers of nuclear proliferation required global collaboration and transparency.

Bohr's efforts to promote international cooperation in the post-war era were not limited to his work on nuclear energy. He was also a vocal advocate for the establishment of the United Nations and for the inclusion of scientists in discussions about global security and peace. In 1950, Bohr wrote an open letter to the United Nations, in which he called for the creation of an "open world" in which nations would share scientific and technical knowledge freely and work together to address common challenges. His vision of an open world was based on the belief that scientific progress could contribute to human welfare only if it was accompanied by mutual understanding and collaboration among nations.

In his later years, Bohr continued to be active in both scientific research and public life. He remained involved in the Institute for Theoretical Physics, which was later renamed the Niels Bohr Institute in his honor, and he continued to contribute to the development of quantum mechanics and related fields. Bohr also remained committed to his efforts to promote peace and international cooperation, and he received numerous accolades for his contributions to science and society.

Niels Bohr passed away on November 18, 1962, in Copenhagen, but his legacy lives on. His work laid the foundation for much of modern physics, and his ideas continue to influence our understanding of the quantum world. Bohr's contributions to science were not limited to his discoveries; he also played a crucial role in shaping the direction of scientific research and in promoting the responsible use of scientific knowledge. His legacy is one of intellectual curiosity, rigorous inquiry, and a deep commitment to the betterment of humanity.

In summary, Niels Bohr was a towering figure in the history of science, whose contributions to atomic theory, quantum mechanics, and the philosophy of science had a profound and lasting impact. His work on the Bohr model of the atom and the development of quantum mechanics revolutionized our understanding of the microscopic world and challenged the classical notions of reality. Bohr's principle of complementarity and the Copenhagen interpretation of quantum mechanics continue to shape our understanding of the quantum realm. Beyond his scientific achievements, Bohr was a tireless advocate for the peaceful use of scientific knowledge and for international cooperation in the pursuit of global security and peace. His legacy is one of intellectual rigor, ethical responsibility, and a deep commitment to the advancement of human knowledge.

Chapter 50: Levitt, Karplus, & Warshel

Michael Levitt, Martin Karplus, and Arieh Warshel are three pioneering scientists whose groundbreaking work in computational chemistry has profoundly influenced the way we understand complex molecular systems. Their innovative research, which earned them the Nobel Prize in Chemistry in 2013, revolutionized the field by allowing scientists to model and simulate chemical reactions at the molecular level using computer programs. This work not only provided deep insights into the fundamental processes of life but also opened new avenues for drug discovery, materials science, and a wide range of other scientific disciplines. The story of Levitt, Karplus, and Warshel is one of collaboration, innovation, and perseverance in the face of scientific challenges that many thought insurmountable.

Michael Levitt was born in Pretoria, South Africa, in 1947. From a young age, Levitt exhibited a keen interest in science and mathematics, which eventually led him to study physics at King's College London. His academic journey was marked by a strong curiosity about the fundamental principles of life, and he soon found himself drawn to the burgeoning field of molecular biology. Levitt's interest in molecular biology was sparked by the realization that the complexity of biological systems could be understood in terms of the physical interactions between molecules. This interdisciplinary approach would become a hallmark of his scientific career.

In the late 1960s, Levitt moved to the Laboratory of Molecular Biology (LMB) in Cambridge, England, where he worked under the guidance of the renowned scientist Francis Crick, one of the co-discoverers of the structure of DNA. It was at the LMB that Levitt began to develop the first computer simulations of molecular dynamics. He realized that the behavior of complex biological molecules could be modeled using principles from physics and chemistry, but this required sophisticated computational techniques that had not yet been fully developed. Levitt's early work in this area laid the foundation for the field of computational chemistry and established him as one of its leading figures.

Martin Karplus, born in Vienna, Austria, in 1930, also had a deep fascination with the fundamental principles of science. After fleeing Nazi-occupied Austria with his family, Karplus grew up in the United States, where he pursued his studies in chemistry. He earned his Ph.D. from the California Institute of Technology (Caltech), where he studied under the legendary chemist Linus Pauling. Karplus's early work focused on quantum chemistry, and he made significant contributions to the understanding of molecular structures and chemical bonding. However, like Levitt, Karplus was intrigued by the possibility of using computers to model the behavior of molecules, and he soon became a pioneer in the field of theoretical chemistry.

In the 1970s, Karplus and his collaborators developed some of the first computer programs capable of simulating the motion of atoms and molecules over time. These simulations, known as molecular dynamics simulations, allowed scientists to study how molecules interact with each other, how chemical reactions proceed, and how biological processes occur at the molecular level. Karplus's work in this area was groundbreaking, as it provided a new way to study complex chemical systems that were previously inaccessible to experimental techniques. His contributions to the development of computational chemistry earned him widespread recognition and established him as one of the foremost theoretical chemists of his time.

Arieh Warshel, born in 1940 in Kibbutz Sde Nahum, Israel, shared a similar passion for understanding the molecular mechanisms of life. After earning his Ph.D. in chemical physics from the Weizmann Institute of Science in Israel, Warshel moved to the United States, where he worked with Martin Karplus at Harvard

University. It was during this time that Warshel made some of his most significant contributions to the field of computational chemistry. Building on the work of Levitt and Karplus, Warshel developed new methods for simulating chemical reactions, particularly those involving enzymes, which are the proteins that catalyze biochemical reactions in living organisms.

One of Warshel's most important contributions was the development of the Quantum Mechanics/Molecular Mechanics (QM/MM) approach, a hybrid method that combines the accuracy of quantum mechanics with the efficiency of classical molecular mechanics. This approach allows scientists to model the behavior of large biological molecules, such as enzymes, with unprecedented precision. By using quantum mechanics to describe the behavior of atoms involved in a chemical reaction and classical mechanics to describe the rest of the molecule, the QM/MM approach provides a powerful tool for studying complex biochemical processes. Warshel's work in this area was instrumental in advancing our understanding of how enzymes function and how chemical reactions occur in biological systems.

The collaboration between Levitt, Karplus, and Warshel was marked by a shared vision of using computational methods to tackle some of the most challenging problems in chemistry and biology. Their work was not without obstacles, as the field of computational chemistry was still in its infancy during the 1970s and 1980s. The computational resources available at the time were limited, and many in the scientific community were skeptical of the idea that computer simulations could provide meaningful insights into complex molecular systems. Despite these challenges, Levitt, Karplus, and Warshel persevered, and their efforts eventually paid off as their methods became more sophisticated and widely adopted.

The impact of their work on the field of chemistry and beyond has been profound. The computational techniques developed by

Levitt, Karplus, and Warshel have become essential tools in a wide range of scientific disciplines. In drug discovery, for example, computational chemistry allows researchers to model how potential drug molecules interact with their targets, such as enzymes or receptors, at the atomic level. This enables the design of more effective and selective drugs, reducing the need for costly and time-consuming experimental testing. In materials science, computational methods are used to design new materials with specific properties by simulating the behavior of atoms and molecules under different conditions. These applications demonstrate the broad utility of the techniques pioneered by Levitt, Karplus, and Warshel.

The contributions of Levitt, Karplus, and Warshel have also had a significant impact on our understanding of fundamental biological processes. By providing detailed insights into the mechanisms of enzyme catalysis, protein folding, and molecular recognition, their work has deepened our knowledge of the molecular basis of life. This has led to new approaches for treating diseases, understanding genetic disorders, and developing biotechnological applications. Their work has also influenced the way scientists think about molecular systems, emphasizing the importance of an interdisciplinary approach that integrates principles from physics, chemistry, and biology.

In recognition of their contributions to the field of computational chemistry, Michael Levitt, Martin Karplus, and Arieh Warshel were awarded the Nobel Prize in Chemistry in 2013. The Nobel Committee cited their development of multiscale models for complex chemical systems as the basis for the award, highlighting the significance of their work in advancing our understanding of molecular processes. The Nobel Prize not only recognized their individual achievements but also underscored the importance of computational chemistry as a field that bridges the gap between theory and experiment.

The legacy of Levitt, Karplus, and Warshel extends beyond their scientific contributions. They have inspired generations of scientists to embrace computational methods as a powerful tool for exploring the complexities of the natural world. Their work has demonstrated that even the most challenging scientific problems can be addressed through innovation, collaboration, and a willingness to explore new approaches. As computational resources continue to advance, the methods they developed will undoubtedly continue to play a central role in shaping the future of science and technology.

In conclusion, the work of Michael Levitt, Martin Karplus, and Arieh Warshel represents a milestone in the field of computational chemistry. Their pioneering efforts to develop computer simulations of molecular systems have transformed our understanding of chemistry and biology, providing new insights into the fundamental processes of life. Their contributions have had far-reaching implications for drug discovery, materials science, and a wide range of other scientific disciplines. The Nobel Prize awarded to Levitt, Karplus, and Warshel in 2013 serves as a testament to the significance of their work and the lasting impact it has had on the scientific community. Their legacy is one of innovation, perseverance, and a deep commitment to advancing our understanding of the molecular world.

Epilogue

As we conclude this exploration of some of history's most brilliant scientific minds, we are reminded of the profound impact these individuals have had on our world. The stories of Nobel Prize-winning scientists are not just chronicles of discovery and innovation; they are narratives of human determination, courage, and the relentless pursuit of truth. Their journeys, marked by moments of inspiration and periods of relentless experimentation, are testaments to the transformative power of science.

Throughout the pages of this book, we have seen how Albert Einstein's theories reshaped our understanding of time and space, how Marie Curie's groundbreaking work with radioactivity opened new frontiers in both physics and medicine, and how James Watson, Francis Crick, and Maurice Wilkins unraveled the structure of DNA, laying the foundation for modern genetics. We have explored the discoveries that have revolutionized entire fields—from the quantum leaps of physics and chemistry to the intricate understanding of biological processes.

But beyond their scientific achievements, these Nobel laureates have also left us with valuable lessons about curiosity, perseverance, and the spirit of inquiry. They remind us that science is not a solitary endeavor but a collaborative effort that thrives on shared knowledge, debate, and a willingness to challenge the unknown. Many of these scientists faced significant obstacles, from limited resources to skepticism from their peers, yet they persevered, driven by a deep curiosity and a desire to understand the universe.

Their stories also serve as a powerful reminder that science is an ever-evolving field. Each discovery builds upon the work of countless others, creating a continuum of knowledge that stretches back centuries and extends into the future. The Nobel Prize, in honoring these achievements, celebrates not only the individuals but also the collective human endeavor to push the boundaries of what is known and to expand our horizons.

As we look forward, the legacy of these Nobel Prize-winning scientists continues to inspire future generations of researchers, thinkers, and dreamers. Their contributions remind us that there are always new questions to be asked, new challenges to be faced, and new discoveries to be made. In a world that is constantly changing, the spirit of scientific inquiry remains a guiding light, showing us the path forward and encouraging us to explore the mysteries that still lie beyond our reach.

The stories in this book are not just historical accounts; they are a call to action—a reminder that the pursuit of knowledge is a journey without end. The scientists we have profiled here have shown us that no matter how much we learn, there is always more to discover, more to understand, and more to explore. Their lives and work are a testament to the boundless possibilities of the human mind and spirit.

As we close this chapter, let us carry forward the lessons and inspiration drawn from these remarkable individuals. Let us continue to ask questions, seek answers, and pursue knowledge with the same passion and dedication that these Nobel laureates have exemplified. For in doing so, we honor their legacy and contribute to the ongoing story of science—an ever-unfolding narrative that shapes our world and our understanding of it.

The journey of discovery never truly ends. It continues with each new generation of scientists, innovators, and thinkers who dare to imagine what lies beyond the known and venture into the unknown with curiosity and courage. This is the enduring legacy of the Nobel Prize-winning scientists whose profiles we have shared—a legacy that will continue to inspire and illuminate the path forward for all who seek to understand the wonders of our universe.

The End.